Cover Photos of the Authors

Far left column
from top to bottom:
Ruth Nomura Tanbara
Gladys Ishida Stone
Mary Mariko Ogura

Second column from left
from top to bottom:
Chisako Joyce Hirabayashi
Tai Shigaki
Kimi Yamada Yanari
Martha Inouye Oye

Second column from right
from top to bottom:
Maye Mitsuye Oye Uemura
Toshiko Baba Yoneji
Alice Abe Matsumoto
Haruko Kuramoto Hashimoto

Far right column
from top to bottom:
Esther Torii Suzuki
Mary Takao Yoshida
Yoshi Uchiyama Tani

Reflections

Memoirs of Japanese American Women in Minnesota

John Nobuya Tsuchida, Editor

Pacific Asia Press
Covina, California

1994

CONTENTS

PREFACE

December 7, 1991 was the 50th anniversary of Pearl Harbor. The commemoration of this important and yet tragic event in the history of the U.S.-Japan relations resurrected among Japanese Americans many sad memories of the 1940's. A group of retired Japanese American women began to feel that unless they recorded their life histories, their children and grandchildren, who grew up in the Midwest, would never fully understand how Issei (pre-World War II Japanese immigrants) and Nisei (U.S.-born children of Issei) had struggled, suffered, and overcome racial prejudice in order to achieve the current socio-economic status of Japanese Americans.

Ruth Tanbara, who voluntarily relocated with her husband from California to the Midwest in 1942, was going to commemorate in 1992 her 50th year in Minnesota. At a luncheon meeting on March 9, 1991, she and 11 Nisei women decided to write autobiographical essays about their experiences on the West Coast and in Minnesota before it became too late to do so. During World War II, these women, along with 110,000 Japanese Americans, were evacuated from the West Coast following the Japanese attack on Pearl Harbor. All of the Nisei women, except Ruth, were subsequently interned in concentration camps for varying periods of time without due process of law. Within a few years, however, they were allowed to relocate to the Midwest and the East to resume their college education or to seek employment.

This group of Minnesota Nisei women chose to undertake this book project for three reasons. In the first place, they wanted to document their deep appreciation for Minnesotans who had welcomed and accepted Japanese Americans from the West Coast States. Secondly, the Nisei women, who are advanced in years, wished to record, for the sake of their posterity, their experiences and the struggles of their immigrant parents from Japan. Lastly, the women authors were interested in recounting how they were affected by the war between the United States, their native country, and Japan, their parents' homeland, and how they had overcome racism and its nefarious effects through education, hard work, and perseverance. The authors were interested in helping educate children, youth, college students, and the general public in order to prevent any minority group from being subjected to such blatant acts of racial discrimination as the wartime exclusion and internment of innocent and loyal Japanese Americans.

During one of the board meetings of the Japan America Society of Minnesota held in the spring of 1991, Ruth Tanbara casually asked me if I would help compile the Nisei women's memoirs into an anthology. Not realizing then that it would eventually become a 500-page book, I offered to help with the worthwhile project. I did not know how to say no to the highly respected octogenarian dean of the Japanese American community in Minnesota. Ruth sent letters to 75 Nisei women residing in the Twin Cities area, inviting them to participate in the book project. Twenty people initially expressed an interest.

On July 31, 1991, we held our first meeting in the craft room of Wilder Park Towers, Ruth Tanbara's retirement condominium building in St. Paul. I gave the participants a general outline to follow in writing their autobiographical essays, asking them to finish a chapter for each of our subsequent meetings. By August 5, 1992, we met ten times and 14 Nisei women completed their essays.

Unfortunately, Kimi Hara who was the first Nisei to relocate from the West Coast to Minnesota after the outbreak of the war, was unable to finish her memoir due to illness and injuries. No history of the Japanese Americans in Minnesota would be complete without recording what she has done not only for her community but also for the State of Minnesota. Trained as a registered nurse in Seattle, Washington, prior to the war, Kimi came to Rochester, Minnesota, to work as a night supervisor in the Obstetrics Department at St. Mary's Hospital. She received a Bachelor of Science degree in Nursing Education in 1953 and a Master's degree in Nursing Administration in 1957, both at the University of Minnesota. Between 1955 and 1973, she taught emergency childbirth procedures at the Minnesota Bureau of Criminal Apprehension and the State Patrol Division. For 18 years from 1963 through 1980, Kimi worked as a nursing education specialist at the Minnesota Board of Nursing, supervising nursing education programs, administering the scholarship/financial aid program, assisting with the administration of the licensure examinations, and handling all disciplinary cases filed with the Board.

In the Japanese American community, Kimi Hara provided both Issei and Nisei with invaluable medical advice and service, particularly in the immediate postwar period. Those Issei who were not fluent in English highly appreciated her medical assistance offered by means of Japanese. Since its establishment in 1949, Kimi has been active in the Twin Cities Chapter of the Japanese American Citizens League, where she has served as scholarship chair to raise funds for scholarships awarded to college-bound Japanese American high school graduates. She has been also active on the Normandale Japanese Garden Committee and in the Japan America Society of Minnesota, where she served as chair and president, respectively. There are few people in the Minnesota Japanese American community who have not been helped directly or indirectly by Kimi Hara.

This book will present a rich social history of Japanese Americans who have been an integral part of Minnesota since 1942 when the Military Intelligence Service Japanese Language School was moved from the Presidio of San Francisco to Camp Savage. The anthology will also epitomize Minnesotans' longstanding tradition to provide a refuge with open arms for those who were displaced, persecuted or discriminated against elsewhere. The 14 Nisei women's memoirs will shed light on how individual citizens of Japanese ancestry were uniquely affected by World War II at the personal level on account of their ethnic background and American racism, as well as how they have successfully coped with adversities in their own ways. Finally, this book will make a valuable contribution to the literature on Japanese Americans, in that the 14 autobiographical essays focus on the Japanese American women's experiences in Minnesota, which are quite different from those of evacuees who eventually returned to the West Coast in the postwar period.

I have been fortunate to be part of the Nisei women's book project.

Minneapolis, Minnesota   John Nobuya Tsuchida

ACKNOWLEDGMENTS

I owe a debt of gratitude to two dozen people who made the production and publication of this book possible. First of all, I must express my sincere gratitude to Ruth Tanbara for asking me in the spring of 1991 to edit and compile an anthology of autobiographical essays which a group of Japanese American women in the Twin Cities area were planning to write in commemoration of the 50th anniversary of Pearl Harbor. Although there were times when I did regret having agreed to undertake what turned out to be a large-scale project, it was an honor and privilege to work with her and 13 other women to produce an anthology of their valuable memoirs.

Joyce Hirabayashi, Alice Matsumoto, Mary Ogura, Martha Oye, Tai Shigaki, Dr. Gladys Stone, Esther Suzuki, Ruth Tanbara, Yoshi Tani, Maye Uemura, Linda van Dooijeweert, Kimi Yanari, Toshi Yoneji, and Mary Yoshida all wrote excellent autobiographical essays in a timely and conscientious manner. These authors are all Nisei (U.S.-born children of pre-World War II Japanese immigrants), with the exception of Linda van Dooijeweert, a Sansei (grandchild of Japanese immigrants), who wrote an essay on behalf of her deceased mother, Haruko Hashimoto. I wish to thank the 14 contributors for sharing their experiences, both joyful and painful, during and after World War II, which will contribute to enhancing the public's understanding of Japanese Americans, as well as the absurdity and the injurious effect of racial prejudice. Without their willingness to impart their memoirs, this book would never have been produced.

With respect to the mechanical part of the book production, I am deeply indebted to my staff at the Office for Minority and Special Student Affairs (OMSSA) at the University of Minnesota. Barbara Chapin not only word-processed many essays, but also devised the basic format of the book and placed a few hundred photographs throughout the anthology. Christine Murakami Noonan was instrumental in laying out the final manuscript. She proofread the entire manuscript, helped make punctuation more uniform in all the memoirs, and made many valuable editorial suggestions. Barbara Chapin and Christine Murakami Noonan designed the book cover. Cathy Wong and Lois Kempenich also word-processed many essays at the draft stage. Erin Kaser proofread several draft essays and conducted some archival research for the editor. Finally, Dawn Sharp proofread all the memoirs at the final draft stage. But for my staff's expertise and dedicated service, I would not have been able to complete this book in a timely manner.

This anthology's quality and value were greatly enhanced by a few hundred rare and old photographs inserted throughout the memoirs. Deborah Eagle served as an official photographer for this project, reproducing almost all the photographs and producing all but two current portraits of the authors. Donna Kelly assisted her with the reproduction of dozens of photographs at the final stage of the project.

Finally, I would like to thank Daniel Chen, president of Pacific Asia Press, for publishing this anthology. I remain grateful for his foresight and wisdom in detecting the educational value of the book.

University of Minnesota   *John Nobuya Tsuchida*
Minneapolis, Minnesota

January 1994

鳳凰語言學校
Phoenix Language Center
707 W. Valley Blvd. # 22
Alhambra, CA 91803
(626) 759-8166

INTRODUCTION

Japanese American History: An Overview
By John Nobuya Tsuchida

As of 1990, 847,562 Japanese Americans resided in the United States, accounting for only 0.3 percent of the nation's total population.[1] As high as 76 percent of the Japanese Americans were concentrated in the Western States, particularly California and Hawaii, which claimed, respectively, 37 percent and 29 percent of this ethnic group.[2] Minnesota, in contrast, had 3,581 residents of Japanese ancestry, or 0.4 percent of the total.[3] Historically, the Japanese Americans were always numerically insignificant. However, they often found themselves caught in the cross fire of the economic, diplomatic and bellicose rivalry between the United States and Japan during the first half of the twentieth century. Most, if not all, ethnic minority groups in this country have been subjected to various forms and degrees of discrimination by the dominant society at one time or another. Nevertheless, the Japanese Americans are unique in that they were the only American minority group in modern U.S. history that the federal government indiscriminately incarcerated en masse without due process of law.

During World War II, the U.S. government, as opposed to individual Americans or private oganizations, flagrantly violated the Japanese Americans' Bill of Rights not because of what they had done, but on account of their race. In the wake of the Japanese Navy's surprise attack on Pearl Harbor, the U.S. government forcibly evacuated 110,000 Japanese Americans from their West Coast homes and interned them for the duration of the war in concentration camps which were euphemistically referred to as "Relocation Centers." Without conducting individual reviews of the accused,[4] the government executed the evacuation and internment program of a thitherto unheard-of magnitude because of "race prejudice, war hysteria and a failure of political leadership."[5] Such a blatant infringement upon the constitutional rights of resident alien Japanese and U.S. citizens of Japanese ancestry naturally could not have happened in a vacuum without widespread culture of racial prejudice condoning the discriminatory treatment of a nonwhite ethnic group. The Japanese American history is fraught with incidents of racial discrimination against Issei (pre-World War II Japanese immigrants) and Nisei (U.S.-born children of Japanese immigrants). Discriminatory laws, acts and practices aimed at the Japanese American community since the 1890's had contributed to creating a milieu where Japan's hostile act against the United States could easily trigger virulent retaliatory measures against the Japanese Americans who were misidentified with the enemy. It, therefore, would behoove us to briefly examine the pre-World War II history of Japanese Americans with a view to understanding their traumatic wartime experience in a proper historical context.

1. Immigration Period, 1884-1924

Japanese were the second Asian group to immigrate to the United States. Attracted by high wages paid by the sugar industry, they first went to the Kingdom of Hawaii in 1884 as contract immigrants under the auspices of the Japanese government. As a labor shortage grew grim on the West Coast in the wake of the 1882 Chinese Exclusion Act, Japanese immigrants began arriving in the continental United States in the 1890's.

When the United States annexed Hawaii following the Spanish American War of 1898, an American law prohibiting indentured immigration also applied to the islands, voiding the labor contracts under which the Japanese were toiling on the sugar plantations. Because Hawaii became a part of the United States, Japanese laborers now could remigrate freely to the West Coast states where wages were substantially higher than on the islands.

Due to remigration from Hawaii and undocumented migration from Canada and Mexico, the Japanese population in the continental United States grew rapidly from 1,979 in 1890 to 78,268 in 1906, when 59 percent of this ethnic group resided in California.[6] Alarmed by the large influx of nonwhite immigrants, Californians quickly rekindled their anti-Asiatic hostility which had culminated two decades earlier in the exclusion of Chinese from the United States. The San Francisco earthquake of 1906 triggered a series of anti-Japanese incidents. Amidst the chaos caused by the virtual devastation of the city, several Japanese residents were assaulted, while Japanese-owned businesses were boycotted and extorted.[7]

In October 1906, the San Francisco Board of Education passed a resolution to segregate Chinese, Japanese, and Korean pupils from the white student body by requiring the Asians to attend the Oriental Public School. The Board alleged that the conflagration ensuing the earthquake had destroyed a number of schools, creating overcrowded classrooms, and that Japanese were too old and immoral to attend the same schools as American children. However, the resolution was actually aimed at only 93 Japanese pupils enrolled at 23 different schools, of whom 25 were native-born U.S. citizens. Furthermore, no more that 12 Japanese students were 18 to 20 years of age. They could have lawfully attended public schools which under the existing law could admit any students aged six through 21. The Japanese government lodged a protest with the U.S. government, asserting that the Board's segregation order was a discriminatory measure in violation of the Japan-U.S. Treaty of Commerce and Navigation of 1894.[8]

The intervention by President Theodore Roosevelt, a Republican, initially met stiff resistance from the San Francisco Board of Education which was controlled by the Union Labor Party. It was not until the federal government promised to take three concrete steps to curb Japanese immigration that the Board agreed to rescind the resolution. First, Congress enacted in February 1907, a more restrictive immigration law, "An Act to Regulate the Immigration of Aliens into the United States." Section 1 of the Act authorized the President to deny entry into the continental United States to aliens possessing passports issued by their governments for going to any country other than the United States or to any insular possession of this country, such as Hawaii, if the aliens' arrival was predicted to be injurious to American labor.[9] And Section 36 provided that all aliens who shall enter the United States except at its seaports or other entry points designated by the Secretary of Commerce and Labor "shall be adjudged to have entered the country unlawfully and shall be deported...."[10] Three weeks after the passage of this immigration law, the Board revoked the segregation order relative to Japanese students, but enforced the resolution against Chinese and Korean children.[11]

Second, President Roosevelt issued an Executive Order in March 1907, specifically banning the entry into the mainland of Japanese immigrant laborers from Hawaii, Canada and Mexico.[12] The Executive Order also applied to Koreans, since Korea had become a Japanese protectorate following the Russo-Japanese War of 1904-1905. The 1907 immigration law and the presidential decree effectively curtailed Japanese remigration to the continental United States from the three sources.

Third and last, the U.S. government, not content with merely prohibiting the flow of Japanese subjects into the mainland from Hawaii, Canada and Mexico, now sought to ban the influx of Japanese immigrant laborers directly from Japan. By March 1908, U.S. Ambassador to Japan Thomas O'Brien and Japanese Foreign Minister Tadasu Hayashi reached through the exchange of memoranda an informal agreement on how to curtail Japanese immigration to the United States.[13] Under this arrangement, commonly known as the "Gentlemen's Agreement," the Tokyo government voluntarily restricted the emigration of Japanese laborers by refusing to issue them passports for the United States.

Nevertheless, the Gentlemen's Agreement permitted the parents, wives and children of resident immigrants to enter this country for family reunification. The Japanese immigrants took advantage of this provision to send for so-called "picture brides" who, prior to their departure from Japan, had been married by proxy to their bridegrooms who were living on the other side of the Pacific. Such marriages arranged by matchmakers on the basis of the potential couples' photographs were not only legal in Japan, but also consistent with the Japanese cultural norm.[14] Between 1911 and 1920, 34,216 Japanese women came to the United States, raising the number of women in the mainland from 985 in 1900 to 38,303 in 1920, when the women constituted 35 percent of the Japanese American population.[15]

As increasing numbers of Japanese women arrived in the United States where they quickly developed families, anti-Japanese forces began denouncing the immigration of picture brides as immoral, un-Christian, and antithetical to American values. The Japanophobes also criticized the influx of these women as a violation of the Gentlemen's Agreement on the ground that they became "immigrant laborers" upon arrival in this country. Most of the picture brides, the critics alleged, worked side by side with their husbands in farming, small businesses and domestic service, in addition to being mothers and homemakers. Moreover, the anti-Japanese agitators vituperated the high birth rate of Japanese immigrant women, who, by virtue of being in the child-bearing age, naturally had superior reproductive capacity relative to the national average. What the opponents of Japanese female immigration feared the most was the inevitable consequence that the women would sooner or later have Nisei who were automatically U.S. citizens enjoying the same constitutional rights as any fellow citizens, and that Issei would settle down, develop families, and perpetuate the Japanese presence in American society.

With a view, however, to preventing the violent anti-Chinese movement of the late nineteenth century from being resurrected against the Japanese, the Imperial government abruptly discontinued in 1920 the issuance of passports to picture brides. When they stopped coming to the United States, 42.5 percent of Japanese immigrant men were still single.[16] Unless they chose to return to Japan, it was practically impossible for these men to ever marry in this country, for many states had anti-miscegenation statutes forbidding interracial marriages between whites and Asians.[17] To make matters worse, Congress in 1922 enacted the Cable Act which was aimed at discouraging American-born women of Asian ancestry from marrying Chinese or Japanese men, who were ineligible to become U.S. citizens through naturalization, by stripping American women of their citizenship should they marry such ineligible aliens. Section 3 of the Act provided in part that "any woman citizen who marries an alien ineligible to citizenship shall cease to be a citizen of the United States." Furthermore, Section 5 made such a woman ineligible for naturalization during the continuance of her marriage with the ineligible alien."[18] In 1936, the League of Women Voters successfully waged a legislative campaign to have Congress repeal the Cable Act, because it discriminated against women in general by imposing on them an undue burden to which no male citizens were subjected.[19]

The premature cessation of female immigration, coupled with the state and federal anti-miscegenation legislation, deprived many Japanese men of their fundamental right to marry. However, the Japanese community, unlike the Chinese counterpart, received a significant number of women who later had tremendous impact on the educational attainment of their American-born children, as well as on the Nisei's attitudes towards education. Younger than their husbands by up to ten years,[20] the picture brides generally had higher levels of formal education; many had a high school education. Because of their educational backgrounds, the Japanese mothers inculcated in the Nisei the importance of education, particularly in the face of widespread discrimination against Asiatics.

Before World War II, Japanese Americans were subjected to many forms of racial discrimination which not only severely abridged their constitutional rights, but also harshly affected this ethnic group economically, educationally, socially, and psychologically. In 1913, the California Legislature enacted an Alien Land Law aimed at prohibiting Japanese immigrants from owning real property or leasing agricultural land for over three years.[21] The denial of landownership and long-term leasehold was predicated upon the Mongoloid people's purported ineligibility to become naturalized U.S. citizens. When the Alien Land Law went into effect in 1913, Japanese farmers in California owned 26,707 acres and had 254,980 acres under lease, which respectively accounted for only 0.2 percent and 2.3 percent of the state's total arable land exceeding 11,000,000 acres.[22]

In order to strengthen the 1913 Alien Land Law, the anti-Japanese forces, such as the Native Sons and Daughters of the Golden West, the American Legion and the California Oriental Exclusion League, successful placed an amendment on the ballot of the 1920 general election. The voters of California overwhelmingly approved the initiative, which went into effect as the Alien Land Law of 1920.[23] Besides banning any type of land leasing by Japanese immigrants, the law prohibited them from purchasing land under the names of their Nisei children and from serving as their guardians in connection with such real property. The law provided not only criminal penalties for the violations thereof, but also an escheat procedure to confiscate land which had been acquired in contravention of the Alien Land Law.[24] Between 1912 and 1923, Arizona, Washington, Oregon, Idaho, Texas, and Nebraska enacted similar alien land laws to squeeze the Japanese out of the agricultural industry which claimed over 44 percent of the Japanese American labor force in 1920.[25]

Takao Ozawa, an alien Japanese, instituted a test case in 1914 for the specific purpose of rendering the various states' alien land laws inapplicable to Japanese by proving that he was eligible to become a naturalized citizen of the United States. In 1922, the U.S. Supreme Court held in *Ozawa v. United States* that since the nationalization acts had traditionally granted naturalization to only "aliens being free white persons, and to aliens of African nativity," the Japanese race, which was neither white nor black, was ineligible for naturalization.[26] With their validity thus confirmed by the nation's highest court, the alien land laws in the Western States effectively excluded Japanese immigrants from the agricultural industry except as farm laborers or sharecroppers. Many of those who had been precluded from farming became gardeners in large urban areas such as Los Angeles and San Francisco.[27]

In the wake of the Supreme Court decision in *Ozawa v. United States*, Congress legislated the exclusion of Japanese immigrants on the basis of their inability to become naturalized U.S. citizens. Instead of granting Japan an annual quota of 146 immigrants, which was equivalent to 2 percent of the Japanese population in the continental United States in 1890,[28] Congress favored the total cessation of Japanese immigration after the fashion of the 1882 Chinese Exclusion Act. Section 13 (c) of the 1924 Immigration Act provided in part: "No alien ineligible to citizenship shall be admitted to the United States...."[29] It was not until 1952 that Japanese immigration was resumed on a small scale.

2.   War Years

The most outrageous act of racism against Japanese Americans was committed during World War II. In the heat of extreme hostility toward this ethnic group triggered by the Japanese bombing on Pearl Harbor on December 7, 1941, the U.S. government uprooted 110,000 West Coast Japanese Americans in the spring of 1942 and detained them in 16 concentration camps for the duration of the war without due process of law. Located in desolate, inhospitable parts of the interior, the 16 detention facilities consisted of three kinds: (1) ten large Relocation Centers run by the War Relocation Authority (WRA) to incarcerate most of the evacuated Japanese American families; (2) four internment camps administered by the Justice Department to detain so-called dangerous enemy aliens who were in fact nothing more than ordinary community leaders; and (3) two citizen isolation centers maintained by the WRA to separate suspected Nisei "troublemakers" from the rest of the internees in the Relocation Centers.[30] Approximately 70 percent of the detainees were native-born U.S. citizens who were mostly between the ages of ten and 30.[31] During the wartime incarceration, 5,981 babies were born and 1,862 internees including new-born babies died in the concentration camps.[32]

As a result of the evacuation and internment, the Japanese Americans not only sustained severe financial losses, but also experienced abrupt and prolonged disruption of their education, not to mention the destruction of their economic base and the loss of self-esteem arising from the extraordinary humiliation and degradation the harsh war measures had inflicted on them. The Japanese American community's property losses alone amounted to $370 million, which would have been worth $2 billion in the early 1980's due to inflation alone.[33] Under the Japanese American Evacuation Claims Act of 1948, many of the former internees were compensated between 1949 and 1965 strictly for "damage to or loss of real or personal property" incurred in connection with the evacuation.[34] On account of the claimants' inability to produce such documentary evidence as receipts for their lost or damaged property, they were awarded only $37 million in inflated postwar dollars for 26,568 claims which had initially sought $148 million.[35] With inflation factored in, the Japanese Americans received under the Evacuation Claims Act no more than five cents for every dollar lost.

Behind the barbed wire, Nisei children continued their education under extremely adverse conditions. Since the government had not contemplated the education of the youngsters as one of the top priorities in interning the West Coast Japanese Americans, approximately 30,000 students resumed their studies in partitionless barracks with little or no furniture. The War Relocation Authority hastily hired some 100 white teachers, whose attrition rate quickly turned out to be quite high because of the severe and primitive environment in the concentration camps. In order to alleviate the dearth of certified teachers, the WRA used over 100 college-educated Nisei internees as assistant teachers.[36] The Japanese American teachers received $19 per month, the maximum salary available to the internees.[37] Some schools had makeshift science laboratories with little or no equipment; others had no typewriters for typing classes. The curriculum was limited due to the lack of qualified teachers, whereas textbooks and other instructional materials were always in short supply.[38]

One of the WRA reports vividly depicted as follows the inauspicious circumstances under which the detained Nisei children had to study in 1942:

> Sometimes the teachers had a desk and chair; more
> often she had only a chair. In the first few weeks

many of the children had no desks or chairs and for the most part were obliged to sit on the floor—or stand up all day.

Textbooks and other supplies were gradually arriving. Laboratory and shop equipment and facilities, however, were still lacking. No center had been able to obtain its full quota of teachers.[39]

Bruce Kaji, a prominent retired Nisei banker, testified at the August 6, 1981 hearing of the Commission on Wartime Relocation and Internment of Civilians held in Los Angeles:

The lack of qualified evacuee teachers, the shortage of trained teachers was awful. I remember having to read a chapter a week in Chemistry and discovering at the end of the semester that we had finished one full year's course. There was a total loss of scheduling with no experiments, demonstrations or laboratory work.[40]

Notwithstanding such constraints as were imposed on the detainees' schools, all of them, with the exception of those in the Tule Lake Relocation Center, received accreditation, while the students were able to transfer most of the credits to regular schools outside the concentration camps.[41]

In the face of the hopeless situation existing behind the barbed wire, the Japanese immigrant parents, especially mothers, encouraged their American-born children to make education their top priority. Consequently, over 7,000 Nisei graduated from high school while in captivity.[42] As many as 4,300 relocated from the detention centers to the Midwest and the East Coast to pursue higher education.[43] The National Japanese American Student Relocation Council and several church groups, most notably the American Friends Service Committee, assisted many of these Nisei students in finding institutions willing to admit them, and in providing the students with scholarships, living quarters, and part-time jobs while attending college.[44]

Dr. Gladys Ishida Stone, a Professor Emeritus of Sociology at the University of Wisconsin-River Falls, was one of the daring Nisei college students who relocated in early 1942 to the potentially hostile parts of the country to attend college. Her mother, a graduate of Ochanomizu Women's College in Tokyo, insisted that her children get a college education, even though an end to the massive detention was nowhere in sight. Gladys Ishida was released from the Amache Relocation Center in Granada, Colorado, to enroll at Washington University in St. Louis, Missouri, where she received a B.S. in Business Administration. She later earned an M.A. in International Relations at the University of Chicago, and a Ph.D. in Far Eastern Studies at the University of Michigan. Dr. Ishida Stone ascribes part of her academic success to her mother's constant admonition to get a good education, as well as the tremendous sacrifice her widowed mother made to enable her daughter to concentrate on her studies.[45]

Despite the outrageous violations by their own government of their Bill of Rights, about 33,000 Nisei men joined the Army to perform combat duties and intelligence activities during the war years.[46] Amidst the general public's tenacious and deep-rooted distrust of Japanese Americans' loyalty to the United States, these Nisei men in the armed forces chose to prove once and for all their patriotism with their deed and blood.

Approximately one half of the Japanese American soldiers served in the 442nd Regimental Combat Team (RCT), a famed all-Nisei unit, to fight the Nazis in Europe.[47] The Nisei distinguished themselves as incomparably valorous and skilled fighters in seven major campaigns, in which they sustained 9,486 casualties including 680 fatalities.[48] One of the 442nd's outstanding exploits was the rescue in October 1944 of 211 Texan soldiers in the 1st Battalion of the 141st Infantry Regiment, the 36th Division, who had been pinned down by the German artillery in the Vosges Mountains, Southern France. In saving the "Lost Battalion," the Japanese American soldiers suffered 814 casualties, including 140 deaths, an outlandishly heavy toll for the number of the rescued.[49] The 442nd RCT received as a unit seven Presidential Distinguished Unit Citations, 87 Division Commendations and 36 Army Commendations, as well as 18,143 individual decorations consisting, among others, of one Congressional Medal of Honor, 52 Distinguished Service Crosses, 560 Silver Stars, 4,000 Bronze Stars, and 9,486 Purple Hearts.[50] The all-Nisei Regiment thus became the most decorated Army unit of a comparable size during World War II.

Military Intelligence Service Specialists, commonly known as MIS'ers, were another group of Nisei soldiers who made great contributions to America's war efforts. Between 1941 and 1946, some 6,000 Nisei men received intensive training in the Military Intelligence Service Language School, which was initially opened in San Francisco one month prior to the Japanese attack on Pearl Harbor and then moved to Minnesota in June 1942 after even Nisei soldiers in U.S. Army uniform became excludable from the military zone along the Pacific Coast. During the War, 3,700 of these MIS'ers were assigned to numerous combat zones in the Pacific Theater of Operations extending from the Aleutian Islands to New Zealand, as well as in the China-Burma-India Theater and the Philippines.[51] They rendered invaluable services to the Allied Forces by decoding intercepted enemy communications, translating captured documents and battle plans, and interrogating Japanese prisoners of war. Major General Charles A. Willoughby, General Douglas MacArthur's Chief of Intelligence, extolled the accomplishments of the Nisei soldiers in the Military Intelligence Service:

> Never before in history did an army know so much concerning its enemy, prior to actual engagement, as did the American Army during most of the Pacific campaigns.[52]

Nicknamed as the "eyes and ears of the Allied Pacific Forces,"[53] the Japanese American MIS'ers were credited with shortening the Pacific War by two years, thereby saving one million lives.[54] Due to the confidential nature of military intelligence, however, documents pertaining to the Nisei language specialists' activities were not declassified until the mid-1970's.[55]

Nisei soldiers' unparalleled feats in combat and intelligence notwithstanding, many Midwestern and Eastern colleges refused to admit qualified Japanese American students released from the concentration camps, partly on the pretext that these institutions had classified defense contracts and partly due to pressure from local Japanophobic groups and organizations. The University of Minnesota was one of such schools. In November 1943, the Regents of the University passed a resolution prohibiting the admission of Japanese American students.[56] Professor George Hoshino of the School of Social Work at the University of Minnesota was dismayed upon discovering in 1983 the existence of such a regental resolution. In his October 10, 1984, letter to this author, Professor Hoshino adroitly expressed his disbelief and indignation:

> I am an MIS'er, although I went through Snelling rather late, in 1945, after I, along with several hundred other Nisei, got diverted at the last minute from being sent as replacements for the 442nd who were then getting involved in the Battle of the Bulge....
>
> But, I recall being irked because, although an American citizen by birth and a member of the U.S. Army, I probably would have been denied admission to the University had I applied. It is even more ironic that I am now a tenured professor on the University's faculty.[57]

Professor Hoshino was a valedictorian at his high school on the West Coast. If he had applied for admission to the University of Minnesota in 1945 while he was stationed in Fort Snelling receiving MIS training, he would have been rejected solely on the basis of his ancestry.

However, thousands of Nisei men and women obtained from the War Relocation Authority leave clearance to move out of the Relocation Centers and acquired a higher education in the Midwest and on the East Coast. Furthermore, thousands of other Japanese American men, who had served in the Armed Forces of the United States during World War II, attended college on GI Bills in the post-war period. With the Japanese Empire vanquished, the American public grew more tolerant of Japanese Americans, while many policy makers were beginning to feel guilty about the indiscriminate exclusion and detention of the entire West Coast Japanese American community. Although the harsh war measures had wreaked havoc on the majority of Japanese American internees, significant numbers of Nisei built self-confidence and regained self-esteem through their distinguished military service under the most trying circumstances, as well as through their academic success demonstrated in many Midwestern and Eastern institutions of higher learning immediately following their mass incarceration. Once given opportunities to develop their potential, these highly motivated Nisei with proven discipline and perseverance quickly excelled in whichever fields were opened to them.

3.   Postwar Period

When President Harry S. Truman presented the 442nd RCT with the seventh Presidential Unit Citation in 1946, he congratulated the Nisei soldiers:

> You fought for the free nations of the world... you fought not only the enemy, you fought prejudice — and you won.[58]

Although Japanese Americans' victory over racial prejudice in American society has not been as total and decisive as President Truman may have imparted, they have slowly but steadily eradicated racism. Shortly after the war, Japanese immigrants and Nisei challenged the unconstitutionality of California's Alien Land Laws. By 1952, they successfully fought legal battles in *Oyama v. California, Sei Fujii v. State of California*, and *Haruye Masaoka v. State of California* to have both the U.S. and California Supreme Courts hold that the Alien Land Laws were unconstitutional as violative of the equal protection clause of the Fourteenth Amendment.[59]

To toll a death knell for the Alien Land Laws, the Japanese American Citizens League (JACL) spearheaded a campaign to repeal through the initiative the legislation which had seriously undermined Japanese American farming activities for decades by denying the immigrant generation landownership and leasehold. Reflecting a drastic change in popular sentiments toward this persecuted and yet superpatriotic group, such traditionally anti-Japanese organizations as the American Legion, California State Grange and labor unions now endorsed the JACL's repeal measure, Proposition 13. California voters approved the proposition by a two to one margin in the November 4, 1956 general election.[60]

Unlike the repeal of the Alien Land Laws which represented a symbolic victory for the Japanese American community, the passage of the Immigration and Nationality Act of 1952, widely known as the Walter-McCarran Act, was far more significant for alien Japanese residing in the United States and for all Asian immigrants for that matter. Thanks to the Japanese American Citizens League's energetic and astute lobbying, Congress inserted in the legislation a provision making all aliens eligible for naturalization. Section 311 of the Act provided in pertinent part:

> The right of a person to become a naturalized citizen of the United States shall not be denied or abridged because of race or sex or because such person is married....[61]

Although the Walter-McCarran Act thus removed all racial barriers to naturalization, it retained a substantial racial obstacle to Asian immigration to the United States.

The 1952 Immigration and Nationality Act established a quota system based on national origins, which favored European immigration at the expense of Asians and Pacific Islanders. The annual quota of any European nation, for example, equaled one-sixth of one percent of the number of that nation's citizens residing in the continental United States in 1920. Any country or quota area within the Asia-Pacific triangle, on the other hand, was given the annual quota of only 100, the minimum quota provided for in the Act.[62]

It was not until the enactment of the 1964 Immigration and Nationality Act that the discriminatory quota system based on national origins was finally abolished. Section 2(a) of the Act provided in part:

> No person shall receive any preference or priority or be discriminated against in the issuance of an immigrant visa because of his race, sex, nationality, place of birth, or place of residence....[63]

The Act provided every nation with the same maximum allowable quota of 20,000 per year. However, the new nondiscriminatory quota system did not take effect until July 1, 1968.[64] Moreover, the 1964 Immigration and Nationality Act, which was aimed primarily at family reunification, hardly benefited Japanese Americans, for few of them had immediate family members in Japan who would have qualified for immigrant visas.

Japanese Americans' latest accomplishment in the area of civil rights was the passage of the Civil Liberties Act of 1988. Despite a widely anticipated veto, President Ronald Reagan signed the Act into law in August 1988,[65] largely due to the political astuteness of the Japanese American Senators and Representatives, as well as to systematic and skillful lobbying by the Japanese American Citizens League and grass-roots groups like the National Coalition for Redress/Reparations. The law was aimed at providing the survivors of the wartime internment, grossly underestimated at 60,000 then, with $20,000 each in personal compensation for the grave injustice to which they were subjected by their own government.[66] Moreover, the Act offered a Congressional apology on behalf of the American people for the blatant violations of the Japanese Americans' constitutional rights. In Section 2. **STATEMENT OF THE CONGRESS**, the Congress of the United States acknowledged:

> [A] grave injustice was done to both citizens and permanent resident aliens of Japanese ancestry by the evacuation, relocation, and internment of civilians during World War II.... The excluded individuals of Japanese ancestry suffered enormous damages, both material and intangible, and there were incalculable losses in education and job training, all of which resulted in significant human suffering for which appropriate compensation has not been made. For these fundamental violations of the basic civil liberties and constitutional rights of these individuals of Japanese ancestry, the Congress apologizes on behalf of the Nation.[67]

Unfortunately, however, there was a huge discrepancy between what Congress had initially intended to do and the subsequent legislative action.

The Civil Liberties Act authorized the total appropriation of $1.25 billion over a ten-year period to carry out the legislative intent, provided that the annual appropriation could not exceed $500 million in any fiscal year. Section 105(a)(1) provided in part:

> [T]he Attorney General shall, subject to the availability of funds appropriated to the Fund for such purpose, pay out of the Fund to each eligible individual the sum of $20,000....[68]

However, few people foresaw the possibility that the Act itself could be meaningless as it related to monetary compensation unless Congress annually appropriated sufficient funds for this purpose. When President Reagan disclosed on January 9, 1989, his budget for fiscal 1990, it allocated only $20 million to provide compensation for merely 1,000 individuals under the Civil Liberties Act. The House of Representatives subsequently increased redress appropriations to $50 million to provide compensation for 2,500 victims of the wartime incarceration 85 years of age and over.[69]

Surprisingly, the Senate Appropriations Subcommittee appropriated no funds for fiscal 1990, but voted on September 12, 1989, to make funding for the Civil Liberties Act a three-year entitlement program beginning in fiscal 1991.[70] Under this arrangement, the redress compensation program would no longer be subjected to the whims of Congress each year at the time of appropriations bills.

At the urging of Senator Daniel Inouye, the Senate approved an entitlement program which would automatically receive $1.25 billion over three years for redress payments.[71] Senator Inouye emphasized the advantage of the entitlement program:

> I believe that this approach ensures that all internees will receive payments as quickly as possible. It also avoids a difficult annual appropriations struggle, pitting reparations payments against funding for other government programs.[72]

Since the House and Senate differed on funding for the Civil Liberties Act, a conference committee had to work out a compromise for final approval. On October 19, 1989, the Senate-House conference committee approved the Senate version of a federal entitlement program.[73]

On October 26, 1989, the House of Representatives approved by a 323-81 vote a conference report on the $17.2 billion appropriations bill for Commerce, Justice, State and Judiciary, which contained the entitlement program for the redress payments.[74] The Senate approved the conference report on November 8,[75] and the appropriations bill was signed into law by President George Bush on November 21.[76]

The long overdue personal compensation for the survivors of American's concentration camps finally became a reality. During this legislative labyrinth, however, about 200 prospective beneficiaries were passing away every month.[77] Approximately 40,000 former internees died before the enactment of the Civil Liberties Act of 1988. An additional 5,000 eligible persons are estimated to have died by the time the first reparations checks were mailed out in October 1990.[78] Representative Robert Matsui, one of the four Japanese American members of Congress who had tirelessly, fearlessly and successfully fought for the passage of the redress bill, poignantly expressed the sentiments of the Japanese American community:

> My heart sinks for the many internees who don't live to see their payment. Once again, we have been forced to accept a postdated check—one that unfortunately will never reach thousands of internees who will die before the first payments are made.[79]

For many former internees, justice done too late was no justice at all. Thanks to liberalized eligibility for redress payments, however, the Office of Redress Administration in the U.S. Justice Department disbursed nearly $1.6 billion by October 8, 1993, to provide over 79,000 victims with $20,000 compensation.[80] In Minnesota, 305 Japanese Americans received redress checks by September 30, 1993.[81]

4. Conclusion

The Japanese Americans, like many of their nonwhite predecessors, have long toiled under racial discrimination in American society. Their predicament was further compounded by the deteriorating U.S.-Japan relations culminating in World War II in the Pacific Theater of Operations. The Japanese American experience was unique in that the U.S. government imprisoned 110,000 innocent and loyal citizens and permanent residents of Japanese ancestry in American concentration camps in flagrant disregard of their constitutional rights. Their history became even more unique when the Japanese Americans refused to succumb to their unconstitutional incarceration and succeeded 46 years later in having the U.S. government apologize for its wartime violation of their Bill of Rights and appropriate $1.6 billion for redress payments. Such a Congressional acknowledgment of governmental wrongdoing perpetrated during World

War II and the costly legislative remedy half a century later are unheard-of in the bicentennial history of the United States or any other nation in the world.

Depending on one's perspective, the Japanese American community's successful redress campaign in the late 1980's may be interpreted differently. It may mean that the United States is big and honest enough to admit and correct its own mistakes no matter how costly redress may be, and that justice eventually prevails in American society. Or it may be argued that the enactment of the 1988 Civil Liberties Act was an exception to the rule, and that reparation provided by the Act was too little too late. Whichever view one may subscribe to, the fact remains that the U.S. government deprived the Japanese Americans' constitutional rights by indiscriminately incarcerating them during World War II without due process of law, and that Congress passed a redress bill almost half a century later to apologize for the unconstitutional wartime internment of the Japanese Americans and to provide the surviving former internees with redress payments which would ultimately reach $1.6 billion by the end of the 1994 fiscal year.

The Japanese Americans' cataclysmic wartime experience should not be regarded as a thing of the distant past or a tragedy peculiar to this small ethnic group. Similar transgression by the U.S. government of the Bill of Rights could have happened or could happen in the future to other minority groups, racial or otherwise, under different circumstances. The Iranian crisis of 1980 and the Gulf War in 1991 are cases in point. American democracy did and could malfunction from time to time, especially with respect to nonwhite minority groups. We must use the Japanese American experience as a lesson to prevent the derailment of the U.S. Constitution and American democracy and to guarantee justice and equality for all.

NOTES

[1] U.S. Bureau of the Census, *1990 Census of Population: General Population Characteristics, United States,* Table 3A. Race and Hispanic Origin: 1990 (Washington D.C.: Government Printing Office, 1992), p. 3.

[2] _____ , *United States Department of Commerce News* (June 12, 1991), Table 3C. Race and Hispanic Origin for the United States and Regions: 1990; Table 5B. Asian or Pacific Islander Persons by Group for the United States and States, no pagination.

[3] _____ , *1990 Census of Population: General Population Characteristics, Minnesota,* Table 3. Race and Hispanic Origin: 1990 (Washington, D.C.: Government Printing Office, 1992), p. 17.

[4] U.S. The Commission on Wartime Relocation and Internment of Civilians (hereafter CWRIC), *Personal Justice Denied* (Washington, D.C.: Government Printing Office, 1982), pp. 2-3.

[5] *Ibid.*, p. 18.

[6] Japan. Naikaku Tokeikyoku, *Nihon Teikoku Tokei Nenkan, 1891* (Tokyo: Naikaku Tokeikyoku, 1891), p. 65; _____ , *Nihon Teikoku Tokei Nenkan, 1907* (Tokyo: Naikaku Tokeikyoku, 1907), p. 67.

[7] Yamato Ichihashi, *Japanese In the United States* (New York: Arno Press and The New York Times, 1969), pp. 234-236.

[8] Japan. Gaimusho, *Nihon Gaiko Bunsho: Taibei Imin Mondai Keika Gaiyo* (Tokyo: Gaimusho, 1972), pp. 140-143.

[9] An Act to Regulate the Immigration of Aliens into the United States, 20 February 1907, *The Statutes at Large of the United States of America from December, 1905, to March, 1907* (Washington, D.C.: Government Printing Office, 1907), Vol. 34, Pt. 1, p. 898.

[10] *Ibid.*, p. 908.

[11] Japan. Gaimusho, *Nihon Gaiko Bunsho: Annexes to Summary of the Course of Negotiations between Japan and the United States concerning the Problems of Japanese Immigration in the United States* (Tokyo: Gaimusho, 1973), p. 21.

[12] Executive Order 589 (March 14, 1907), *Presidential Executive Orders*: Numbers 1-7,403 (June, 1845 - June, 1936) (New York: Dobbs Ferry, 1980), no pagination; U.S. Bureau of Immigration and Naturalization, *Immigration Laws and Regulations of July 1, 1907* (Washington, D.C.: Government Printing Office, 1908), p. 40.

[13] Gaimusho, *Nihon Gaiko Bunsho: Annexes to Summary ..., Annex No. 17: Gentlemen's Agreement*, pp. 35-112.

[14] Zaibei Nihonjinkai, *Zaibei Nihonjinshi* (San Francisco: Zaibei Nihonjinkai, 1941), p. 90.

[15] Ichihashi, *Japanese in the United States*, pp. 70-72.

[16] U.S. Bureau of the Census, *Abstract of the Fourteenth Census of the United States, 1920*, Table 52. Marital Condition of the Population 15 Years of Age and Over, by Classes, for the United States: 1890 to 1920 (Washington, D.C.: Government Printing Office, 1923), pp. 216-217.

[17] For anti-miscegenation statutes, see Megumi Dick Osumi, "Asians and California's Anti-Miscegenation Laws," in Nobuya Tsuchida (ed.), *Asian and Pacific American Experiences: Women's Perspectives* (Minneapolis: Asian/Pacific American Learning Resource Center, University of Minnesota, 1982), pp. 1-37. California, for example, had such anti-miscegenation statutes prohibiting white-Asian marriages between 1880 and 1948, It was not until 1967, however, that the United States Supreme Court in *Loving v. Virginia* invalidated all the anti-miscegenation statutes still extant in 16 states as being violative of the equal protection and due process clause of the Fourteenth Amendment.

[18] Public Law No. 346, *The Statutes at Large of the United States of America from April, 1921 to March, 1923* (Washington, D.C.: Government Printing Office, 1923), p. 1022.

[19] Frank F. Chuman, *The Bamboo People: The Law and Japanese-Americans* (Del Mar, California: Publisher's Inc., 1976), pp. 165-166.

[20] Evelyn Nakano Glenn, *Issei, Nisei, War Bride: Three Generations of Japanese American Women in Domestic Service* (Philadelphia: Temple University Press, 1986), p. 43.

[21] California Statutes, Chapter 113, Sections 1 and 2, *The Statutes of California and Amendments to the Codes Passed at the Fortieth Session of the Legislature, 1913* (Sacramento: Superintendent of State Printing, 1913), pp. 206-207.

[22] Ichihashi, *Japanese in the United States*, p. 193.

[23] Chuman, *The Bamboo People* ..., pp. 77-79.

[24] Alien Land Law, *California Statutes, 1919-1921* (San Francisco: Bancroft-Whitney Company, 1921), pp. LXXXVII-XC.

[25] U.S. Bureau of the Census, *Fourteenth Census of the United States Taken in the Year 1920*, Table 5. Total Persons 10 Years of Age and Over Engaged in Each Specified Occupation, Classified by Sex, Color or Race, Nativity, and Parentage, for the United States: 1920 (Washington, D.C.: Government Printing Office, 1923), Vol. 4, pp. 342-343.

[26] *Ozawa v. United States*, 260 U.S. 178, 195, 198 (1922); Bill Hosokawa, *Nisei: The Quiet Americans* (New York: William Morrow and Company, Inc., 1969), p. 91. In 1870, Congress extended the privilege of naturalization to "aliens of African nativity and to persons of African descent."

[27] For Japanese gardeners in California, see Nobuya Tsuchida, "Japanese Gardeners in Southern California, 1900-1941," in Lucie Cheng and Edna Bonacich (eds.), *Labor Immigration under Capitalism: Asian Workers in the United States before World War II* (Berkeley, Los Angeles and London: University of California Press, 1984), pp. 435-469.

[28] Ichihashi, *Japanese in the United States*, p. 318; Hosokawa, *Nisei* ..., p. 111. All European nations received annual immigration quotas equal to 2% of the numbers of their citizens residing in the continental United States as reported in the 1890 U.S. census.

[29] Immigration Act of 1924, Chapter 190, Section 13(c), *The Statutes at Large of the United States of America from December, 1923, to March, 1925* (Washington, D.C.: Government Printing Office, 1925), Vol. 43, Pt. 1, p. 162.

[30] For the two isolation centers at Moab, Utah, and Leupp, Arizona, see Michi Weglyn, *Years of Infamy: The Untold Story of America's Concentration Camps* (New York: William Morrow and Company, Inc. 1976), pp. 125-132.

[31] Dillon S. Myer, *Uprooted Americans: The Japanese Americans and the War Relocation Authority during World War II* (Tucson: University of Arizona Press, 1971), pp. 30, 32.

[32] CWRIC, *Personal Justice Denied*, p. 150.

[33] Nobuya Tsuchida, *American Justice: Japanese American Evacuation and Redress Cases* (Minneapolis: Asian/Pacific American Learning Resource Center, University of Minnesota, 1988), p. 1.

[34] Public Law 886, Chapter 814 (July 2, 1948), *United States Statutes at Large* (Washington, D.C.: Government Printing Office, 1949), Vol. 62, Pt. 1, pp. 1231-1233.

[35] CWRIC, *Personal Justice Denied*, p. 118; Hosokawa, *Nisei* ..., pp. 445-446.

[36] Myer, *Uprooted Americans* ..., pp. 48-51. Before World War II, there were very few Nisei teachers and many potential teachers were discouraged from majoring in education, because Japanese Americans were practically excluded from the teaching profession. For the *de facto* preclusion of Japanese Americans from teaching jobs in the prewar period, see Harry H.L. Kitano, *Japanese Americans: The Evolution of a Subculture* (Englewood Cliffs, New Jersey: Prentice-Hall, Inc., 1976), p. 97.

[37] Myer, *Uprooted Americans* ..., p. 52.

[38] CWRIC, *Personal Justice Denied*, pp. 170-171.

[39] Report of the War Relocation Authority, October 1 - December 31, 1942, pp. 14-15, as quoted in CWRIC, *Personal Justice Denied*, p. 170.

[40] Testimony, Bruce Kaji, Los Angeles, August 6, 1981, p. 272, as quoted in CWRIC, *Personal Justice Denied*, p. 171.

[41] CWRIC, *Personal Justice Denied*, p. 171.

[42] Myer, *Uprooted Americans* ..., p. 48.

[43] Roger Daniels, *Concentration Camps USA: Japanese Americans and World War II* (Hinsdale, Illinois: The Dryden Press, 1971), p. 100. Many Nisei who had already been in college when the War started were allowed to move out of the West Coast military zone to resume their studies while they were still in the Assembly Centers, makeshift detention facilities where Japanese Americans were held prior to the completion of the ten Relocation Centers.

[44] CWRIC, *Personal Justice Denied*, p. 181; Weglyn, *Years of Infamy* ..., pp. 105-107.

[45] Gladys Ishida Stone, "A Testimony by Gladys Ishida Stone," in Nobuya Tsuchida (ed.), *Asian and Pacific American Experiences: Women's Perspectives* (Minneapolis: Asian/Pacific American Learning Resource Center, University of Minnesota, 1982), pp. 99-101.

[46] CWRIC, *Personal Justice Denied*, p. 253. Since the Navy and the Marine Corps had traditionally excluded Japanese Americans from military service, the Army was the only branch of the U.S. Armed Forces willing to induct Nisei men. Hosokawa, *Nisei* ..., p. 360.

[47] Allen R. Bosworth, *America's Concentration Camps* (New York: W.W. Norton & Company, Inc., 1967), pp. 17-18.

[48] Chester Tanaka, *Go for Broke: A Pictorial History of the Japanese American 100th Infantry Battalion and the 442nd Regimental Combat Team* (Richmond, California: Go for Broke, Inc., 1982), p. 143.

[49] Hosokawa, *Nisei* ..., pp. 405-406.

[50] Tanaka, *Go for Broke* ..., p. 146.

[51] CWRIC, *Personal Justice Denied*, pp. 254-255.

[52] Hosokawa, *Nisei* ..., p. 398.

[53] John Weckerling, *Japanese Americans Play Vital Role in United States Intelligence Service in World War Two* (San Francisco: Diversified Business Forms, Incorporated, 1983), no pagination.

[54] Joseph D. Harrington, *Yankee Samurai: The Secret Role of Nisei in America's Pacific Victory* (Detroit: Pettigrew Enterprises, Inc., 1979), p. 15.

[55] *Ibid.*, pp. 11, 363.

[56] Letter from Carol E. Kraus, Executive Assistant, the Board of Regents of the University of Minnesota, to Professor George Hoshino, School of Social Work, University of Minnesota (March 22, 1983).

[57] Letter from Professor George Hoshino to Dr. Nobuya Tsuchida, Director of the Asian/Pacific American Learning Resource Center, University of Minnesota (October 10, 1984).

[58] Tanaka, *Go for Broke* ..., pp. 170-171.

[59] *Oyama v. California*, 332 U.S. 633 (1948); *Sei Fujii v. State of California*, 38 Cal. 2d 718 (1952); *Haruye Masaoka v. State of California*, 39 Cal. 2d 883 (1952).

[60] Chuman, *The Bamboo People*, p. 221-222.

[61] Immigration and Nationality Act, Chapter 477, Section 311, *United States Statutes at Large* (Washington, D.C.: Government Printing Office, 1953), Vol. 66, p. 239.

[62] *Ibid.*, Sections 201 and 202, pp. 175, 177.

[63] Immigration and Nationality Act, Section 2(a), *United States Statutes at Large* (Washington, D.C.: Government Printing Office, 1966), Vol. 79, p. 911.

[64] *Ibid.*, Section 1(c) and Section 2(a), pp. 911-912.

[65] California. Office of the Attorney General, *Civil Rights Newsletter*, Vol. 2, No. 4 (Fall, 1988).

[66] Civil Liberties Act of 1988, Section 105(a)(1), *United States Statutes at Large* (100th Congress Second Session, 1988), (Washington, D.C.: Government Printing Office, 1990), Vol. 102, Pt. 1, pp. 905-906.

[67] *Ibid.*, Section 2, pp. 903-904.

[68] *Ibid.*, Section 105 (a)(1), pp. 905-906. The term "Fund" refers to the Civil Liberties Public Education Fund which was established to oversee the disbursement of restitution funds. See the Civil Liberties Act of 1988, Sections 104, 106, and 108.

[69] *The Rafu Shimpo* (August 1, 1989); *The Pacific Citizen* (September 1, 1989).

[70] *The Rafu Shimpo* (September 12, 1989).

[71] *The Pacific Citizen* (October 6, 1989).

[72] *Ibid.*

[73] *Ibid.* (October 27, 1989).

[74] *The Rafu Shimpo* (October 26, 1989).

[75] *Ibid.* (November 9, 1989).

[76] *Minneapolis Star Tribune* (November 21, 1989).

[77] *The Los Angeles Times* (September 6, 1989).

[78] *Ibid.* (October 27, 1989).

[79] *Ibid.* (October 20, 1989).

[80] *The Rafu Shimpo* (October 9, 1993.)

[81] *The Pacific Citizen* (October 8-14, 1993).

Illustration by Moto Tani

A STORY TO TELL

Homeless, we were once,
Forced out from our West Coast homes –
Americans, all,
But there were those who proclaimed,
We looked like the enemy.

Barbed-wire fences –
On the outside, stood armed guards –
Prisoners, were we –
Yet, we managed to survive,
Unbroken, like the bamboo.

Justice did prevail –
World War II is history,
Freedom lost, regained,
Minnesota, "Home sweet home" –
We have a story to tell.

Yoshi Uchiyama Tani

RUTH NOMURA TANBARA

The "Indra Pura" ship brought my parents, Frank Jiro Nomura and Kiyo Takeda Nomura, to America from Japan on January 6,1903. Father was born in Tokyo on October 19, 1874. He passed away on September 12, 1956. Mother was born in Tokyo on January 30, 1882, and died on September 2, 1980. In Tokyo, Father graduated from a boys intermediate school and also studied English in a special evening course. Mother completed courses in a girls secondary school. As was the custom in those days to learn the homemaking arts, she went to the home of Viscountess Okabe in Tokyo for one year to study etiquette, dress, homemaking and the arts. They were married in 1902.

At the turn of the twentieth century, socio-economic conditions in Japan were gloomy due to high taxes, overpopulation, compulsory military service, and discontent over the class system. Furthermore, farmers suffered a frequent rice crop failure. Faced with the possibility of famine, the Nomura family decided to share the small estate among the sons. They heard about America being "the land of opportunity" and an "adventure to seek a better way of life." So my parents decided to come to America on their honeymoon. They arrived in Portland, Oregon, where very few Japanese lived. However, they found housing at the Japanese Methodist Episcopal Mission where the Rev. Sugihara's family assisted immigrants in locating housing and employment. With his knowledge of English, Father was able to communicate well enough to find employment in restaurant work.

My parents planned to go to Chicago and en route made a stopover in Minneapolis to see friends from Japan who were working as bus boys in the Nicollet Hotel during the busy college homecoming season. Father stayed in Minneapolis and worked with them. The winter was so severely cold in Minnesota that my parents changed their original plans of going to Chicago. In 1904, they returned to Portland, where the climate was mild and Mt. Hood reminded them of Mt. Fuji.

As employment opportunities for Asians were scarce, Father found employment in the dining room of the Calumet Hotel and assisted the chef. Mother, wanting to learn American ways of homemaking and cooking, went to the home of Dr. and Mrs. Milo Kirkpatrick and assisted in their home. They were so kind and patient as to teach her the American customs. Later my parents purchased a home which was a privilege to non-citizens in those days. In the years following, the children were born and the Kirkpatricks suggested Christian names for Paul, Ruth, and Howard. My sister, Martha, passed away at eight months.

Dr. Jessie McGavin, a physician in Portland, took care of my family through the years. She named my sister Elsie. Since there were very few Japanese families in the early days, the folk knowledge of medical care was shared among themselves. As the families became established, however, Dr. McGavin served as the family physician for many of the Japanese in Portland.

Father opened the Mt. Fuji Grocery Store on Russell Street on the east side of Portland, and my uncle Yoshizo Takeda came from Japan to help. It was not a cash-and-carry store as today, and customers were so dilatory in paying their accounts that the store was closed a few years later. Having the increasing responsibility of raising a family of four children, coupled with his dedication to the education of his children, Father was employed for many years at the Northern Pacific Terminal Company doing maintenance work and later porter service. He retired before the evacuation in 1942 with honors and many friends.

Ruth Tanbara's father, Frank Jiro Nomura, operated Mt. Fuji Grocery on Russell Street in Portland, Oregon, 1910.

After my brother Paul completed his courses at Benson Technical School, he opened the Walnut Park Fruit and Vegetable Market on North Union Avenue. All members of the family helped in the store. However, that was the period of the Great Depression in the 1930s when the banks were closed and the economy was at a low ebb. It was a difficult time for everyone, but accorded us a valuable experience of helping our family and many others to survive.

My parents were asked by other Japanese families and state agencies to care for those children whose mothers were ill or passed away in childbirth or accidents. Some of the children were orphans. So through the years, besides their own four children, my parents took care of 13 other children at different times, some for short periods and others for years. Mother was featured in an article with a

3

photo, entitled "The Mothers of the Nations of the World," in the May 7, 1938, issue of the *News Telegram*, a Portland, Oregon paper, in recognition of her courage, sacrifice and devotion.

In 1952, Mother and Father celebrated their 50th anniversary at a special dinner at my home in St. Paul.

Ruth Tanbara's parents, Frank Jiro and Kiyo Nomura (second from right and far right), celebrated their 50th anniversary at their daughter's home in St. Paul, Minnesota, 1952. Ruth is standing behind her husband, Earl, seated at the end of the table.

When the Immigration and Naturalization Act was passed in 1952 repealing the Japanese Exclusion Act of 1924, Mother studied with me at home and passed the citizenship examination to become a naturalized U.S. citizen on May 15, 1957, in St. Paul. She was proud to go to the election booth for the county, state and general elections from 1960 on.

"It's a girl!", exclaimed my parents when I was born on October 15, 1907, in the family home located in the Sunnyside district of Portland. It was a moment of joy. Since my brother was born two years before, my parents now had a son and daughter. It was a very happy event! Later the family moved to the northeast section of

Portland to be near the public schools. I attended Albina Homestead Elementary School and Jefferson High School which was highly rated at that time. I did not join the clubs at school, because I was studying piano with my teacher, Lois Oakes Abbot. With practice sessions, music lessons, recitals and homework, my time was well occupied.

Ruth Tanbara with her mother, Kiyo Nomura, in Portland, Oregon, 1907.

Frank Jiro Nomura is holding his newly born daughter, Ruth, in Portland, Oregon, 1907.

On Saturdays, I studied the Japanese language with my brothers. A college student from Japan was our instructor, since there were no special language schools in Portland then. He taught us the vocabulary, pronunciation and writing the characters with a brush. During the week, Mother taught the polite forms of greeting, prayers, table graces, courtesies and the customs when attending memorial services at Buddhist and Christian churches. I learned some of her special prayers by heart and sincerely regret I did not record all of them, for they were truly beautiful poetic gems from the heart. At

Ruth Tanbara was born on October 15, 1907, in this house in Portland, Oregon.

home we always spoke in Japanese since Mother wanted us to be able to converse in her native language.

The neighborhood where I lived was cross-cultural in character with families of German, Russian, French and English backgrounds. My friends, therefore, taught me many of their customs and skills in handwork like crochet, embroidery, and cooking. They also taught me simple everyday phrases in their native tongues, so I could understand when their parents spoke to me. Many neighbors had large families with six or seven children, each of whom helped with family chores, studied hard and took time to play. They were great gardeners and raised most of their fruits and vegetables, and preserved them by canning or pickling as freezers were not available in those days.

Ruth Tanbara with her parents, Frank Jiro and Kiyo Nomura,
and brothers, Paul and Howard (center), in Portland, Oregon, circa 1912.

There were only two other Japanese families living about ten blocks from my home, so we joined with them on special holidays and community picnics. Frances Maeda and I became good friends and attended the Japanese Methodist Mission. We taught Sunday School classes for the children from Japanese families. During our growing years, I enjoyed many happy get-togethers with the Kobayashi girls whose parents were also from Tokyo, Japan. Even though we live in different cities today, we still continue our friendships.

During the summer months, following my graduation from high school, I enrolled in a secretarial course at Northwestern School of Commerce in downtown Portland. After completing the course, I was employed as a typist for the S. Ban Company, a Japanese import and export firm.

Early in the spring of 1926, there was an essay and subscription contest for Nisei students sponsored by the Nichibei Newspaper Company of San Francisco. The Japanese American newspaper had a circulation not only in California, but also in Washington and Oregon. Mr. Kyutaro Abiko, the publisher of the *Nichibei Newspaper*, and Mrs. Yona Abiko had a vision that the Nisei could serve as a "bridge of understanding" between Japan and the United States. The Abikos thought it essential that the Nisei study and tour Japan to be knowledgeable about the land of their ancestors. So they organized study tours in 1925 and 1926 through a subscription contest. Ten Nisei delegates would have an opportunity to go to Japan, meet the people, study its civilization, visit schools, museums, temples and organizations, and see the scenic beauty of the country as well as the well-tilled soils of the farmlands.

I was fortunate enough to be selected as the delegate from Oregon with the second *Nichibei Kengakudan*. Mrs. Yona Abiko, the wife of the publisher, was our teacher and guardian. Well educated and cultured, she was fluent in both Japanese and English. She was the sister of Umeko Tsuda, the founder of the well-known Tsuda College for Women in Tokyo. Mr. S. Hara was the business manager of the tour. My mother and sister Elsie were on the trip as passengers. On March 2, 1926, we embarked from San Francisco on the SS *Korea Maru* of the Nippon Yusen Kaisha (Japan Mail Steamship Company). It took 18 days to cross the Pacific with a short stopover in Hawaii.

During the days on board the ship, Mrs. Abiko taught the group about Japan, so we would be informed of its history. She explained the daily schedule of the three-month tour on which we would be visiting museums, temples, some companies, families, and schools.

Ruth Tanbara with other members of the second Nichibei Kengakudan aboard the Korea Maru shortly before embarkation from San Francisco, California, 1926.

She also taught us the Japanese customs of greeting, manners, and etiquette at the table, and reminded us to take off our shoes when we entered Japanese homes and temples. Each day on the tour, there was an assignment to write our daily impressions and experiences to send to the newspaper for publication. The Royal Typewriter Company loaned me a portable typewriter for the trip. It was also one of my assignments to demonstrate the typewriter when we visited some of the high schools. The students were fascinated with the American typewriter—something new in Japan. They enjoyed typing their names and kept them as souvenirs. It is interesting to note today that many of the typewriters in the United States are made in Japan.

I had an interesting experience in Tokyo when my uncle, Saburo Nomura, who was a graduate of Oxford University in England and teacher of English at the Gakushuin (Peers School for Boys), invited me to one of his classes to give a short talk. He asked me to wear the uniform coat of the school, so that I would not be conspicuous in the classroom and during the session. I was seated in the back row. After introductions, I gave a short talk in English and explained about life in America. The students were very attentive and expressed their appreciation in English. I suggested that they visit the United States whenever there was an opportunity, so they could use their knowledge of English in daily conversations with the people and tour some of the American cities. It was parents day at the Gakushuin and I remember the red carpet was rolled out at the entry for the mothers.

The 1926 trip to Japan on the second *Nichibei Kengakudan* when I was in my teen-age years enriched my life and gave me a deep appreciation of Japan, its people, arts and civilization. It encouraged me to study the language, flower arrangement, holiday festivals, the tea ceremony, daily customs, Japanese cooking and serving, music, arts and crafts, particularly pottery, painting and calligraphy. It was an opportunity to meet my dear relatives who in turn were interested in learning about life in America. The tour group returned to the United States on May 28, 1926, on the SS *Siberia Maru*. With the wind currents in our favor and taking the northern route, the return trip took only 11 days. Talks of the trip and impressions of Japan were scheduled with young people's groups in the San Francisco Bay Area and Los Angeles.

It was during this trip that my parents and relatives gave me my first Japanese *kimono*—complete to the brocaded *obi* (sash), *tabi* and *zori* (footwear). The family crest was stenciled on the kimono with its long sleeves for formal wear. When I wore it for the first time, I experienced a new appreciation in being of Japanese ancestry.

I encouraged all Nisei to visit Japan so they could enjoy the experiences of seeing the country, appreciate the culture of their parents, and become well-informed interpreters of the two nations.

In the fall of 1926, I enrolled at Oregon State Agricultural College in Corvallis, Oregon, now renamed as Oregon State University. I was the first Nisei woman student from Portland to enroll at the College. I remember that Mildred Bartholomew of the Methodist Church extended a warm welcome and helped me during my freshman year to get acquainted with the campus. In addition to student life, I received a number of requests from church and school groups in the local community to give talks on my recent trip to Japan.

Corvallis is located about 87 miles from Portland, and not having a car in those days, we traveled by train and went home only on holidays. I lived in Margaret Snell Hall, the women's dormitory for upperclassmen. My roommate at college was Mabel Chin Quong, a Chinese American sophomore coed from Portland. We became good friends and enjoyed being roommates for four years. I had a pleasant visit with her in California in 1990. Nori Shimomura, a Nisei friend from Portland, enrolled at Oregon State the following year and roomed with us as a freshman. She was a very brilliant student, and everyone enjoyed her friendship.

Ruth Tanbara attired in kimono which her parents and relatives gave her during the trip to Japan, 1926.

During my freshman year, I was registered in Business Administration. However, I changed my major after meeting Dean Ava B. Milam of the School of Home Economics, who had traveled extensively in Japan, Korea and China and established Home Economics courses in some of the colleges over there. She explained the opportunities and the challenges to teach Home Economics and Nutrition in women's colleges in Japan. I communicated with my parents and with their approval, I switched my major to the professional curriculum in Home Economics for teaching and took courses in Chemistry, Bacteriology, Physiology, and Nutrition. In addition to my class schedule, I worked as a part-time secretary in the Dean's Office. It was during my junior and senior years at Oregon State College that I was invited to membership in Phi Kappa Phi, all-college National Honor Society; Omicron Nu, National Honor Society in Home Economics; and Kappa Delta Pi, National Education Honor Society. In 1930, I received a Bachelor of Science degree in Home Economics. This academic training proved to be an asset throughout my life.

Ruth Tanbara received a B.S. in Home Economics from Oregon State College in Corvallis, Oregon, 1930.

Though offered a position to teach in Japan, I did not accept it since my parents felt I should stay in the United States. I decided to take the position offered by the Women's Home Missionary Society of the Methodist Church in Portland which had established a preschool course for children of Japanese families. There was a need to teach the children in English, because their parents spoke only Japanese in their homes. The parents were concerned that their children would not be able to understand English when they enrolled in public schools. There were about 50 children and the classes met in the mornings during the week in the newly constructed Manley Community Center in the Southwest section of Portland. The Women's Home Missionary Society provided a large red bus and Mr. Oba was the driver. Each morning during the week, the children had a round-trip ride from their homes. It was an enjoyable experience for all of us. When I attended the 1990 Portland reunion, I met a number of the class members who were now in their 60s and all successful in their professions. We enjoyed being together in Portland since some had come from Hawaii and New York.

After the morning preschool sessions, I worked as one of the secretaries in the Japanese Consulate General in Portland. Later I

Ruth Tanbara taught preschool children of Japanese ancestry at the Manley Community Center in Portland, Oregon, circa 1931.

changed to a position in the Portland YWCA where Miss Grace Steinbeck was the Executive Secretary. She served for several years as General Secretary in the YWCA program in Foochow, China. She was an excellent director and the first to employ a Nisei on the YWCA staff.

In September 1935, with a friendship and courtship of several years, I was married to Earl K. Tanbara of San Francisco, who was the Advertising Manager of the Dollar Steamship Company with its headquarters in San Francisco. So I moved to Berkeley, California, where I enjoyed meeting new friends, took a part-time position with the International Institute of San Francisco, working as a social worker in the Japanese community.

Ruth and Earl K. Tanbara were married in Portland, Oregon, 1935.

With my background in Home Economics, I was asked by the Japanese Wholesale Grocers Association in San Francisco to assist Mr. S. Akiya of San Francisco, a highly skilled chef in Japanese cooking. He catered the special menus for the Japanese Consulate's banquets and receptions. The assignment was to work with him as he prepared the foods by experience, and to standardize the measurements in English using the teaspoons, tablespoons, cups, pints and quarts as used in American cooking. After attending the interesting weekly demonstrations for over a year and tasting all the delicacies, I completed the manuscript. The book, entitled *Japanese Food Recipes*, was published in English with complete Japanese foods, menus, vocabulary and sketches to illustrate cutting, serving and arrangement of foods for dinners, picnics and special holidays. The book was published in 1940 by the Kokusai Shuppan Insatsusha, Tokyo, Japan. It is one of the early books on Japanese cooking in English. It helped introduce Japanese recipes and methods in English for the Nisei to continue using Japanese food products.

With my special interest in handicrafts, I enrolled in a course taught by a Miss Thomsen in Oakland, California, and learned to sew hand-stitched leather dress gloves for ladies and men with imported leathers from England, France and South Africa. The gloves were die-cut by a highly skilled glove cutter, and by taking individual hand patterns, we were able to fit gloves for each person. The hobby became so popular that classes were scheduled in my studio in the Women's City Club in San Francisco. Many orders were received from dress shops nearby to match colors, designs and lengths. I taught a number of Nisei women to sew the gloves and they assisted me in filling the orders. They enjoyed the work since they could do the sewing in their homes.

The World's Fair in San Francisco on Treasure Island in 1939 brought many friends to visit the spectacular event and I enjoyed going to the Fair with them. The exhibits and programs of each country were educational, artistic and beautiful. It was one of the highlights of my life to be able to go to the World's Fair so close to home!

It was about this time that the Dollar Steamship Company, a privately owned firm, became the merchant marine of the United States and its name was changed to the American President Lines. This was a critical period in our lives since Earl's position was changed about a year later. He decided to go to Japan and was assigned by a

Japanese firm to go on a trade mission to India. His travels brought him many interesting experiences which I enjoyed through his letters and photographs. As travel between the United States and Japan became more restricted each month, everyone encouraged Earl to return home. He was fortunate to obtain passage on the last steamship returning to San Francisco in late 1939.

On December 7, 1941, World War II was declared, and my classes in glovemaking were terminated, so I closed the studio and stored the equipment. After the war ended, our furniture and household goods which had been stored with friends were shipped by the U.S. government to our home in St. Paul.

Since I did not go to camp, this chapter explains my role in helping evacuees from the internment centers resettle in Minnesota. December 7, 1941, was a quiet Sunday in Berkeley, California, and I had just returned from teaching a Sunday School class at the Japanese Berkeley Community Church. When I heard the news on the radio, I was shocked and did not believe it, thinking it was part of a story being broadcast. When the news was repeated over and over, I realized the seriousness of the broadcast. I knelt down and prayed that the terrible destruction in Hawaii by Japan's surprise attack would end. I hoped for understanding for the Japanese people in the United States, since I realized we would be affected, even if we were American citizens by birth. The question repeated in my mind over and over was how and why could Japan do this terrible act. When Earl returned from his golf game, he was also shocked to learn the news and called his family and friends trying to figure out why this had happened. It was truly the saddest day for our family, relatives, and friends. It was beyond our comprehension that Japan would launch such a foolish surprise attack without the formal declaration of war. We felt deep compassion for the people in Hawaii and the terrible destruction of the warships there.

My Caucasian friends were very concerned and called on us the following Monday to express their sincerity and to offer any assistance when needed. I realized that we of Japanese extraction would be affected in some serious way, because it would be difficult to differentiate Japanese Americans who are U.S. citizens and the Japanese from Japan who could not become naturalized in those days. So I started packing the household goods and recording everything which we would have to take care of, especially for our aging parents. My Nisei friends called on us and we shared the same concerns. After the 8 p.m. curfew was imposed on all persons of Japanese ancestry, we abided by all the rules and regulations. My non-Japanese friends offered any assistance to help us in this crisis.

After President Franklin D. Roosevelt officially declared war on Japan on December 7, 1941, he issued Executive Order 9066 on February 19, 1942, which gave the Secretary of War and the Military Commanders the power to exclude all persons of Japanese ancestry from designated areas in order to provide security against sabotage.

In the wake of this order, the subject of evacuation became the widespread topic of conversation, and the Tolan Hearings were scheduled in San Francisco which were government-sponsored meetings to consider the possibility of evacuation. I attended some of the Tolan Hearings in February 1942. I remember the Japanese Americans at those meetings were a very young, naive group in their late 20's and early 30's, compared to the mature Italian and German leaders attending the Hearings. Italian Americans explained to me that the U.S. government would never evacuate them, since it would have to move most of the people in San Francisco. Even Mayor Angelo Rossi was of Italian descent. German American community leaders felt the same, so they reassured me, "Don't worry. Evacuation from the West Coast would not happen."

But it did happen to the Japanese Americans—through fear, prejudice, and hostile public sentiment against us. We were highly visible and fewer in number compared to the other two nationality groups. From week to week, we received military orders and lived under the curfew regulations. We also had to give up our cooking knives, personal cameras, guns or hunting equipment to the local police station, and these things were never returned to us. Because it was difficult to differentiate the Chinese Americans from the Japanese Americans, my Chinese friends wore large buttons which read "I AM CHINESE."

Orders were received that we could evacuate voluntarily on 48 hours notice if we would move 150 miles inland from the coast by March 2, 1942. In consultation with my husband's parents, we decided to move to a friend's farm in Reedley, California, which is about 15 miles from Fresno in the San Joaquin Valley and 150 miles from the coast. With the help of our loyal Caucasian friends, we stored our household goods, closed our businesses, and settled our accounts within that 48-hour period. I placed our silver and little jewelry with a signed statement of contents in the safety deposit vault of a local bank. Arrangements were made with a local shipping company to move to Reedley our basic things—a stove, a refrigerator, bedding, kitchenware, and personal clothing. I will always be grateful to our non-Japanese friends who helped pack our belongings, took care of our Mahogany furniture in their homes, and assisted in renting our six-room house to a couple studying for their advanced degrees at the University of California, Berkeley. The tenants welcomed the home where their children could live, since many of the homes and apartments did not allow children.

Another Japanese American family from Alameda, California, voluntarily evacuated with us to Reedley. They were Mr. and Mrs. George Rokutani, their three-year-old daughter Barbara, and Mr. Rokutani's mother. They were also friends of the Japanese American family in Reedley. The two cars with our families and personal belonging arrived safely in Reedley in the early hours the next day— to freedom again. However, the sad thought lingered with me throughout the trip that I would never be returning to my Berkeley home.

The genuine kindness of the Kitahara and Minami families of Reedley in befriending us to their ranch during this crisis will always be remembered and deeply cherished.

Reedley is one of the fertile agricultural areas in California where peaches, Santa Rosa plums, oranges, and table grapes are produced. We stayed in Reedley for five months, during which time we just began to learn about farming with the help of our friends and the staff of the U.S. Department of Agriculture. Then, one hot day in July when the temperature hovered around 117 degrees in dry heat, another military order was issued to move all Japanese Americans in the Pacific Coast states to the Relocation Centers. We had planned to go to one of the centers with our family. However, during the registration process, the Provost Marshall of the U.S. Army stationed in Reedley gave Earl and me the option to go to the Eastern or Midwestern part of the United States and help build community acceptance and resettle Japanese American internees from the Relocation Centers on a volunteer basis. We were in our early 30's, married and had been employed, so we chose to relocate to the Midwest. We were willing to work even as a cook or gardener to make ends meet, avoiding to go on welfare.

The sociologists at the universities on the West Coast did not want another Indian reservation problem. Therefore, we were planning to go to Lincoln, Nebraska, where Earl had been offered a teaching position at the University of Nebraska. However, the Chief of Police in Lincoln warned us not to come, since he was of German extraction and it was becoming unsafe even for him to stay there during the war. He feared that we might suffer more due to our higher visibility. We were also concerned about our safety, because we knew of one case where a Nisei dentist had voluntarily evacuated to Texas where he was immediately imprisoned until his identity as a good American citizen was established by the FBI. Another Japanese American family went to a city in Ohio, where the mother who had fallen seriously ill was denied hospitalization because she was an enemy alien.

I remember selling our car in haste outside the local bank to the first customer for $250. It was an almost new Chevrolet. We had to travel by train since the Army officer felt it would be safer. The rationing of gas would not permit such a long journey, and many gas stations would not have sold gasoline to people with Japanese faces.

WESTERN DEFENSE COMMAND AND FOURTH ARMY

Office of Assistant Chief of Staff, Civil Affairs Division

WARTIME CIVIL CONTROL ADMINISTRATION
1231 MARKET STREET
SAN FRANCISCO, CALIFORNIA
Telephone KLONDIKE 2-2611

July 24, 1942

TO ALL PEACE OFFICERS AND
ALL OTHER PERSONS CONCERNED:

     1. The bearers, persons of Japanese ancestry, of this travel authority are;

Earl Tanabara	Male	36 yrs.	Citizen
Ruth Tanabara	Female	34 yrs.	Citizen

who are now residing at Route 1, Box 319, Reedley, California.

     2. The bearers will be permitted to travel to St. Paul, Minnesota, for the purpose residence.

     3. Travel will commence on or before August 3, 1942. Travel within the Western Defense Command will be by public carrier and by the most direct route possible without stop-overs en route, except for those necessitated by carrier schedules.

     4. This travel permit is granted upon condition that bearers will not, after leaving the Western Defense Command area, return thereto without written permission from Wartime Civil Control Administration or higher headquarters.

     5. It is requested that all persons concerned facilitate the travel of the above named persons.

For the Assistant Chief of Staff, C.A.D.

Herman P. Goebel, Jr.
Major, Cavalry
Chief of Regulatory Section

The Wartime Civil Control Administration issued Ruth and Earl K. Tanbara a travel permit to relocate from Reedley, California, to St. Paul, Minnesota, July 24, 1942.

We called Mr. Henry Matsushita, a family friend, who offered his home in St. Paul, Minnesota. Because my brother Paul was already enrolled in the Military Intelligence Service Language School at Camp Savage, we decided to go to St. Paul, where we arrived after a long train ride on August 9, 1942. Mr. Matsushita was the chef for the president of one of the railroad companies. Since, however, he was an alien, he could not ride the trains during the war. So he was employed as a chef for Father Jennings of St. Mary's Church near the St. Croix River.

When the military ordered all persons of Japanese ancestry to leave Reedley for the Poston Relocation Centers in Arizona, the members of the churches in Reedley prepared hundreds of lunches for the evacuees before they departed on the trains. I will always remember the many kindnesses extended to the evacuees. Also, when Earl and I were leaving Reedley, Mr. Jacob Aurenheimer, a Mennonite, drove us 15 miles to Fresno to board the train for St. Paul, Minnesota. He used his precious gasoline ration for this round trip. We will always be grateful for his thoughtfulness.

On the long train journey to Minnesota, many thoughts came to us. We realized that the concern and care of our loyal friends in Berkeley, Reedley, Oakland, Portland and San Francisco gave us the courage to meet our new challenge. Their support and help in making this transition gave us inner strength to do our very best in the resettlement program before us. Our special thanks go to the California families of Thomas, Edith and Irene Jones, Dean and Netty Jane Langworthy, Claudia and Ben Murphy, Ruth and Henry Harvey, and the Sweetmans, as well as to individuals like Ruth Kingman, Annie Clo Watson, Claire McAllister, Merren Morton of Oakland, and others.

I had letters of introduction and references from various organizations, as well as from such individuals as Miss Grace Steinbeck of the YWCA in Portland where I had served on the staff, Miss Annie Clo Watson of the International Institute of San Francisco where I was a part-time social case worker, and Dean Ava B. Milam of the

School of Home Economics at Oregon State College, my alma mater. Earl also possessed reference letters from several firms and from Mr. Robert Stanley Dollar, President of the Dollar Steamship Lines where Earl had been employed as Advertising Manager for over ten years, and from Mr. Henry R. Harvey of San Francisco, a longtime business friend. These letters and clearance from the FBI all helped establish our introduction to our new community in Minnesota.

Our main assignment was to build community acceptance. So each week, Earl and I were invited to different church groups, youth groups, schools, colleges, and farming communities to give talks on Japanese Americans. Sometimes the weather was 26 degrees below zero with the sun shining, and we were not prepared for it since we had been living in hot, sunny California. We did not have a car, and there were no buses then—we traveled by trolley. I remember our first trip to South St. Paul took over an hour. As there were only ten Japanese families living in St. Paul before the war, many Minnesotans were not acquainted with American citizens of Japanese extraction.

We had many interesting experiences. One of my brothers was stationed at Camp Savage, receiving intensive training in the Military Intelligence Service Language School. On Sundays, we would invite him and his friends for a home-cooked dinner. One of the neighbors complained to the FBI that we were entertaining Japanese soldiers. The FBI came to visit us, and the late Colonel Kai Rasmussen from Fort Snelling called on the homes in our neighborhood and explained to the residents that the soldiers were American soldiers receiving training in the U.S. Army's Military Intelligence Service Language School. He suggested that I place a service flag in our window to show that we had a relative serving in the U.S. Army.

Many families and students wrote to us from the Relocation Centers. There were ten centers in different parts of California, Utah, Arizona, Idaho, Arkansas, Wyoming, and Colorado. As the internees wanted to resettle in Minnesota, we made contacts with colleges and potential employers. Many Japanese Americans were highly trained

YOUNG WOMEN'S CHRISTIAN ASSOCIATION

MEMBER OF THE YOUNG WOMEN'S CHRISTIAN ASSOCIATIONS OF THE UNITED STATES OF AMERICA

941 SOUTH FIGUEROA STREET - Phone TRinity 0461 - LOS ANGELES

April 6, 1942

To Whom It May Concern:

This note is to record that Mrs. Earl Tanbara has been known to me for twelve years through her active work in the Young Women's Christian Association of Portland, Oregon, as a member of the staff and as a personal friend in the years since we have both moved away from Portland.

I can most heartily commend Mrs. Tanbara to those in the community in which she may be living in these coming months as one who can be counted upon to assist in any constructive work for girls, women, and children because of the experience she has had in working in the Y.W.C.A. and because of her fine, cooperative spirit and desire to be of service to others. She is unusually fine in secretarial work and in the field of hand-work and crafts, having been a student in home economics in college.

I hope that those to whom she may present this letter will welcome her and help her to be of service or to secure a position in those fields in which she feels she can contribute most.

Very sincerely,

Grace C. Steinbeck

Grace C. Steinbeck,
General Secretary.

The Young Women's Christian Association's reference letter for Ruth Tanbara, April 6, 1942.

23

International Institute
FOR SERVICE TO IMMIGRANTS AND NEW AMERICANS
1000 WASHINGTON STREET :: SAN FRANCISCO, CALIFORNIA
TUxedo 1212

March 26, 1942

TO WHOM IT MAY CONCERN:

   Ruth Nomura Tanbara (Mrs. Earl) has been known to the International Institute for approximately five years. During one year she was employed as a member of the staff, working in the capacity of social worker among the Japanese people.

   She is a woman of refinement and of exceptionally good educational background. She is highly skilled in her own profession which is in the field of home economics.

   Before she came to the International Institute, she worked for a number of years on the staff of the Young Womens Christian Association in her home town of Portland, Oregon. She has been trained and has lived as an American citizen. I consider her not only a woman of fine character but also a loyal American and I recommend her to anyone who may desire her services.

        Respectfully yours,

        Annie Clo Watson

The International Institute of San Francisco also wrote a letter of recommendation in behalf of Ruth Tanbara, March 26, 1942.

OREGON STATE COLLEGE
SCHOOL OF HOME ECONOMICS
CORVALLIS, OREGON

June 15, 1942

TO WHOM IT MAY CONCERN:

This is to indicate to you that Ruth Nomura Tanbara was one of our honor students in Home Economics at Oregon State College. Ruth did not only excellent work as a student, but she won the respect and admiration of the staff and students because of her charming personality. Since her graduation she has done some excellent work in Portland and also in California. I believe her teaching and other professional experience qualify her admirably for teaching.

Very sincerely,

Ava B. Milam, Dean and
Director of Home Economics

ABM:d

Dean Ava B. Milam of Oregon State College provided Ruth Tanbara
with a nice letter of character reference, June 15, 1942.

THE ROBERT DOLLAR CO.

DOLLAR LINE
ROBERT DOLLAR BUILDING
SAN FRANCISCO

CABLE ADDRESS "DOLLAR"
CODES
BENTLEY PHRASE CODE
A B C 5TH EDITION
UNIVERSAL TRADE CODE
FIVE LETTER WESTERN UNION

March 8, 1939

TO WHOM IT MAY CONCERN:

The bearer of this letter, Mr. Earl Tanbara, was in our employ for about eleven years, up to the time our personnel was turned over to American President Lines, Ltd. in conformity with agreement made with United States Maritime Commission.

During the time he was employed by us, Mr. Tanbara was connected with the Passenger Department of our business. In recent years he was in charge of the Advertising Division. During these years of service, Mr. Tanbara had the opportunity, and took advantage of it, to become thoroughly familiar with our services, Trans-Pacific and Round-the-World, and also the ports of call served by our liners, together with the many points of interest in the various countries visited by our ships during their voyages.

Mr. Tanbara is a graduate of an American University and has excellent knowledge of the English language. He has a pleasing personality and his relations with the traveling public and his fellow employees have always been upon a most pleasant basis.

His integrity, as well as his interest in and application to his duties, are of the highest character.

I take pleasure in recommending Mr. Tanbara to any company that may be in position to avail itself of his services.

Am sure the knowledge of and experience in the Passenger branch of the transportation industry which he gained during the years he was in our employ should be very valuable to his employers.

Please feel free to communicate with me personally should you desire any further information relative to Mr. Tanbara's qualifications.

Yours very truly,

THE ROBERT DOLLAR CO.,

By

President

President Robert Stanley Dollar of the Robert Dollar Company wrote a reference letter for Earl K. Tanbara, March 8, 1939.

26

INDEPENDENT PRESSROOM

INCORPORATED

PROCESS COLOR PRINTERS

COMPLETE SERVICE ON ALL DIRECT ADVERTISING

TELEPHONE SUtter 8670
300 BROADWAY · SAN FRANCISCO
June 10, 1942

TO WHOM IT MAY CONCERN:

The undersigned wish to certify that they have known the bearer of this letter, Earl K. Tanbara for more than ten years, and that they have known his wife, Ruth Tanbara since their marriage some seven or eight years ago.

Our acquaintance with the Tanbaras has been more than a casual one. We have enjoyed their friendship and confidence. We know them well enough to be competent to judge their loyalty and to be able to estimate their character and ability with what we feel sure is a high degree of accuracy.

The Tanbaras are both completely loyal American citizens. They have a genuine feeling of patriotism that is stronger than that of the average citizen. In the past few months they have made great sacrifices cheerfully, with a feeling in doing so they were making their necessary contribution to this country's war effort.

They are both exceptional persons. They are both University graduates. They are both entirely honest and trustworthy. They are industrious and exceptionally competent. They deserve the trust and confidence of everyone.

This letter is entirely voluntary on the part of the undersigned; it was not solicited by the Tanbaras, but it is written by us in the hope that if they ever need to use it, that it may help these very good friends of ours.

Sincerely,

HRH:om

Henry R. Harvey
Ruth M. Harvey

Henry R. Harvey, a long-time business friend of Earl K. Tanbara's, and his wife, Ruth M. Harvey, provided the Tanbaras with a fine letter of character reference prior to their departure for Minnesota.

27

and skilled in their professions—there were auto mechanics, cooks, dentists, stenographers, doctors, nurses, dressmakers, engineers, beauticians, teachers, artists, etc.

In the beginning, we helped by opening our small home to families and students, but the numbers increased beyond our expectations. It, therefore, became necessary to form a resettlement committee and the Council of Human Relations was organized. Serving on the committee were social workers, board members of the YWCA, the YMCA, the International Institute and Family Service Agency, church leaders, college faculty members, and interested community people. Mr. Warren Burger was an outstanding attorney in St. Paul at that time and served as the first Council chairman. In 1986, he retired as Chief Justice of the U.S. Supreme Court. When I retired in 1972 after 30 years with the YWCA, I received a congratulatory letter from Chief Justice Warren Burger.

Dr. Charles Turck, President of Macalester College, was the second chairman of the Council. Macalester was the first college to accept Nisei students. Mrs. Ruth Abernathy was the first Executive Director of the Council of Human Relations which assisted all minority groups with their problems. Mrs. Ruth Gage Colby, a St. Paul volunteer, gave many hours of dedicated service to help the Nisei solve problems of employment and housing.

Japanese language classes were offered at the University of Minnesota for enlisted men, and Grace Kurihara, who had studied the language for many years in Japan, was one of the instructors. Fuji Shigaki also taught there. Mrs. Colby helped recruit some of the instructors. The St. Paul Resettlement Committee leased a small hotel where the present Civic Center is located, and Mrs. Tomiko Ogata was the director. She managed the housing and prepared the meals at a nominal fee for the families who came directly from the Relocation Centers. She also advised them about adjustment to living in Minnesota with the harsh winters and humid summers. Japanese American relocatees thus had their housing, employment and other immediate needs met.

I was then on the part-time staff of the St. Paul YWCA. Many Nisei girls were seeking household employment, since they were going to school and needed a place where they could get room and board. Through the YWCA, a committee was formed to help establish standards for the household employees by defining their respon-

*Chief Justice of the U.S. Supreme Court Warren Burger sent Ruth Tanbara
a congratulatory letter on the occasion of her retirement from the St. Paul
YWCA. In the postwar period, when he was practicing law in St. Paul,
Burger served as the first chair of the Council of Human Relations
which helped many Japanese Americans resettle in Minnesota.*

sibilities, work hours, salaries, duties, and free time. The committee also found families which were seeking replacements for their regular maids and cooks, who had gone to work in the defense industry. Committee members contacted the families, helped with the interviews and worked out details of placement.

It is interesting to note that through this experience of household employment, the Minnesota Tests for Household Skills were prepared by University of Minnesota faculty members: Professor of Home Economics Education Clara Brown Arny, Director of Family Life Dorothy T. Dyer, and Instructor of Home Economics Margaret F. Proshek. The tests included child care, cleaning, laundry and foods, and were published in 1952 by Science Research Associates, Inc. of Chicago, Illinois.

Many Nisei girls came to the Twin Cities because their boyfriends or brothers were stationed at Fort Snelling. With the help of the International Institute, we planned social get-togethers with the group and had the first New Year's Eve party in 1942. Many weddings of Nisei brides and enlisted grooms were held in the chapel at Fort Snelling. Earl and I were often invited to substitute for their parents who were not able to attend from the Relocation Centers.

I remember an interesting episode that happened when the late Bishop Emeritus Philip McNairy of St. Mark's Cathedral in Minneapolis was the third chairman of the Council. The Rev. McNairy was the minister of Christ Episcopal Church in downtown St. Paul during the war years. One time he asked if there were specific problems encountered by Japanese Americans, and I explained the need to find a barber so that the Nisei male students could get a hair cut. The barbers turned down the Japanese American men. We also needed to find employment for trained and experienced beauticians. The Rev. McNairy expressed this need in his sermon and found members of his church who were willing to open their shops for these services. Subsequently, some Nisei beauticians were offered employment.

Many new problems confronted us each day. I remember being interested in purchasing a modest home which was owned by a physician who was willing to sell, but hesitated because the neighbors objected to living nextdoor to a Japanese American. The doctor also felt he might lose some of his patients. Another instance occurred during the arrangements for my father's funeral in 1956. We had a difficult time finding a funeral home in St. Paul where we could have the visitation services, a cemetery where he could be cremated, and a crypt where his remains could be stored. Earl asked our minister, the Rev. Arthur Foote of the Unity-Unitarian Church of St. Paul, who contacted the funeral homes and found one (Godbout Mortuary) which opened its doors to anyone seeking its services. It was a beautiful dignified chapel and the staff person in charge was kind and understanding. The Rev. Foote also contacted the cemeteries, and Lakewood Cemetery in Minneapolis welcomed everyone. We did discover there were some cemeteries in 1956 where only Caucasian bodies were buried. Policies have since changed in Minnesota with regard to cemeteries and mortuaries, and there is no such discrimination today.

Our first task was to help the Japanese American students resettle since they wished to continue their education. In order to help them defray their school expenses, we found odd jobs for them around the house and gardens. The students had a good command of English. We received many letters from the Relocation Centers, as well as from young adults who were interested in coming to Minnesota. Leading educators in California universities were against the mass evacuation of Japanese Americans, but accepted it only as a military necessity. They served on the National Japanese American Student Relocation Council of California.

Though the weather was truly cold in Minnesota, in general the hearts of the people were warm and gracious. Many opened their homes, and churches welcomed the Nisei to adjust their religious and social life. We were in communication with our friends who resettled in other states, and in comparison, Minnesota was outstanding in accepting the Japanese Americans.

Minidoka march 31 '43.
Hunt.
Idaho

Mr & Mrs Tanhara,

Dear friend, How are you.
Mrs Tanbara might know me. my son
Geo. M. Suzuki will be over there
in few days. He is still Green boy.
please kindly Guide him or lead him
to live to follow the Road as Christian
So far as you can.

yours Trully
Kinichi, Suzuki
Mrs Namiye. Suzuki

He will leave here to-morrow april 1.

Before George Suzuki left the Minidoka Relocation Center in Idaho for St. Paul to attend Macalester College, his parents, Kinichi and Namiye Suzuki, had sent this letter to Earl K. and Ruth Tanbara asking them to help and guide their son.

Personally, evacuation was no doubt a tragic experience which caused a lot of sadness and bitterness, and I sincerely hope it will never happen to any group or persons.

In retrospect, as one writer described it, "we were a part of a huge human drama where there was no script because it was unprecedented to have compulsory evacuation in the United States of U.S. citizens." At that time, our parents, some of whom had lived in the United States for 40 years, could not become U.S. citizens because laws did not allow it. However, the laws were changed in 1952 to enable first-generation Japanese to become naturalized citizens if they met the residency requirement and passed the examinations on American history and government, as well as the U.S. Constitution.

"There was not time for a dress rehearsal of this drama, everything was trial and error and the villain was race prejudice, fear, war hysteria, intolerance and discrimination as well as political and economic pressures."

"The scenes were endless ... many books have been written and films produced and now after 50 years, the curtain goes up on the final act. We must remember the United States was founded on the premise that individuals of different races, cultures and religious beliefs could live together harmoniously to create a strong, just and tolerant nation." With our voluntary resettlement program over, I continued to work on my Master's degree at the University of Minnesota and to serve on the program staff of the St. Paul YWCA for 30 years.

After the atomic bombings of Hiroshima and Nagasaki on August 6 and 9, 1945, peace was declared ending World War II on V-J Day, August 15, 1945. In the immediate postwar period, most Japanese Americans and their families returned to the West Coast to start rebuilding their lives. However, many remained in St. Paul and Minneapolis to continue their education or to raise their families; many advanced in their occupations and professions. They became longtime residents of Minnesota, where they have since been participating in and contributing to the community with their special skills and interests. It is estimated there are approximately 3,000 Japanese Americans residing in Minnesota today (1992).

Earl and I took a brief trip to San Francisco and Berkeley, visiting our former neighborhood and renewing friendships with those who had taken care of us for the duration of the evacuation. We did keep in touch with them through correspondence during the three years. It was a real homecoming and most enjoyable. We tried to visualize the idea of returning to California to live and start all over again. It was a very difficult decision and required a great deal of thought.

We sold our home and property during the war years and purchased a home in St. Paul. Earl had a position as sales manager for Larry's Glass Company, and with construction in sight after the war, business seemed promising in Minnesota. Air travel with its speed and time-saving conveniences had taken over steamship travel. We also shared the responsibility of caring for our parents who were in their retirement years and lived nearby in St. Paul. My parents lived in Chicago, but came to visit us often. I was on the program staff of the St. Paul YWCA enjoying the responsibility of directing 60 Adult Education classes and World Fellowship which was the international program of the YWCA established in 1991 in 76 countries around the world.

We enjoyed the trip to the West Coast, but somehow in estimating the advantages and disadvantages, my husband and I decided to stay in Minnesota. As the years passed by, we realized it was the wisest decision. Minnesota adopted us and became our home.

With staff requirements for graduate study, I enrolled at the University of Minnesota in the Department of Home Economics Education with a major in Adult Education and a minor in Social Group Work. Professor Clara Brown Arny was my adviser. I attended classes regularly, continued with my YWCA assignments and wrote my Master's thesis entitled "Development of a Plan for Instruction in Foods and Nutrition Appropriate for Adult Groups and College Students Interested in Personal and Family Living." There were no photo copy machines in those days, so I remember typing my own thesis of 154 pages to save expenses. On July 16, 1953, I received a Master of Science degree and was invited to Phi Upsilon Omicron, the National Honor Society in Home Economics at the University.

Ruth Tanbara received a Master of Science degree in Home Economics from the University of Minnesota in St. Paul, Minnesota, 1953.

In 1955, I attended the World's YWCA Council meetings in London, England, where the YWCA celebrated its 100th anniversary. The 17-day meetings were held at Royal Holloway College in Surrey near London. It was an enriching experience to meet YWCA delegates from many countries around the world, to learn about their programs, and to study their postwar problems and plans for the future. It was gratifying to renew friendships with staff members from Hong Kong and Japan who had come to the St. Paul "Y" at different times to observe and study.

Ruth Tanbara (center) attended the World's YWCA Council meetings held in London, Great Britain, to celebrate the YWCA's centennial, 1955.

After the World's Council meetings in London, I continued my journey to the European Continent and visited Paris and West Berlin. I went on a special bus tour of West Berlin, but we were not permitted to get off the bus in some areas. I met Kaethe Raweil who was a classmate when we were studying at the University of Minnesota in 1952. She was a social worker in West Berlin and was going to Frankfurt to attend a conference. So I stopped there with her to see the city, and enjoyed a special music concert one evening. I went on to visit Lotte Linn, a friend of mine from St. Paul, who was visiting her mother. They invited me to the Harz Mountains for a weekend and we enjoyed the musical concerts at tea time. Many guests were vacationing in the beautiful mountain area. I remember the name Harz as the place where there are too many canary birds. Then I proceeded on to Stuttgart to visit Fuji Shigake Zerick. Her husband Tom was an officer in the U.S. Army stationed in Stuttgart. We had a pleasant tour seeing the palaces there. I continued my trip to Munich, where I met Miss Tan Jen Chiu of Hong Kong. She had attended the Council meetings in London, so it was like a reunion to see her. We toured the city and enjoyed the museums. I also met a music teacher who guided me through the lovely gardens and places of interest. One could see the destruction of many buildings, including the hotel where I was staying, caused by the bombings during the War.

The World Fellowship Committee of the St. Paul YWCA had the assignment not only to study the programs of YWCA's in other countries, but also to raise an annual pledge of $2,000 for the international movement. The local committee, composed of 25 active, devoted members, sponsored in the fall season the annual Holiday Market, one of the largest Christmas bazaars in St. Paul directed by staff member Barbara Swanson. The committee also sponsored the Annual Minnesota Apple Sale and the publication of the first and second editions of *World Fellowship Cook Book*. Favorite recipes from local, national and international YWCA members were gathered. I will always remember the dedicated work the volunteers performed in selecting and testing the recipes. After the printer completed the recipe pages, loyal volunteers spent hours binding the pages with the plastic binders to save additional expenses. It was a wonderful learning experience. The committee members organized the distribution of 2,000 copies of the first 1959 edition and 4,000 copies of the second edition published in 1963.

The artistic skills shared by volunteers in the Craft Workshop each week preparing for the annual Holiday Sale in November were an inspiration for all. Truly noteworthy was their enthusiasm to carry the project through each year with unusual handicrafts to benefit the YWCA.

I was also assigned to the YWCA Religious Interests Committee to serve as a program resource in stimulating religious interests by working through various program areas of the Association and cooperating with other community religious groups. The Lenten Worship series each year with religious leaders in the community brought many employed women from downtown offices to share in the devotional hour.

I truly enjoyed my work at the St. Paul YWCA assisting dedicated volunteers and sharing their talents, interests, and time to carry out the programs of the organization, and offering a variety of classes in the Adult Education Program with trained, experienced teachers in the home arts such as sewing, tailoring, weaving and quilting, and in such business skills as typing, accounting and shorthand. We also offered classes in gardening, flower arrangement, gourmet cooking, oil and watercolor painting, pottery, wood carving, special holiday classes in Christmas crafts and gifts, and many others.

After the resettlement of evacuees from the interment camps was completed, in addition to my work, my interest and time was devoted to serving on various volunteer community committees as a volunteer to help with the relocatees' postwar adjustments. The organizations I was invited to join as a Board member included: the St. Paul-Nagasaki Sister City Committee, Family Service Agency of Greater St. Paul, Japan America Society of Minnesota, Altrusa Club of St. Paul, and Minnesota Museum of Art.

I enjoyed the associations with many volunteers and realized, as an unidentified author once wrote, that "[c]ivilization is maintained by individuals who live for others, who radiate kindness and friendship and live beyond themselves to add something to your contentment and happiness for others."

Fond memories will always be remembered of the first Festival of Nations in 1947 when the Japanese Americans were invited to participate. During the preliminary preparations, it was a wonderful opportunity to meet people from many countries around the world who were now living in Minnesota, to view the exhibit plans of their arts, handicrafts and folk dances, and to sample their delicious native foods. The participants were originally from 39 countries—some were second-, third-, and fourth-generation Americans all taking part in a Festival of Nations for everyone to enjoy.

I thought that the Japanese exhibit and food market plans should be of the highest quality, since it was to be our first venture. Earl and I drove down to Des Moines, Iowa, to visit Mrs. Tomoko Yamamoto. Before World War II, she was the leading teacher in San Francisco in the art of flower arrangement, *bonkei* (tray-landscapes with white sand), and the formal Japanese tea ceremony. During the War, she was residing near her family in Des Moines. We invited

Mrs. Yamamoto to the Festival of Nations in the spring to demonstrate these arts in the Japan exhibit booth. She accepted the invitation. We reserved a room in the YWCA Residence which at that time was located on Fifth Street across from the St. Paul Auditorium where the Festival was held. It was a convenient place for her room and meals in the cafeteria.

Tomoko Yamamoto from Des Moines, Iowa, demonstrated the art of flower arrangement and bonkei (tray-landscapes with white sand) during the first Festival of Nations in St. Paul, Minnesota, 1947.

It was a rare privilege to have her at the Festival and to introduce the quality of her work. Mrs. Yamamoto was a lovely person and had a beautiful philosophy which she combined in her conversation and demonstrations. She was a charming, friendly person and an excellent teacher. She truly presented the Japanese arts at their best. Japanese *ondo* dances were performed by 50 Twin Cities ladies in colorful Japanese *kimonos*. Our parents and many Nisei volunteers participated in the food booth, preparing *sukiyaki* (tender beef cooked in mild soy sauce with fresh vegetables), rice, a light lettuce salad with vegetables, and, on Friday evenings, the ever popular shrimp *tempura*. This was also an opportunity for Nisei women to

The Japanese American community participated in the Grand Parade with a jinrikisha at the Festival of Nations in St. Paul, Minnesota, 1947. The participants are, left to right, Aiko Ogata, Toshiko Teramoto, Joan and Barbara Rokutani, Haruko Hashimoto, and Tom Kurihara.

prepare Japanese foods in quality and quantity. Nisei men, on the other hand, exhibited archery, *judo* (form of wrestling), and *kendo* (fencing).

It was at this time that a deep interest developed in Minnesota in things Japanese, such as studying the Japanese language. Subsequently, Japanese classes were offered in some high schools and colleges—the University of Minnesota in Minneapolis and Macalester College in St. Paul, to name a few. Specialists from Japan taught classes in the art of flower arrangement, tea ceremony, brush painting, music, Japanese *haiku* poetry, Japanese drama, and the colorful informal cherry blossom dances. Preparation of Japanese foods became one of the popular classes at the St. Paul YWCA. Requests came for children's programs, such as interpretation of the Doll Festival Day for Girls in March, the Boys Festival in May, kite flying, the Moon Festival and other colorful celebrations of Japan.

I enjoyed the opportunity to teach Japanese flower arrangement which I had studied in Portland during my youth and later in Berkeley with teachers from Japan. I was invited to give flower arrangement demonstrations at local garden clubs. Tours to the Orient became very popular, and I served as a tour leader in 1964 and later for a number of enjoyable trips through the Orient.

There developed a very deep interest in Japanese gardens and many people read excellent books on the subject in the St. Paul Public Library. Landscape architects came from Japan to teach the principles of Japanese gardening. Mr. Koichi Kawana was the landscape architect of the Japanese Garden at the Minnesota Landscape Arboretum of the University of Minnesota at Chanhassen, Minnesota. Mr. Masami Matsuda from Nagasaki, Japan, designed the Ordway Memorial Japanese Garden in Como Park, St. Paul, whereas Mr. Takao Watanabe from Tokyo, Japan, was the landscape architect for the Normandale Japanese Garden in Bloomington, Minnesota. After the fashion of these Japanese gardens, a number of local residents designed and built gardens on their property because of their simplicity of combining stones, water, pine and few flowers such as iris to cre-

Ruth Tanbara teaching flower arrangement in St. Paul, Minnesota, 1945.
(Photograph by Betty Engle of the St. Paul Pioneer Press.
Reprinted with permission.)

ate a tranquility with nature. With the acceptance of "things Japanese," by Minnesotans, there was a deep feeling of reciprocal appreciation for the different cultures of the people of Minnesota, the "Land of Ten Thousand Lakes."

It was in 1955 that the St. Paul-Nagasaki Sister City Committee was organized by Mr. Louis W. Hill, Jr. St. Paul was a Japanese city's first sister city in the United States. In 1956, President Dwight D. Eisenhower launched the sister city program which was "founded on the concept that citizens of this country represent the great strength of the United States and could and should make contributions to improve the image and understanding of our country to the peoples of other nations ... it was to involve people at all levels of our society in 'personal diplomacy.'" The program has been strengthened with the successive administrations, and today there are over 868 affiliations between American cities and foreign cities around the world. It has been an enriching experience to serve on this committee from the beginning. In 1987, Mr. Hill received a medal, Order of the Rising Sun Gold Rays with Rosettes, from the Government of Japan for his contribution to the U.S.-Japan relations.

In cooperation with Nagasaki, the Sister City Committee has sponsored over the years many exchange visits by mayors and citizens of both cities. The committee also cooperated with the International Sister City Organization in undertaking Youth Art Contests, promoting peace, and sponsoring student exchange programs. With picnics, tours, and home stays, the committee extended hospitality each summer for the students from Junshin Women's Junior College in Nagasaki which is affiliated with the College of St. Catherine in St. Paul. Every year, Junshin sends many students to St. Paul to further their study of English and American culture.

The Japan food booth of the annual Festival of Nations held in the Civic Center of St. Paul is the annual fund-raising project of the Sister City Committee. From 1982 through 1988, Anice Hirabayashi, Mary Kimball and I served as co-chairpersons, working with over 50 volunteers on the four-day Japan food booth project. More than 80,000 people, including some 16,000 students from all around the state come and attend this colorful international event. In recent years, the success of the project made it possible for us to bring Mr. Masami Matsuda, a landscape architect from Nagasaki who had designed the Ordway Memorial Japanese Garden in St. Paul's Como Park. He came five times with assistants to supervise and work on the details of the garden which was completed in 1992. Mr. Matsuda is of the opinion that "[g]ardens are never finished since trees and plants keep growing and need seasonal care."

From 1982 through 1988, Ruth Tanbara co-chaired the St. Paul-Nagasaki Sister City Committee's Japan food booth during the annual Festival of Nations in St. Paul, Minnesota. This photograph, taken in 1982, features, left to right, Dr. Gladys Stone, Yoshi Tani, Anice Hirabayashi (co-chair), Ruth Tanbara, and Mary Kimball (co-chair).

The Sister City Committee also sponsored a special Nagasaki Kite Festival in Landmark Center with many colorful kites displayed from the ceiling of the Cortile.

The Family Service Agency of Greater St. Paul, one of the non-profit social work agencies of the United Way, assisted Japanese Americans in relocating from the internment camps during the war. The Agency's staff members served on the resettlement committee to help meet the evacuees' immediate needs. Through the resettlement committee, a small hotel was leased where the St. Paul Civic Center now stands, and the evacuees found temporary lodging, meals, and employment opportunities as they arrived from the camps. After my retirement from the YWCA in 1972, I was invited to serve on the Board of Directors of the Family Service Agency for six years.

Mr. and Mrs. Charles Meech of Minneapolis were instrumental in establishing the Japan America Society of Minnesota in 1972, in the wake of a tea party honoring the visit of His Excellency

Nobuhiko Ushiba, Ambassador of Japan to Washington, D.C. Mr. Meech was an executive of Minneapolis Honeywell Company. He and his wife lived in Japan part of the year, and shared their knowledge of Japanese culture with many members of the Japan America Society. Mr. Arnulf Ueland was the first Honorary Consul of Japan at Minneapolis. I was elected to the first Board of Directors along with 14 other members, and through the years I served as a program chairperson, secretary, publicity chairperson, and photographer for the Society.

Membership in the Altrusa Club of St. Paul, a national women's service organization, was extended to me in 1965. It is composed of women leaders who either represent women's professions or hold executive positions established firms. It was a pleasure to attend the dinner meetings and work on the Club's community service programs with the friendly members for six years.

One of my early volunteer assignments for the Minnesota Museum of Art was to arrange flowers for an exhibit on April 26, 1950, when Mr. Bernard Leach, a famous potter from St. Ives, Cornwall, England, was invited to St. Paul to lecture at the Museum and exhibit his famous pottery. He had lived in Japan and studied with Shoji Hamada, a famous Japanese potter in Mashiko, a well-known pottery village north of Tokyo. It was one of the most delightful experiences and an honor to arrange flowers in Mr. Leach's exquisite pottery. The genuine, rare containers in their simplicity and somber colors added real quality to the arrangements.

The Museum's first program on Japan was the "Twilight Tea" on April 28, 1968. In collaboration with a very active group of Japanese Americans from the St. Paul-Nagasaki Sister City Committee and YWCA friends, the Museum organized the program. Exhibits of pottery, lacquer ware, fans, and a Girl's Day Doll Festival set were displayed. Also included were demonstrations in calligraphy, brush painting, *origami* (artistic paper folding). And the premier showing of the film, *My Garden Japan*, brought over 900 guests to the evening program, wrote Mrs. Patricia Heikenen, a Museum staff member, in her letter of acknowledgment to the volunteers. Special Japanese delicacies of *sushi*, *monaka* cakes and green tea were served for the first time in St. Paul. In 1972, I was invited to serve on the Board of Trustees of the Minnesota Museum of Art and was later appointed to serve as an Honorary Life Trustee. The program featuring Hanae Mori, a famous Japanese designer in Tokyo and Paris, and her entourage brought an outstanding style show of gowns and models. It was the highlight of the 1978 Annual Spring Benefit, and brought a record attendance to the dinner program at the Radisson Hotel in St. Paul.

With my special interest in modified Japanese flower arrangement, I had the pleasure of arranging flowers on Sunday mornings in the sanctuary of the Unity Church-Unitarian for over 35 years. With an increase in church attendance, it became necessary to have two Sunday morning services. However, making flower arrangement for the early service was inconvenient for me. Mrs. Antoinette Sargent, a long-time member of the Unity Church, and I decided to offer a class teaching flower arrangement for the church sanctuary. We offered four classes, without charge, on Saturday mornings, with the understanding that students would volunteer to do the arrangement every Sunday for a month. Nineteen members, both men and women, enrolled in the class. Some of the members became so interested in this art that they continued their study and made flower arrangement their profession. Doing a modified version of Japanese- and Western-style flower and foliage arrangements brought opportunities to demonstrate and share this art with friends at various garden clubs, classes, and meetings.

In 1869, Mark Twain wrote in *Innocents Abroad* that "[t]ravel is fatal to prejudice, bigotry and narrow mindedness ... broad, wholesome, charitable views cannot be acquired by vegetating in one's little corner of earth." I was reminded of this quotation when a friend expressed a widespread interest in travel to the Orient. So in August 1964, I organized a tour through a local travel agency. It was like a new adventure for me; I had not been to Japan since 1926 and many changes had taken place in travel, accommodations, and services. With excellent travel guides in each country and many YWCA friends

*Ruth Tanbara teaching a flower arrangement class
in the St. Paul YWCA Adult Education Department, circa 1957.
(Photograph by the St. Paul Pioneer Press. Reprinted with permission.)*

through our World Fellowship program, the itinerary was well planned. There were 12 people in our group, all members of the St. Paul YWCA. The members of the tour were: Bertha Ask, Betty Bachmann, Gertrude Hartung, Clara Hovland, Evelyn Mitsch, Evelyn Olson, Margaret Pursley, Elizabeth Reynolds, Irene Tacke, Edith Wallenberg, and Lucille Wells. I was their escort.

The 34-day tour included Tokyo, Nikko, Kamakura, Hakone, Shizuoka, Hamamatsu, Nagoya, Yokkaichi, Toba, Matsuzaka, Kyoto, Takarazuka, Kobe, Beppu, Shimabara, Unzen, Nagasaki, Osaka, Taipei, Hong Kong, Bangkok, Honolulu, and San Francisco.

It was an enjoyable trip. I had many interesting experiences meeting people, visiting schools and large chinaware, textile and electrical appliance companies, and made lasting friendships. I mention this first tour, because it was the best and the service was excellent wherever we went. In 1992, the same tour would probably cost three times more than what we paid in 1964.

On the 1970 tour, we went to the Osaka World Fair. We stayed in Kyoto, and a bus drove us to the fairgrounds each day. Through the years, I had been to the World Fairs in San Francisco, Seattle, Washington, and Montreal, Canada, but the Osaka Fair was the most modern and many new inventions were displayed from each country.

Some of our tour members returned home, but Evelyn Mitsch, Lillian Quarfoot and I continued on to New Delhi, India. Dorothy Cotter, a former staff member of the St. Paul YWCA, was on the program staff of the YWCA in New Delhi. She invited Evelyn Mitsch and me to conduct a Christmas craft workshop for the New Delhi YWCA to help raise funds for its program. We took many craft items and held a workshop for two days for the ladies there. Most of them were Americans, i.e., wives of American corporate or government officials in the Indian capital.

I remember it was very hot in New Delhi, about 114 degrees Fahrenheit with very dry heat. Our hostess had boiled gallons of water and cooled it in the refrigerator. We consumed most of it on the first day. We visited Agra to see the famous Taj Mahal, a most beautiful palace at dawn, and especially lovely in the evening at moonlight.

Since we were halfway around the world, we returned home through Iran where we visited the grand palaces and gardens. The Shah was still in power then. We saw some Iranian students rushing to their classes and noticed ladies in their somber black garments with their heads and faces covered. Large beautiful Persian rugs were displayed in rows of tents where merchants were hustling for sales. I stayed behind our guide for fear of getting lost in the rug displays. There is much to be done to modernize the country and make improvements for the health of the people.

Our next stop was in Athens, Greece, where my University of Minnesota classmate, Olympia Kokevi, took us on a tour of her work in Athens. We visited the YWCA building which housed the

School of Social Work. The excellent guides renewed our study of Greek mythology. We were impressed by the Parthenon and the Acropolis. Greece is a wonderful country to visit. Its climate is like that of San Francisco, the temperature is mild the year around, and fruits, especially oranges, are abundant. I do hope to visit Greece another day.

Then we went on to Rome, Italy. We took tours seeing the famous Coliseum and other historic sites, had time for leisurely walks along the boulevards, and enjoyed pizzas at their best.

Finally, we flew to London. We went on scheduled tours and found things quite changed from the time I was there in 1955. Nonetheless, it was interesting to tour the city and countryside. Everything seemed much more expensive and services were limited. We saw The Changing of the Guard at Buckingham Palace and other tourist attractions, shopped at Harrods and enjoyed English tea at our hotel. Our return flight home was via Detroit, and somehow after being around the world, it was wonderful to be back in St. Paul.

The 1973, 1975, and 1984 tours to the Orient were with smaller groups, but enjoyable since the itineraries were limited to fewer cities and we stayed longer in each place. We took time to enjoy our friends and relatives and to walk through some of the famous gardens of Japan, to visit museums and temples and to do a little more shopping.

In 1985, I went on a special Japan Air Lines tour and joined my sister Elsie and her husband, Jack Shiozaki, in Nagasaki. We later went to Hong Kong together. This was the 30th anniversary of our sister city relationship with Nagasaki, and 28 people from St. Paul were on a special scheduled tour there to celebrate. Nagasaki officials planned a wonderful program to welcome the group with lunches, dinners, receptions and official meetings. We saw the famous fall Okunchi Festival at its best! My special tour arrived a week before the Nagasaki Celebration, so I had the opportunity to visit some of my friends in Nagasaki: Dr. and Mrs. Yoshiro Tsuji, who had a fellowship for one year at the University of Minnesota; Miss Chiyoko Tsuruta, a faculty member of Kwassui Women's College in Nagasaki who had visited St. Paul; Mr. and Mrs. M. Taneguchi; and Dr. and Mrs. M. Iwanaga, whose family visited St. Paul a number of times and dedicated a memorial in Como Park for their late son. We spent an interesting day in Arita, Japan, and visited the famous ceramist, Yokoichi Gagyu, and watched the process of making pottery in his studio.

During the 30th anniversary celebration in Nagasaki, we had the pleasure of visiting the home and garden of Mr. Masami Matsuda, the designer and landscape architect of the Ordway Memorial Japanese Garden in Como Park, St. Paul. As I look at my album of pictures which I had taken on that occasion, Mr. and Mrs. Matsuda's gracious hospitality extended to our group will long be remembered.

In 1990, the Japanese American community in Portland, Oregon, had a reunion for its residents and former residents. Over 927 attended the three-day meeting, August 3-5, at the Red Lion Hotel in Lloyd Center. A very special program was planned and it was a real pleasure to meet longtime friends. The preschool children, whom I taught at the Manley Community Center back in the 1930s, had all grown up and were successful in their professions. I had not been in Portland for a long time. Once I attended the 45th reunion of my 1930 class at Oregon State University, and the second time I visited Mrs. R. Maeda, a longtime family friend. It was wonderful to see the changes in the city and the improvements made to add beauty to the landmarks. Mt. Hood looked at its best, and the Japanese Garden up near Council Crest was authentic and lovely. It was wonderful to be back, and I was happy that I was "Made in Portland."

Mark Twain was right when he said that "travel is wholesome, refreshing and the best education to broaden one's views."

Believe it or not, Earl and I met through the San Francisco YWCA. My sister and I were going to Los Angeles to visit my college roommate who was married and living there. On the way, we stopped in San Francisco to visit Miss Sumi Yamamoto, a long time friend who was the Executive Director of the San Francisco Japanese YWCA. Sumi was originally from Idaho. When she attended Linfield College in Oregon, she stayed with my family during Christmas and other holiday seasons in Portland. On that particular day, Sumi was very involved in a YWCA Board of Directors meeting and could not get away for lunch or sightseeing as we had originally planned. She asked Earl Tanbara to drive us to Golden Gate Park and other scenic parts of the city during his lunch hour. I remember he was very courteous and the lunch was enjoyable. It was probably a year or so later that Earl came to Portland on a business trip and called me. So my brothers and I took him for sightseeing in Portland as a return favor. He visited several times, driving hundreds of miles from Berkeley.

Earl was born in Pleasanton, California, on December 5, 1905. His parents, Mr. Miyota Tanbara and Mrs. Takeno Tanbara, were originally from Okayama, Japan. Earl had one sister, Grace. He attended Montezuma Private School for Boys in Los Gatos, California, Santa Cruz High School, Los Gatos High School, College of Pacific, and the University of California, Berkeley, where he earned his B.A. in Economics in 1927. In his early years, Earl was very active in baseball and belonged to the San Jose Asahi Team and toured Japan to play exhibition baseball. In Wakayama, it was reported that Earl hit a grand slam, and that a marker was labeled: "Earl Tanbara hit here." He enjoyed golf and played regularly with his business associates and Japanese American friends. Once he hit a "hole in one" on the Lake Chabot course in Oakland and was recorded in the *Pacific Citizen*—a real golfer's dream. He participated in the Twin Cities JACL tournaments and won a number of silver trophies.

For indoor recreation, Earl was an avid contract bridge player, enjoyed playing in the San Francisco city-wide tournaments with Mr. Taki Domoto, and won many honors as recorded in the San Francisco newspapers. He taught me to play contract bridge, and I remember playing Duplicate Bridge with Earl in the San Francisco

JACL tournament in which we won a silver trophy. I appreciated Earl teaching me to play bridge, for through the years, I have enjoyed playing on social occasions with friends.

In May 1935, we became engaged. The announcement was made by my parents at a dinner in our home in Portland. In those days, we had go-between friends (*baishakunin*). Mr. Harold Toda of Portland represented my family, and Mr. Dwight Takashi Uchida of Berkeley with the Mitsui Company was Earl's family representative. Mr. Uchida was also a friend of my family, since his family had lived in Portland before he was transferred to San Francisco.

We were married on September 16, 1935, at the Centenary Wilbur Methodist Church in Portland with the Rev. Thomas Acheson officiating, assisted by the Rev. S. Kawashima of the Japanese Methodist Church. We were the first Nisei couple to be married in an American Church in Portland. Most weddings were at the Japanese Methodist Church or the Buddhist Temple. The board members of the Portland YWCA where I served on the staff as membership secretary all came to help with the reception. It was a beautiful wedding. One friend, Mrs. Wheeler, brought ivory-colored gladiolas from her garden, and many Japanese friends made *osushi* to add to the festivities. We left the next morning for Vancouver, British Columbia, on our honeymoon.

Earl was employed by the Robert Dollar Steamship Company with Around the World Travel Service on the President Steamships. He was the Director of the Advertising Department at the company's head office in the Dollar Building in San Francisco. He was responsible for all phases of advertising from the printed travel brochures, sailing schedules, menus, calendars, bridge playing cards, magazine and newspaper stories, and billboards, and often gave travel presentations with films to different organizations. He enjoyed his work and his associates over ten years.

In the January 5, 1974 issue of the *Pacific Citizen*, its editor, Harry Honda of Los Angeles, wrote that "Earl was one of the foun-

*Before World War II, Earl K. Tanbara worked as
Director of the Advertising Department at the
Robert Dollar Steamship Company in San Francisco, California.*

dation stones of the Japanese American Citizens League (JACL)."
During the early years of the paper, Earl was the managing editor as
well as the editor of the *San Francisco JACL Newsletter*, the *Pacific
Citizen's* precursor. He also gave the paper its present name, the
Pacific Citizen. In addition to his work on the resettlement of the
Nisei in Minnesota, he helped organize the JACL in Minnesota and
the Twin Cities JACL Credit Union. Earl also served on the Board
of Directors of the International Institute of Minnesota. He believed
in low-cost funeral arrangements and contributing memorials to help
community organizations, and served on the Board of Directors of
the Minnesota Memorial Society for many years.

In later years, Earl commented that Minnesota was a good
place for our youth and education. He hoped that young Nisei (he
always said "I'm one of the older Nisei"), Sansei and their posterity
would keep alive some of the Japanese traditions and customs which
had been introduced through the evacuation process. He also stated
that despite the hardships experienced by the early Issei immigrants,
the anti-alien land laws, the Depression, World War II, the evacua-

Earl K. Tanbara on a trade mission to India, circa 1939.

tion en masse, the personal tragedies and losses, we still came out as winners, and that late as it was in coming, the naturalization of the Isseis attested to their loyalty to the United States. Earl really believed in the JACL's creed that Japanese Americans should strive to become "Better Americans in a Greater America."

Earl passed away on January 4, 1974. In his eulogy for my late husband, the Rev. Roy Phillips said that Earl was remembered by many of his friends for his wonderful sense of humor and "his ability to see life, to live it fully and to enjoy it." So his absence is truly missed. In 1974, the Twin Cities JACL established the Earl Tanbara Memorial Scholarship Fund in his memory to help Japanese American students continue their college education.

*Ruth and Earl K. Tanbara representing Japan in the Grand Parade
at the Festival of Nations in St. Paul, Minnesota, 1973.*

My younger brother Howard graduated from Oregon State College with a degree in Pharmacy. He had a pharmacy in Portland before the war. After resettling in St. Paul, he passed the Minnesota state board examinations and worked as a registered pharmacist for many years with a local firm.

At one time, all my immediate relatives resided in Minnesota, but through the years, many of them moved to other states. My sister Elsie's family moved to Chicago, Indiana, Iowa, and California, whereas my brother Paul was employed with a firm in Chicago. Grace, Earl's sister, resides in San Francisco, and her son Tom's family lives in Virginia. I miss my parents and Earl's parents, who have passed away. At this writing, my late brother Howard's family lives in the Twin Cities, and includes Mrs. Emi Nomura, her two children Judy and Philip, and her five grandchildren, Christine, Lisa, Steven, Mari, Jennifer and Philip, and great-grandson Alexander. I have many pleasant memories sharing holiday dinner parties, birthdays and visits with my relatives in the Twin Cities, Chicago, San Francisco and Vienna, Virginia. Though distance keeps us apart, we are in touch by phone, correspondence and occasional visits. I enjoy my relatives and have a great regard for them, and they have all been wonderful to me.

Since Earl sold his business at Pyramid Products Company and retired, I also retired from my position in 1972, after 30 years on the program staff of the St. Paul YWCA. The YWCA members and friends planned a very special retirement celebration and in 1973 dedicated a Japanese garden in the patio of the YWCA building as a tribute to my years at the organization.

In 1973, the St. Paul YWCA dedicated to Ruth Tanbara a Japanese garden in the patio of the YWCA building as a tribute to her 30 years of service to the organization.

Reflections

In 1942, Alice L. Sickels, Executive Director of the International Institute of Minnesota, wrote her book, *Around the World in St. Paul*, which included the history of the Nisei, a new ethnic group coming to St. Paul during World War II (pages 200-210), along with their photos (page 149). It seems fitting to add a sequel to her story, relating what happened to the Nisei during the next 50 years.

She had foresight and courage to welcome the group at a time in our history when the United States was at war with Japan, following the Japanese attack on Pearl Harbor in Hawaii. She understood the difference between the Japanese nationals of Japan and the Japanese Americans who were U.S. citizens by birth, although their parents were from Japan and could not become naturalized citizens even after residing here over 40 years. She understood the problems of relocation and adjustment and assigned members of her social work staff to cooperate in the resettlement program.

After the exclusion orders against Japanese Americans were revoked in January 1945, many Nisei and their families returned to the West Coast to start life anew. However, a number of families decided to stay in the Twin Cities, their adopted home, and to continue their education, raise their families and contribute their interests and special skills to add to the life in the community through participation in local programs and events.

During an informal luncheon in St. Paul on March 9, 1991, a group of 12 Nisei women gathered to celebrate their first 50 years in Minnesota. In our casual conversation, we decided to write our autobiographies as a legacy to our family and friends, and to record it in the history of Minnesota for the warm welcome and hospitality extended to the Japanese Americans.

This was the beginning of our project. Invitations were mailed to 75 Nisei women who lived in the Twin Cities area, or who used to live here but moved out of the state. Actual replies were received by approximately 20 people.

Prof. John Nobuya Tsuchida, Director of the Office for Minority and Special Student Affairs at the University of Minnesota, offered to assist with the book project by meeting with the group and editing our manuscripts. He suggested that some photographs of different events in our lives would add special interest. Monthly meetings were held since July 1991 as an informal class, and no fees were charged. Autobiographies were written according to a standard outline consisting of seven chapters which had been prepared by Dr. Tsuchida. There were 14 members in the active group, and the deadline for the manuscripts and photographs was set for February 22, 1992. The book was initially scheduled for publication by the end of 1992. At each session, volunteers offered and served fresh fruit, rolls, tea and coffee for the early morning classes.

Particular changes in my life style were noted. When I lived in the San Francisco Bay area, my schedule of activities centered around the home, friends, church, teaching Sunday school, going to concerts and attending lectures of special interests at the University of California, Berkeley where some of my former instructors from Oregon State College were on the faculty, and I continued my interest in handicrafts. We were planning to build a house on our property in El Cerrito (near Berkeley). A warrant was issued when we were living in St. Paul that the property was condemned for residential purposes, since the City of El Cerrito was planning to build a high school and needed our one acre of land for the athletic field. Through an attorney in St. Paul, the property was sold to the City of El Cerrito.

From personal involvement to carrying responsibilities of helping other families in the resettlement program, my activities centered around volunteer work, finding housing, employment, social activities, medical care for patients, as well as doing volunteer work with other organizations. My vision and purpose in life developed far beyond my expectations. It gave me the opportunity to meet not only other Japanese Americans from many West Coast cities now residing in Minnesota, but many leaders and groups in the community as we worked together to enrich our community. As one friend commented, "I would never have met you except for the evacuation."

From about 1945, the social life of the Japanese Americans in the Twin Cities centered around the Japanese Community Center located in a large house at 2200 Blaisdell Street in Minneapolis. The property was owned by the Episcopal Diocese of Minnesota, which provided the Director, first the Rev. Daisuke Kitagawa and later the Rev. Andrew N. Otani. The upkeep and program developments were supervised by the Japanese American Board of Management. Other organizations in the Twin Cities met there—the Japanese American Citizens League, the Japanese Christian Church with sermons in Japanese for our parents, and the active Rainbow Club, an interfaith, interracial group. Many programs and social events were offered at the Center and were well attended by families in the Twin Cities. The house required general upkeep, maintenance care, and garden work, and heating was expensive during the winter months. Family members volunteered each week to help take care of the facility.

With increasing responsibilities in their own homes, it became difficult to find volunteers to help at the Center, so the Board of Management decided to give up the building and returned it to the Episcopal Diocese. Later they had an opportunity to sell the property and a building was erected there. It was an interesting gathering place, but when the children grew up and families moved to the suburbs and joined the churches and school groups in their neighborhoods, the Community Center had already met its purpose and was ready to be dissolved. Many played golf, tennis, bowling, fishing and water sports at the lakes nearby, and the residents became integrated in their own communities. Other groups, such as the Minnesota Nikkei Project for aging Issei, were organized. The active Twin Cities JACL often met in the board members' homes and carried on their special activities with dinner meetings in local hotels and restaurants. Others joined the St. Paul-Nagasaki Sister City Committee founded in 1955 and the Japan America Society of Minnesota established in 1972.

For reference and record purposes, the Board of Management presented the records of the Japanese American Community Center on March 5, 1956, to the Director of the Minnesota Historical Society at a special Japanese *sukiyaki* dinner.

I feel confident that settling down in Minnesota was the wisest decision I have ever made. It was a sharing process. I have always enjoyed the cities where I lived. There was a real charm in Portland, Oregon, my birthplace where I resided with my family and spent my childhood, teen and school years. It is a residential city where many people took pride in their homes and rose gardens and the changes of seasons were mild and enjoyable. Mt. Hood was a beautiful sight on a clear day and brought strength and inspiration to us as Oregonians.

After marriage, I lived in Berkeley and the San Francisco Bay area with temperate climate all year round. I was fascinated living in a metropolitan area where there were so many programs and activities offered. I felt it a privilege to live there: just by crossing the Bay, one could visit the magnificent art museums, attend great symphony concerts, go down to the wharfs on sailing days to wish *bon voyage* to people traveling on steamships around the world. Friends were cordial and living seemed more sophisticated there. I particularly noticed that with its 70-degree weather, ladies were always well-dressed going to the City with hats, suits and shoes matching their purses and gloves. It really had a charm of its own to view Golden Gate Park when the rhododendrons were in bloom; to visit the Japanese Garden and Tea House; to ride on the cable cars; to visit Twin Peaks or drive down to Palo Alto to visit the Stanford University Campus; or to attend the big homecoming football games with the University of California. These eight years will always be well-remembered.

Coming on the long train ride to St. Paul, Minnesota, in 1942 during the heat, rainstorms and thunder of early August was quite an experience. It was unusual for me to witness heavy rains during the summer months which do not usually happen in the West. In many ways, it reminded me of Portland in that St. Paul is a residential city where people take pride in their homes and gardens. I was greatly impressed with the flowers and shrubs blooming in great profusion in the early spring, especially the tulips, lilacs, peonies, irises and roses. In due time, I learned to adjust to the changes of seasons in Minnesota which are more severe than in Oregon. I also discovered that even though the temperature in winter goes down far below zero in Fahrenheit, the people of St. Paul extended a warm, cordial welcome. For almost 39 years, Earl and I lived in the Crocus Hill section on South Avon and Linwood Streets, settled down in the community life with friends and relatives, and became Minnesotans as the saying goes: "Home is the place where the heart is."

There were many disillusionments and heartaches which accompanied the wartime evacuation. People were bewildered; many lost their farms, crops, property, equipment, homes, household goods, machinery, and cars. However, I truly believe there have been some compensations:

1. The dispersal of the Japanese American community from the West Coast to the Midwest and East was a "blessing in disguise." It broadened our knowledge of the United States to get away from the ghettos of the West. It also widened educational opportunities for the Japanese American students. The Student Relocation Committee contacted the National Japanese American Student Relocation Council of California which communicated with the colleges in the Midwest and East, so many Japanese American students received scholarships to enroll in some of the top universities.

2. The evacuation also enhanced employment opportunities for college graduates in their respective fields. I recall when I completed my B.S. degree (1930) in Home Economics for teaching, I was denied the opportunity to teach in the public high schools because of my heritage even with better than average scholastic standing. I also re-

member the Japanese American graduates in Engineering at Western colleges with top honors could not find employment in the United States, so they went to Japan or worked in fruit and vegetable stores on the West Coast. Today in the Midwest and East as well as in Western states, Japanese American college graduates have opportunities to teach like any other graduates and to pursue other professions of their choice.

3. Living in the Midwest, we had a better understanding of the problems of other minority groups. We discovered "there are many people in America not only in the Midwest and East, but also in the West who helped us keep faith in the democratic way, and that in this country there is a place for all people of goodwill regardless of their racial heritage."

It is heartwarming to know that today great strides have been made among the Nisei and Sansei. Many Japanese American men and women have achieved highest honors in all fields and professions: sports, music, print and electronic media, art, politics, law, business, education, writing, medicine, science, engineering, research, etc.

It is the Issei that we honor for their foresight and sacrifices to educate their children through the years. They worked hard and gave up many social activities so their children could be well-educated. They understood the value of education to become good citizens of the United States, although they were legally barred from naturalization.

In a democracy, one realizes that education is most important not only because of the knowledge of the 3 R's (Reading, Writing and Arithmetic) which are required subjects for literacy. Opportunities for these subjects should be available and encouraged for everyone to study and become intelligent citizens. Continuing education classes in human relations will also help citizens study and appreciate other points of view, thereby enabling them to use good judgment in relationships with other racial and religious groups to respect, understand and help solve their problems.

In 1933, when I was employed as a part-time secretary in the Japanese Consulate General in Portland, I had the occasion to accompany the Foreign Minister of Japan, Yosuke Matsuoka, to the University of Oregon at Eugene, along with the consular staff. Mr. Matsuoka was a graduate of the University of Oregon and was well known during his student days. As an alumnus of the University, he was invited to address the students at a convocation. The train trip took about three hours, and in our casual conversation he asked me about my plans since I had graduated from college. I was not ready to reply, but asked him what a Nisei should do. He recommended that the Nisei study and get a good education, stay in the United States, and marry another Nisei, and that both become the best examples and help enhance understanding between Japan and the United States. I appreciated his advice so much through the years that it became Earl's and my purpose to be good American citizens as Nisei.

As I write, I think of many deceased friends who contributed their time and skills during the resettlement days and of those who dedicated many volunteer hours to make life abundant. Included among them are:

Alice L. Sickels who cordially welcomed the Nisei to Minnesota 50 years ago.

Dr. Kano Ikeda who, during the resettlement program, helped many of us who were new in the city by providing us with medical advice and service as well as referrals to specialists. Dr. Ikeda was born in Tokyo, Japan, in 1886 and came to the United States in 1904 to study medicine. He received his medical degree from Illinois University in 1914. He was the chief pathologist at Miller Hospital in St. Paul for 30 years. He also served as a pathologist at Children's Hospital, Gillette State Hospital for crippled children, Riverview Memorial

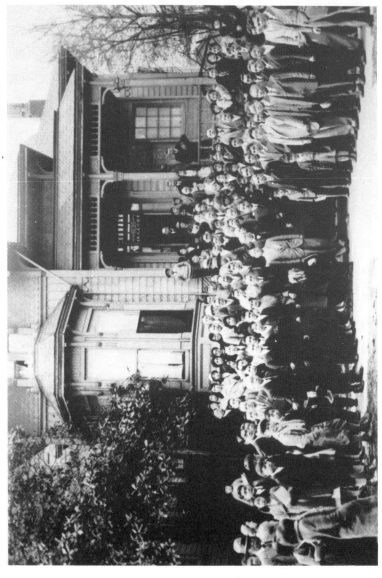

While working at the Japanese Consulate in Portland, Oregon, in 1933, Ruth Tanbara (front row, center, wearing a white bonnet) met Japanese Foreign Minister Yosuke Matsuoka (front row, fourth from Ruth, with a mustachio on) who was a graduate of the University of Oregon. This photograph was taken in front of the Japanese Methodist Episcopal Church in Portland, Oregon, 1933.

Hospital, and the Department of Medical Technology at Macalester College. Dr. Ikeda was outstanding in the field of Pathology and Medical Technology and won many honors for his studies. He was a member of many national and international medical societies. Despite his many responsibilities, he was kind-hearted to all of us evacuees when we needed medical attention. He always made time to provide us with professional help and advice, for which we shall always be grateful. He lived in St. Paul with his wife, Mae, daughter Ethel, son Alden, and three grandchildren. After the Walter-McCarran Act was enacted in 1952 to allow alien Japanese to become naturalized American citizens, Dr. Ikeda was the first Japanese to become a U.S. citizen in Minnesota.

Dr. Kano Ikeda provided many Japanese Americans in Minnesota with medical service and advice during the resettlement period, circa 1945.

Mr. Clemet White of the American Friends Service Committee of Philadelphia who was assigned to Minnesota to assist with the resettlement of Japanese Americans and their families. He was outstanding in building community acceptance for the Japanese American relocatees and made many contacts for housing and employment. Earl was so impressed with the work of the American Friends Service Committee that Mr. White invited him to go to Philadelphia to study this organization's services, particularly its program of resettlement in other locations.

Kay Kushino of Minneapolis who worked many years at Bruce Publishing Company editing text books in Home Economics. She was a dedicated volunteer of the Japanese American Citizens League and the Japan America Society of Minnesota, whose special assignment was in membership and program arrangements. I remember her devoted assistance in the Japan Food Booth of the Festival of Nations and her enthusiastic support of the Japanese potluck dinners for six years for hundreds of women students from Junshin Junior College of Nagasaki who came every summer to further their study of English and the United States at the College of St. Catherine in St. Paul, their sister affiliate.

Evelyn Mitsch who was the mother of a fine family in St. Paul and a special friend of mine. She was active on the St. Paul-Nagasaki Sister City Committee as Secretary and Membership Director for many years. Skilled in the arts, she was interested in Japan and the art of Oriental brush painting which she taught at the St. Paul YWCA. Through her many travels, she made a valuable contribution to strengthening the YWCA program, as well as to enhancing our knowledge about Japan.

Finally, I would like to take this opportunity to express my deepest appreciation to my parents, my late husband Earl, brothers Paul and Howard, sister Elsie, relatives in the United States and Japan, many friends in Minnesota and other places where I lived and visited, associates in volunteer organizations, and all who have made time and life so precious and enjoyable. I also wish to give special acknowledgment to three organizations:

1. The St. Paul YWCA for the copper plaque which reads:

The Ruth Tanbara Japanese Garden
at 65 East Kellogg Boulevard
Donated by YWCA Members of St. Paul
1972
for 30 years on the YWCA Staff
Billie and Jerre Logan and Helen Richardson
Garden Committee

2. Family Service Agency of St. Paul for the special plaque named:

Ruth Tanbara Diamond Award
for Volunteer Contributions
May 20, 1992
From Family Service Agency of St. Paul
on their 100th Anniversary

3. The Beautification and Social Committees at the Wilder Park Towers condominium, where I live and have volunteered caring for the plants and flowers in the atrium since 1980, gave a special tea when I retired from the responsibility on July 13, 1993, and placed a brass plaque, "The Ruth Tanbara Atrium," in the entry on the ground level. Many volunteers assisted me in keeping the green plants healthy and the colorful geraniums always in bloom.

MARY MARIKO OGURA

My father Frank Kyosuke Yokota was born on March 26, 1885, in Aso Village, Kibi County, Okayama Prefecture, Japan. Aso Village is located about 150 miles inland from the seaport of Kobe. The village had approximately 120 families comprising 650 people. Kyosuke was the third of five sons born to Genzo and Nobu Yokota.

The Yokota family's occupation was tobacco farming, and they also grew vegetables for their own consumption. They owned no animals except for one horse. In wealth the family stood a little above average in relationship to the rest of the community.

Educationally, my father went through elementary and middle school (equivalent to high school). He also graduated from a normal school.

In Japan, the eldest son inherited all the family wealth and land, and so my father had to seek his fortune on his own. He chose to set out for America, arriving in August 1907 at the age of 17. Once in America, my father's life followed a pattern very familiar to many Japanese immigrants. Upon arrival, he immediately left for Portland, Oregon, to work for the railroad. A year later, he went to Hood River, Oregon, to work as a domestic in a private home. This was his first intimate look at how Americans lived. From 1910 to 1913, he split his time between Hood River and Underwood, Washington, working as a domestic, on apple orchards and berry farms, and clearing land for cultivation.

In 1912, my father was married to Tatsuye Hirata by "picture." He had not met her as yet, only knowing her by a picture sent to him by his family who had arranged the marriage. In December, 1913, he left America and returned to his family in Japan, where he took up residence with his bride until May 1915 when they returned to Seattle, Washington. During the 15 months they spent in Japan, a daughter was born to them whom they named Tsuyuko. Tsuyuko remained in Japan when my parents came to America. They left her behind because they only planned on returning to America for a few years and they thought it would be better for the child not to risk the voyage.

My mother, Tatsuye Hirata, was born on August 8, 1895, in Tomiyama Village, Kibi County, Okayama Prefecture, Japan. She was the only daughter of Mokusaburo and Saye Hirata who also had two sons. They also were farmers raising rice as a cash crop and vegetables for their own consumption. The Hirata family was also a little above average in wealth. My mother graduated from elementary and middle school and had attended a girls' high school after graduation. When she was married by picture on March 31, 1912, she left her home to reside with the Yokota family in the neighboring village until her husband arrived from America.

After arriving in America in April 1915, my parents worked at a farm in South Park, a suburb of Seattle, Washington. In the fall of that year, they began raising hogs at South Park. Between 1916 and 1919, three daughters were born to them, Priscilla, myself, and Sue. By this time my father gave up the idea of returning to Japan. He felt his daughters would have better opportunities in America than in Japan.

*Mary Ogura's parents, Frank Kyosuke and Tatsuye Yokota,
in Sunnydale, Washington, 1962.*

In 1919, my parents set down permanent roots in America by
buying their own farm in Sunnydale, Washington, also a suburb of
Seattle. There they raised hogs until 1923. The farm consisted of 35
acres of uncleared land, a two-story house and a large barn. We
owned two work horses and a pony named Mary. We were one of
the first Japanese families to settle in Sunnydale.

The period from 1919 to 1924 was a particularly difficult
time for our family. Two children were born and both died during
infancy of childhood illnesses: a girl named Lillian in 1921 and a
boy named Frank in 1923. My parents quit attending church after
Frank passed away. They had attended the Buddhist church before.
During this same period, the Seattle City Council began regulating
the raising of hogs in an effort to force Japanese out of the business.
This culminated in the passage of an ordinance which prevented Japanese from collecting garbage from Seattle's restaurants for hog feed,
while Caucasians could continue the practice. My father said this

was the most difficult period of his life. He had built the facilities to meet the city's regulatory conditions, but was now denied his source of feed. He later wrote, "Swallowing our tears, we finally gave up."

This period was marked by many other anti-Japanese laws, such as the Alien Land Law which threatened my father's right to own our land. To keep it, my father put ownership under the name of our sister, Priscilla. This required the sponsorship of an American attorney. It was a very trying period for all Japanese Americans.

Mary Ogura's sister, Priscilla Yokota, in front of her house in Sunnydale, Washington, immediately prior to the forced evacuation of Japanese Americans from the West Coast in 1942. She is wearing her identification number as a prospective detainee in the Puyallup Assembly Center in Washington.

Although the land at Sunnydale was of poor quality, we cleaned our neighbors' chicken coops in exchange for manure, which we put into the land and began raising vegetables as a cash crop. So it was in 1923 that my parents turned to the occupation that would fill all of our lives until I left to marry in 1938. In 1925, King County school district voted to build Highline High School on part of our land. Ten acres were appropriated from us for this purpose. The school is still being used today. My parents belonged to the PTA and participated in many activities.

My childhood was split between public school and working the farm. There was little time or money for play. But we did have the companionship of each other, for we toiled together in the fields as a family. My parents were very interested in education, and much to their chagrin, I was not a very good student. However, I was good at track, winning many ribbons.

Although there were 27 Japanese families in the community, the neighborhood that we grew up in was almost entirely Caucasian. I attended public school mostly with Caucasians, graduating from Highline High School. On Saturdays we also attended Japanese school. Unlike most Japanese families, we always ate an American breakfast of bacon, eggs and coffee. We also attended Methodist Church although my parents did not. We were on very good terms with our neighbors because Dad saw to it that we helped when there was a need in the community. He acted as the liaison between the white and Japanese communities.

Even though we got along well in the community, we experienced the same discrimination as other Japanese. We were not allowed to swim at the public beaches in the area. Dad dammed the creek that crossed our land and we used to play there; however, I never did learn to swim. Job opportunities for Japanese were limited to domestic service, farm work, or the railroads and saw mills. At school, we were teased and taunted as "Japs" or "Chinks." One of my jobs as a child was to do family grocery shopping several times a week. The store was two miles away and I was always on the lookout for several white kids who loved to lie in wait to tease and ridicule me.

Some time in January 1937, a family acquaintance called my parents to ask whether they would be interested in having one of their daughters meet a young Japanese man who was from the same area of Japan as they. After some discussion, my parents approached me with the idea. I was 19 years old at the time and although I hadn't really dated, I was ready to get on with my own life. So I agreed and met Johnnie Chikao Ogura at our friend's home. Johnnie was on vacation from his job with the Great Northern Railroad. He worked as a waiter on the private car of the president. The railroad crew was based in St. Paul, Minnesota, but traveled a great deal between there and Seattle. We began a long-distance correspondence, with Johnnie visiting me whenever he was in town, which ultimately led us to marry on December 15, 1938.

Mary and Johnnie Chikao Ogura were married on December 15, 1938, in Seattle, Washington.

Johnnie Chikao Ogura was born on March 12, 1903, in Aso Village, Kibi County, Okayama Prefecture, Japan. Although he came from the same village as my parents, the families did not know each other. Johnnie was the third of six sons born to Tetsuyemon and Sae Ogura. The Oguras were also rice farmers. Johnnie completed elementary school and two years of middle school before setting out on his own. In March 1919, he went to Kobe, Japan and got a job shoveling coal on an ocean going steamer. By June 1919, the ship had made the voyage across the Pacific, arriving in Seattle. By this time he had had enough of the sea and decided to jump ship to seek his fortune here.

Johnnie's early years in America followed the pattern of my father. At first he worked in a saw mill away from the general population with other Japanese laborers. This is where he first began to learn English. In 1920, an uncle got him a job in a railroad repair shop in Hilyard, Washington. When his older brother Tomosaburo arrived from Japan, Johnnie gave him his job and took a job as a domestic living with a white family. This job allowed him the time to attend public elementary school to learn better English, which he did even though he was a grown man. From 1922 until 1928, he worked at a series of different jobs: domestic help, chauffeur, waiter, etc. Then in March 1928, he landed the job I mentioned earlier with the Great Northern Railroad. He would end up working for the railroad except for the war years until his retirement in 1970, with 42 years of service.

In 1930, the private car Johnnie worked on was based in Duluth, Minnesota. He met and married a Caucasian woman named

Johnnie Chikao Ogura retired in 1970 from the Great Northern Railroad after 42 years of service. He was presented with a diamond tie tac, and his wife, Mary, received a pin and earring set with a jewelry box at his retirement reception in St. Paul, Minnesota.

Hilda Maki. In 1931, they had a son, whom they named Jim. In 1935, they were divorced. Johnnie took Jim to live with her sister in Superior, Wisconsin, because Hilda had a severe drinking problem. Since his job involved extensive travel, he saw Jim whenever he was in town. In 1937, his boss was promoted to President and Johnnie moved with him to the Great Northern's headquarters in St. Paul.

After a short honeymoon on which I met my husband's friends and brother in Spokane, Washington, we traveled to St. Paul, Minnesota, arriving in time for Christmas of 1938. It was WINTER, need

Johnnie Chikao Ogura worked as a waiter on the private car of the Great Northern Railroad's president. This photograph was taken with his mother-in-law, Tatsuye Yokota, in Seattle, Washington, circa 1940.

76

I say more? We took up residence at the Euclid Hotel on Wabasha and 9th Streets. It was the one hotel that didn't discriminate and accommodated Japanese and Chinese guests. The winter season meant my husband didn't have to travel, and we were together most of those first few months. I remember writing my mother and telling her that "I live in an icebox." One day I went out in the snow and cold and froze my knee caps. Women didn't wear slacks then. I didn't tell anyone and warmed them against the radiator, something I now know is not the thing to do.

When I first came to St. Paul, most people thought I was Chinese and I didn't correct them. I think they thought this because there were several Chinese restaurants here. All told, there were eleven Japanese in St. Paul at the time; one family of four, Johnnie and I, and the rest were Japanese men who were single or married to Caucasians.

By March 1939, Johnnie was beginning to travel again, so I decided to return to Seattle for the summer to help on my parents' farm. I left our things with the hotel manager to wait for my return in the fall. Although my first three months away from my parents' home were in a strange city, in a foreboding climate, away from most Japanese, I was pleased and happy with my new life. Since I had been raised among Caucasians in Seattle, I didn't feel like a foreigner in St. Paul.

Upon my return to St. Paul in September 1939, I was happy to see that Minnesota's weather didn't only consist of ice and snow. Since there was no room at the hotel, we moved to a light house-keeping apartment on 9th Street run by a wonderful German family. The family consisted of father, mother, three girls and two boys. Some of the children were married and lived there with their wives. Their youngest daughter, Violet, was especially fond of me and we were like one big happy family, sharing everything.

With things becoming stable in the fall of 1939, we sent for my husband's son Jim, who arrived in time to celebrate Christmas with us. He was a very good boy and it was good to have him with us. I also found I was pregnant with our first child. These were happy and exciting times for me as we began to establish our own family.

Johnnie Chikao Ogura with his son, James Richard Ogura, at their cabin at Lake Loveless, Wisconsin, 1991.

In July 1940, my first daughter, Mary, was born and I returned to Seattle for a short time to show my parents the baby. After my return to St. Paul, I settled in with my new family as a housewife. Job opportunities were very limited in St. Paul, with most companies having restrictions against hiring Japanese. We continued to live with our German friends on 9th Street.

Life went along quickly until December 7, 1941, when the world seemed to stop. I was home that day. My husband was in Seattle with the railroad. When I heard the news of the attack, I was very depressed. The railroad immediately brought my husband back to St. Paul and the government instituted travel restrictions on Japanese, which meant he had to leave his job with the railroad. The railroad granted Japanese employees leaves of absence so they

Mary and Johnnie Chikao Ogura at the house of Willie and Ruth Akamatsu in St. Paul, Minnesota, 1940.

wouldn't lose their seniority, and allowed them to collect benefits until they found new employment. My husband was without work for ten months until he finally landed a job as a domestic with Howard Kahn in 1942. Mr. Kahn was a journalist who wrote the "Paul Light" column for the *St. Paul Pioneer Press*.

After my husband returned from Seattle in December 1941, we had to turn in our radio and camera to the authorities at the Public Safety Building. We never got these back. We were also subject to a 6:00 p.m. curfew and could not travel outside of the city without first getting official permission. We were told to keep out of public places, so we decided to maintain a low profile.

Back in Seattle, my parents, brother, and sisters were shocked by Pearl Harbor like any other Americans. They were not afraid of an anti-Japanese reaction from their neighbors because of their close relationship with them. However, the real shocker came later when all Japanese, regardless of citizenship, were ordered to evacuate into the internment camps. My parents and siblings were first relocated to Pinedale, California, and later to the Tule Lake Relocation Center in California. They stayed there until 1943 when they were relocated to a camp at Heart Mountain, Wyoming. The move was due to the fact that Tule Lake had been designated for those Japanese American internees who had been considered by the U.S. government as "disloyal" following the administration of flawed loyalty questionnaires.

Mary Ogura's brother, Bill, in Sunnydale, Washington, 1942.

My parents remained there until September 1945. While in camp, they were allowed only two rooms for their entire family. My father worked as a carpenter, fashioning furniture from crates and things.

Back in St. Paul, I remember a time in 1942 when my husband, his Japanese friend, my daughter Mary, and I were out in public. A Caucasian woman came up to us and said what a cute "Chink" baby she was. She went on to say how we must hate and want to fight those "sneaky Japs." We just looked at each other. It was at this time that I decided not to teach my children any Japanese for fear that they would get into trouble.

Mary Ogura's parents, Frank Kyosuke and Tatsuye Yokota, with their daughters, Dorothea (center) and Priscilla, in front of their barracks at the Heart Mountain Relocation Center in Wyoming, Christmas, 1944.

Mary Ogura's parents, Frank Kyosuke and Tatsuye Yokota, hiking with their friend at the Heart Mountain Relocation Center in Wyoming, circa 1944.

Though the war was on, nature continued its miracle of life and late in 1942, I found I was pregnant again. Howard Kahn, my husband's employer, was very kind to us during this period. He wrote an article in his "Paul Light" column about the loyalty of the Japanese Americans mentioning my husband. Another person, Ruth Gage Colby, a volunteer with the War Relocation Authority, worked tirelessly on behalf of Japanese Americans. We were very thankful for their support.

On August 1, 1943, my sister Sue arrived from the Tule Lake Relocation Center to live with us. Through the efforts of Mrs. Colby, she became the first Japanese employee of Brown & Bigelow in St. Paul. My second daughter, Sandy, was born on August 9, the same day that Sue started work. On the train trip to St. Paul, Sue met Shigeo Sato, a young Japanese American GI on his way to Camp Sheridan, Illinois.

By December 1943, with Sue's help, we bought the home where we live today in Hayden Heights on St. Paul's eastside. At that time that was the outer limit of the city, with homes just along White Bear Avenue and open fields beyond them. It was the very end of the trolley car route. Shigeo Sato came to visit Sue while on leave in December 1943, and in July 1944, they were married in Duluth, Minnesota, just before he was shipped overseas. Sue continued living with us until Shig returned at the war's end in 1946. Shig was from California where his parents owned a store until they were interned in one of the relocation camps. He had enlisted just before the attack on Pearl Harbor and didn't go to the camp. Shig was sent to Italy with the now famous "Go For Broke" 442nd Regiment of Japanese Americans. He returned a decorated war hero, receiving the Bronze Star for heroism in combat.

My brother, Bill, arrived from the relocation camp in June, 1944, and attended Bethel College until June 1945, when he was drafted and entered the service. At the end of the war, he returned to Seattle and never came back to Minnesota.

Mary Ogura's brother, Bill Yokota, visiting his father, Frank Kyosuke, in Sunnydale, Washington, following his discharge from the Army, circa 1949.

Mary Ogura's mother, Tatsuye Yokota, with her son, Bill, in Sunnydale, Washington, when he was discharged from the Army, circa 1949.

In the spring of 1944, I got a night job with a plastics company on Chestnut Street in St. Paul. I ran a molder and made everything from casings for incendiary bombs to cups and toilet seats. Sue took care of my children at night. My husband also changed employment as Howard Kahn couldn't pay him enough to make ends meet. He went to work as a housekeeper and cook for Mr. Sydney Dean, a St. Paul businessman who lived on Edgcumbe Road in Highland Park. Mr. and Mrs. Dean were very kind to us also. I continued working until December 1945, when I quit to prepare for the birth of my third child, Bill, in March 1946.

V-J Day brought us all much relief and change. My parents and their remaining children returned to their farm in Seattle to find it ransacked. The government had rented the farm out in their absence. The former tenant was never brought to trial and my parents were never compensated for their losses. Due to his advanced age

Mary Ogura's husband, Johnnie Chikao Ogura, worked as a housekeeper and cook for Sydney Dean, a businessman in St. Paul, Minnesota, 1944.

and declining stamina, my father never returned to farming. He became a gardener for hire until he retired. My mother worked as a domestic. In the post war years, Seattle grew to encompass Sunnydale and his land grew in value. The area around his farm became a residential area with a shopping center. In 1962, he leased the land to a company which built a restaurant and office building on it. He and my mother moved in with their son, Bill. The rent income and Bill's family provided a very comfortable retirement for my parents until their demise.

Shig Sato returned from the Army to begin his life with my sister Sue. They set up residence in St. Paul, while he went back to school to study engine repair. In 1947, they had their first daughter, Ann. They moved back to Seattle for several years and their second son, Steve, was born there. They returned in 1952 to settle in Roseville, Minnesota. They had another son, Duayne, and a second daughter, Lynn, and continue to live in Minnesota. Sue retired from the Postal Service and Shig retired from the Brunswick Corporation.

After the war, my husband was not able to get his old job back with the railroad because a Filipino now had it. He continued to work for the Deans until 1952, when he returned to the railroad. He worked at various jobs, such as janitor, night watchman, and elevator operator, until his retirement in 1970. He continues to enjoy his retirement, and at the age of 89, he is still in good health.

In 1948, I got a job with the Toni Company, which was eventually bought out by the Gillette Company. I worked on the assembly line as a packer and machine operator. Except for one short layoff period, I continued working for Gillette until I retired in 1979 with 31 years of service.

In April 1954, my last child, Michael, was born. All of my five children graduated from high school and institutions of higher education. They have done well. My oldest son, Jim, was a teacher, school principal, and worked for the U.S. Department of Education in Washington, D.C. My oldest daughter, Mary, graduated from the University of Minnesota and now works for the Machinists Union as an administrative assistant. My second daughter, Sandy, attended the University of Minnesota and the University of North Dakota, receiving her degree in Education form the University of Montana. My second son, Bill, graduated from the University of Minnesota after being an outstanding football, basketball, and baseball player at Johnson High School. He, like my eldest son, served in the U.S. Navy. He became a manager with a dairy company and now is a management consultant. My youngest son, Michael, graduated from technical school in Graphic Arts. He worked for Minnesota Mining and Manufacturing Company for several years before returning to school to study computers. He now is a computer consultant.

My sister Sue's children also did well. Their daughter, Ann, attended the University of Minnesota and became a nurse. Their son, Steve, graduated from the University of Minnesota Institute of

*Mary Ogura's son, Michael (back row, left), married Virginia Dahl
(next to Michael) in 1975 in St. Paul, Minnesota.
Seated in the middle are Mary and Johnnie Chikao Ogura.*

*Sandy Ogura and Jim Young flanked by her parents,
Johnnie Chikao and Mary Ogura, and his parents, Lorraine and Bill Young,
at their wedding in St. Paul, Minnesota, 1963.*

Mary Ogura's daughter, Mary (front row, right), married Don Liljedahl
(second row, second from left) in 1961 in St. Paul, Minnesota.
Standing behind her are her sister, Sandy, brother, Bill, and parents,
Mary and Johnnie Chikao Ogura.

Technology, receiving a B.S. in Mechanical Engineering. He joined the U.S. Air Force after graduation and is now a Lt. Colonel. Lynn, Sue's youngest daughter, graduated from Mankato State University with a B.A. in Accounting, receiving a Master's degree in Business Administration from the University of Minnesota. She presently works in management with Katun in Bloomington, Minnesota.

Our family has not been without its close calls and tragedies, however. My son, Jim, broke his neck while in the service in Japan. Fortunately, he recovered fully. My son, Bill, almost lost his life in an auto accident in 1952. He also recovered fully. My sister Sue's daughter Ann died in a car accident at the age of 21. My daughter

Sandy lost two children in childbirth and later lost her 16-year-old son, Peter, in a car accident. The loss of Ann and Peter deeply affected us all and neither will ever be forgotten.

All in all, I look back on my life with satisfaction. Attitudes toward Japanese have changed immensely in my life time. There has been steady progress toward viewing and treating all people as people. War is now viewed as a tragedy for both Japan and the United States. There are many people I would like to thank for helping bring about these changes.

ESTHER
TORII
SUZUKI

I f my parents hadn't been among the determined group of immigrants who practically swam the Pacific Ocean to come to a strange land whose customs and language were as inscrutable to them as vice versa, I would be a Japanese in Japan. Actually, when they arrived on these shores, they might as well have been deaf and mute, for they did not speak or understand English. I marvel at how hard they worked, staying off relief rolls and bringing up law-abiding and respectable offspring.

World War II hysteria on the West Coast which led to the indiscriminate evacuation of 120,000 Japanese and Japanese Americans resulted in their dispersal all over the United States. Consequently, we settled in St. Paul, Minnesota. So instead of living in Little Tokyos on the West Coast, we found ourselves among the Swedish, the Germans, the Norwegians and the Irish, to name a few. It may have been a new experience for us, but the encounter was mutual—Papa planting *daikon* (a large white radish measuring about 19 inches in length) in a residential district, foreign students coming and going, the telephone party line listening in on conversations in Japanese, telephone solicitors getting the reply, "I not interesting"... the impact was real.

My father, Tokichi Torii, was born on January 8, 1881, in Hongu, Wakayama Prefecture, Japan. When Tokichi was three years old, his mother died in childbirth. Since there were no wetnurses in the village or surrounding countryside, his baby sister died also. While his father, a carpenter, worked, he left Tokichi in the care of relatives who used the money to buy white rice for themselves and fed cheaper brown rice to Tokichi. I read someplace that during the Civil War, the prisoners were fed the peelings of potatoes while the guards feasted on the white inside of the potato. Now we know that the vitamins are in the peel. My father lived to 94 years and eleven months while his relatives did not enjoy such longevity.

In one of his childhood stories, Tokichi and his friend, Masaru, walked to a city, where there were *jinrickshaws* (a two-wheeled carriage pulled by one man), something they had seen only in pictures. They pooled their money for their first ride on a moving vehicle. The rickshaw man shouted at Masaru to sit on the seat and not where the feet were to go. Masaru explained, "But I want to go second class." The rickshaw man ran and ran and explained all the sights. Tokichi became motion sick and pleaded with the man to stop, but he was intent on earning his pay.

At age sixteen, Tokichi went to Yokohama to take a civil service examination for the Postal Service. One of the questions was an essay on a famous historic site which was a national treasure. Tokichi told the examiner he had never been there and was informed that he should use his imagination. Tokichi was bright and had plenty of imagination along with a talent in writing, so he wrote a glowing report on a place he had never seen, but wisely ended it, "Ah, I woke up from a wonderful dream." He passed.

At the turn of the twentieth century, the Japanese Government drafted many young men in preparation for the imminent outbreak of hostilities between Japan and Russia. Tokichi decided to emigrate to the United States in 1903. He landed in Vancouver, British Columbia, but eventually moved to Oregon. In Japan, a professor had helped Tokichi with English lessons and Tokichi continued his studies with the help of Noah Webster (dictionary). He worked as a houseboy and gardener, and later became the executive secretary of the Oregon Growers Association. He was one of the three founders of the Japanese Methodist Episcopal Church in Portland, Oregon. His faith sustained him in the years to come.

He went to Japan to pick out a bride just before the Japanese Exclusion Act become effective in June, 1924. He married Tomae Tamaki on May 23, 1924 in Shingu, a city about 30 miles from his birthplace. He was 43 years old and Tomae was 18 years old.

Esther Suzuki (left), nee Torii, with her parents, Tokichi and Tomae Torii, and sisters, Lucy (center) and Eunice (right), in Portland, Oregon, 1931.

Tokichi had three daughters: Esther, Eunice and Lucy. All three graduated from college—two social workers and one teacher.

During the three and a half years of internment at Minidoka, Idaho, he worked two years at $8 a month in the mess hall. In the final year he got a job as a reporter at $12 a month, writing accounts of Nisei soldiers. He enjoyed this as he was exceptionally interested in writing and was good at it.

When V-J Day came and the internment camp was closed, he came to St. Paul and found employment at 64 years of age as a pot and pan washer in the men's dormitory at Macalester College. Since this was part-time, he worked at another part-time job as a janitor at a publishing company. He was active in the Twin Cities Independent Church, a Japanese congregation of all Protestant denominations. He wrote the weekly newsletter and Sunday bulletin in Japanese. During the summers he gardened and all in all enjoyed a long, happy life. He is buried at Lakewood Cemetery in Minneapolis, Minnesota.

Tomae Tamaki, born March 23, 1906, was the oldest of five children. She finished high school, then went to a finishing school which in those days prepared young women for marriage by teaching embroidery, sewing, tea ceremony, and flower arrangement. Her education did not include cooking, so she was married and living in the United States before she learned the rudiments of Meiji era *sushi* making from an older Japanese woman. Her sister told us that Tomae had a teaching certificate which she kept a secret since she didn't want to teach Japanese in the language school. She preferred sewing.

Her sewing skills proved to be a godsend. She made all her daughters' clothes, including coats and sweaters. During her three and a half years in the Minidoka Relocation Center in Idaho, she honed her embroidery skills under a master teacher, embroidering pictures of silk thread on silk cloth. There is an old Japanese saying, "*ude ga aru*," which roughly means "has a flair and a decided skill."

Usually, this has to do with the hands because the literal translation is "she has a wrist."

Esther Suzuki's mother, Tomae Torii (second from left), with her fellow students in an embroidery class at the Minidoka Relocation Center in Idaho, circa 1943. Displayed in the background are their works of art.

Time that could have been spent on works of art was diverted to making Indian moccasin pins (beading on one-inch moccasins of chamois cloth) for a man who paid five cents each. These were sold in souvenir stands, state fairs and the old five-and-ten-cent stores for considerably more. Working late into the night by the one dim, naked light bulb suspended from the ceiling in their 16' x 12' room, Tomae earned my train fare from Macalester College in St. Paul, Minnesota to the concentration camp for a one-week vacation in the summer of 1943. A special visitor's permit was required. She also had to pay for my three meals a day which were measured in nickels. It seemed a lot of money for prison fare. The hours that went into the countless tiny moccasin stitches would be like counting the grains of sand in the desert. For these concentration camps were places in the midst of deserts surrounded by barbed wire fences, sage brush, tumbleweeds and scorching sun and merciless wind. In retrospect, this was the best vacation of my life; being reunited with my family, if for only a week in this one room with five cots with straw-filled mattresses (the room was designed for four cots).

Recently, one woman lovingly told me the story of her mother who had a talent for playing the piano and played every chance she could in order to pay for her daughter's expensive private school tuition. Another woman said that her mother made an exquisite quilt for her dentist to pay for her orthodontic treatment.

Tomae was the first feminist to cross my path. Having a teaching certificate, she was a firm believer in education. Having had a good education herself, she valued this for her three daughters. She was a realist also and did not believe that a woman's role was just to make a "good marriage" by marrying a wealthy man and being sup-

Esther Suzuki's mother, Tomae Torii, in front of her barracks at the Minidoka Relocation Center in Idaho, 1944.

ported for her lifetime. Although she could not help with homework except in Mathematics, she was active in the P.T.A., assuming the chairwomanship for Japan Day by arranging for Japanese dances and refreshments of tea and rice cakes. Some old letters dating from 1933 through 1939 were from the principals of Couch Grammar School, Shattuck Grammar School and Lincoln High School in Portland, Oregon, thanking Tomae for her annual donations of crepe paper art carnations she made for Mother's Day. The proceeds went to the schools' general fund and one letter said the sale that year netted $5.85 (each carnation sold for five cents).

Besides being a strong woman, Tomae had a good heart and believed in sharing what little she had. One recollection is Saturday night meals. When she prepared chow mein, she would have us deliver half of our dinner to a widower with four children who lived six blocks away. Mother believed in sharing above seconds for us. After Tomae's death, a visitor from Japan took flowers to her grave and said he remembered what she had said 30 years before when he was a student in this country, "It doesn't cost anything to be kind." He said that he has tried to live by this simple rule. Another of Tomae's homespun rules was to never look above oneself and envy those who have more, but to look around and see some with less; and being fortunate, do something for them.

Tomae did not apply herself in English class in Japan because she felt this subject would be of little use to her. Little did she dream she would spend the rest of her life (65 years) in the United States with five visits to Japan. After she retired from her job as a seamstress for 26 years in Minnesota, she enrolled in the Minnesota Literacy Program. A volunteer (Tomae's was a retired nurse) came two times a week to her home and tutored her one hour in reading and writing and another hour in conversational English while they drank tea. Tomae completed five levels of English and one year proudly showed her teacher Christmas cards which Tomae had addressed in script. Up until then, she only knew how to print. One year, Tomae, the oldest student in the State of Minnesota, was invited with her tutor and all the other Twin Cities students and tutors

Esther Suzuki's mother, Tomae Torii, taught her granddaughter, Nami Jean (center), and her four friends embroidery every Saturday morning in St. Paul, Minnesota, 1957.

to then Governor Wendell Anderson's mansion for a recognition dinner.

Tomae's most looked-forward-to event besides church was the semimonthly meetings of the Minnesota Nikkei Project which was established in July, 1978, by Nisei for the Issei. The Project started with 26 Issei, but their number has now dwindled to nine, only three of whom are able to participate today. Activities included chair exercises and outings to trout farms, apple orchards, autumn leaf watching, *Noh* drama, *sushi* restaurants and *warabi* (bracken or fern) picking. Winter months were spent in crafts, watching Japanese movies, eating Japanese food and all around socializing. The craft director told me an interesting story. Mother had a best friend that she saw only at Nikkei Project meetings, since they did not go to the same church. Usually, all the Christians sat on one side of the table and the Buddhists on the other, but Tomae twice a month sat on the Buddhist side with her friend who was ten years older.

Esther and George Suzuki (back row, center) with her mother, Tomae Torii (front row, right), and family at the Minnesota Nikkei Project's Open House in Minneapolis, Minnesota, 1986.

At her memorial service in October, 1989, one of Tomae's seven grandchildren, Jay Kirihara, gave the following tribute:

> Grandma wanted Peter to speak at her funeral because she liked Peter's talk at Grandma Kirihara's funeral. Unfortunately, Peter is now in Europe. I know Peter will be honored at Grandma's request. So in Peter's absence, we all put together some thoughts and reflections on Grandma.
>
> I think some of Grandma's happier times were when the whole family got together. I always knew it was a family gathering if *makizushi* was on the menu or if Peter would bring his pants along for alterations. This

summer was especially eventful for Grandma when the entire family was together at Jan and Mitch's wedding.

Another highlight in Grandma's life was her trips to Chicago to see Eunice's family. She would love to go to the Japanese and Chinese restaurants and see her friends.

The Nikkei Project was also an integral part of Grandma's social life. She would look forward to the meetings twice a month, where she could see her Issei and Nisei friends and they would eat traditional Japanese food.

Grandma always loved baseball. She would take us to the Twins' knothole games and she would listen to the games on her radio. Grandma would even stay up past her 7:00 p.m. bedtime to see how the game was going. I never knew why she enjoyed baseball so much, but it really didn't matter; baseball was one of her passions.

Grandma was very progressive in her time. Grandma instilled in her three daughters the importance of self-reliance and independence. This is why she encouraged Esther, Eunice and Lucy to pursue their college education and careers. She was proud of what her daughters have achieved. Grandma saw her vision realized.

Before Grandma died, I got the opportunity to talk a lot with her about her past while she was recuperating from her heart problems. I will always remember something Grandma said, "I'm lucky, you know." I think this statement reflected Grandma's philosophy of life. She felt fortunate to have lived, even though her life was sometimes a struggle and her life was very frugal. But Grandma made the most out of life through her giving nature. She was able to enjoy her grandchildren and her two great grandchildren. So Grandma was right when she would say she was lucky; she was one of the few who really appreciated life.

We will miss Grandma. But when we remember her, we will be inspired with her inner strength and her wonderful outlook on life.

My life has been divided into roughly four 20-year plans. The first 20 years were devoted to the education of myself. The second was filled with marriage, two children and volunteer community work. The third extended into 24 years and four months, when I pursued a career as a social worker. The last 20 years are reserved for more volunteer work, writing memoirs, and enjoying my grandchildren.

Education has been the single most important factor stressed by our parents. From the day that my father escorted me to the front of the kindergarten class and entrusted me to the teacher with these words, "Please, you teachum her English," I have been on a one-track course.

In 1985, the *St. Paul Pioneer Press* had a contest on the topic, "My Favorite Teacher," and chose my essay out of over 200 entries as one of seven to be published. The following was my essay.

"Her Love of Books Lasted"

When I was 12 years old, a child of immigrants, an English teacher in Oregon took notice of me.

Miss Ruth Arbuckle required each student to give a book review. It was shortly after I gave a nervous presentation on "Little Women" that Miss Arbuckle asked me if I would like to belong to a book club. I was overjoyed at this invitation to join such a group.

I went to the first meeting Friday after school, and only Miss Arbuckle was there. I wondered where all the others were. It became apparent that no one was interested except us.

Miss Arbuckle recommended I read a book a week from her list. I looked forward to discuss "Vanity Fair" by Thackeray, Victor Hugo's "Les Miserables," "Pride and Prejudice" and "Elements of Style" by E.B. White, etc.

Sometimes I stayed up until 3 a.m., reading by flashlight under the bedcovers in fear of being discovered by my mother who was a strong believer in a good night's sleep. My sisters remember me in childhood with my nose in a book, unable to help with household chores because I had a weekly deadline.

When summer vacation came, Miss Arbuckle had a longer list for me to read. She didn't know that I spent 10 hours a day picking berries to supplement the meager family income. I came back to school in September, sleepy.

I didn't realize until I was in college how much this special reading course helped me. I had had a private tutor, like Helen Keller with her Ann Sullivan.

I found I was able to answer questions in tests that minority students were failing, because knowledge of the prevailing culture is contained and revealed in books. Recently, I was reminded of Miss Arbuckle when I saw a rerun of "The Corn is Green" in which Katharine Hepburn tutors an illiterate young Welsh miner for acceptance into Oxford.

Miss Arbuckle thought her book club ended with me, but it was my passage into the mainstream of American life and for my children and their children. My granddaughter, who was brought up on books, has written two books dictated to her mother and illustrated by pictures cut out of magazines. She is four years old.

Esther Suzuki visiting Ruth Arbuckle, her former high school English teacher, in Portland, Oregon, 1990.

The November 1991 issue of "Macalester Today" published the following account of how I came to Macalester College in 1942.

I enrolled at Macalester in September 1942 when I was 16. For my first assignment in freshman speech class, I began by declaring, "The happiest day of my life was the day I left for college." But suddenly I remembered my father, mother and two sisters standing on the other side of the barbed wire fence in Oregon, waving goodbye, smiling bravely through their tears. I broke down and couldn't continue.

On May 5, 1942, my family and I were forced to leave our home in Portland, Oregon, for a detention camp in that city. We had been given a week's notice and told we could only bring what would fit in a few suitcases. We had to sell or leave most of our possessions. We sold our piano for $15, but I managed to take some books with me.

My father and mother were from Japan, but my sisters and I were Nisei—born in America of Japanese immigrant parents. We joined 4,000 other Japanese and Japanese-Americans from Oregon and Washington in an "assembly center." It was actually Portland's exposition hall, used for rodeos and the like. We lived communal-style in converted horse stalls, eating in shifts of 2,000 and guarded by armed soldiers. The stalls had not been thoroughly cleaned and wooden planks had been placed over the manure. When it rained, as it often does in Oregon, and the ground got wet, the stench was overpowering.

In all, about 120,000 people of Japanese descent were interned from 1942 to 1945. Over two-thirds of them were U.S. citizens like me and my sisters, Eunice and Lucy. This tragedy was caused by a combination of war hysteria after Pearl Harbor, racial hatred, economic greed for the rich farms that the Japanese had developed from marginal land, and weak political leadership.

In our detention center, days dragged endlessly. I was not allowed to attend my high school graduation that June; instead my high school diploma was mailed to me. Then the pieces of a great cosmic puzzle began to miraculously fit together. The Quakers set up a scholarship fund called the Nisei Student Relocation Fund which awarded me $100. (I was accepted to Willamette University in Salem, Oregon, but Japanese-Americans were not allowed to attend college in the West Coast defense zone.) We had to be accepted by a Midwestern or Eastern college.

Esther Suzuki graduated from Lincoln High School in Portland, Oregon, in 1942. She was not allowed to attend the commencement. Her diploma was mailed to her at the assembly center in Portland.

My high school English teacher, who was also a Quaker, suggested Macalester because she had read a book by Glenn Clark, a Macalester professor. Macalester President Charles J. Turck wrote me a letter of acceptance. Macalester was the first college in Minnesota to accept Japanese-American students.

Before I could be released from detention, I had to send President Turck's letter to the War Department and obtain its approval. I also needed letters of recommendation from three Caucasians attesting to my loyalty and honesty, and letters from the St. Paul police and fire chiefs acknowledging my residence in their city.

Our group of 4,000 was scheduled to be taken by guarded trains from Portland to a permanent concentration camp—it was called a relocation center—in Minidoka, Idaho, at 1 p.m. on September 8, 1942. Just two hours and 15 minutes before the appointed time, a telegram arrived from Washington, D.C., releasing me to attend Macalester. I was the first person to be freed from detention in Portland. We hurriedly repacked my belongings separately and my family gave me the only suitcase we owned.

I was born in Portland and had only visited Seattle, so traveling to Minnesota was a great adventure. When the conductor announced we were crossing the Mississippi—a big thrill since I had read Mark Twain's books—I became excited and raised the curtain. He loudly ordered me to lower it and asked if I knew there was a blackout. I felt everyone was looking at me as though I were a spy.

After a few hours of sleep, I took the Minnesota Multiphasic Personality Inventory the next morning in the Macalester gym. The person administering the test cautioned us to be truthful in answering all 500 questions, saying there was a way of detecting lies. So I truthfully answered "Yes" to questions like, "Do you feel people are out to get you?" and "Do you feel at times that someone is following you?"

One day at the corner of Grand and Snelling Avenues, a lady asked me where she could catch the bus. When I told her, she asked me how long I had lived here and I replied, "Two weeks." She said, "My, you speak good English."

In addition to my degree, I learned a lot at Macalester about human kindness and concern for others, and made friendships which have lasted through the years.

My adviser was Dr. Milton McLean, who was chosen to advise all five Japanese-Americans at Macalester. On Sunday evenings he held open house and all students were welcome to join his family in a light supper and fellowship. My earnings (25 cents an hour) at the Macalester Park Publishing Company owned by Dr. Clark put me through four years. Another faculty member who made me feel at home was Dr. Edwin Kagin, who opened my eyes to a whole different view of religion.

I had a student work contract to type scripts for drama Professor Mary Gwen Owen. One day my youngest sister, Lucy, wrote to say she and my family were all ill with food poisoning. I started to cry. Miss Owen went from her office on the third floor of Old Main down to the basement Grille and bought me an ice cream cone because, she said, "One can't cry and eat ice cream at the same time." When I graduated, she gave me a party at her Wisconsin farm and invited my whole family. (My sister, Eunice, joined me at Macalester in 1944, later transferring to the University of Minnesota, but my parents and Lucy were not released from the concentration camp until the war's end. My parents became U.S. citizens in 1952.)

Margaret Doty, the dean of women, was wonderful. She gave me free tickets to the symphony, and for graduation gave me a year's membership in the St. Paul chapter of the American Association of University Women. She attended my wedding and bought my children birth gifts. At the 25th reunion of our class, Miss Doty was asked to give a few reminiscences. Seeing me, she recalled that the original plan was to have six Japanese Americans at Macalester in 1942—three men and three women. I had never heard that before and said, "I suppose that was so we could date each other." Miss Doty, never missing a beat, replied, "Esther, you were always impudent."

Survival would not have been possible without many thoughtful student friends. When my dormitory closed for the holidays, someone would invite me to her home. One friend's mother felt so badly about my family's internment that she offered to do my laundry. The large oatmeal cookies she baked and packed in the laundry box smelled like the homemade soap she used, but I ate them with relish.

It will take the rest of my life to pay back into the vast well of human kindness that I found at Macalester.

Japanese-American students like me who received assistance a half-century ago have been contributing over the years to the Nisei Student Relocation Commemorative Fund. Since 1983 it has been awarding scholarships to Southeast Asian students whose lives have been disrupted by war, including Vietnamese, Laotians, Hmong and Cambodians.

The chain of helping hands continues.

In June 1946, I graduated *cum laude* with a major in Sociology and with minors in Latin and Home Economics. I was inducted into Pi Phi Epsilon (National Honor Society), Pi Gamma Mu (National Social Science Honor Society) as president, and the Classical Club (for Greek and Latin students) as president.

George Suzuki was released from the Relocation Center in Minidoka, Idaho, to do stoop labor as a beet topper for a Mormon farmer in Idaho. From there he was accepted by Macalester College and he arrived in St. Paul in April, 1943. He earned his tuition by scrubbing floors for a small restaurant in exchange for meals, cleaning oil drums, chauffeuring, and washing glasses at the University Club, from which he was summarily fired when a Filipino who had seniority objected to a Japanese American working there. (Japan had invaded the Philippines in 1942.) George was drafted in 1944 and was accepted into the Military Intelligence Service at Fort Snelling, Minnesota. The Japanese Language School had classes and enforced study for 12 hours a day, excluding time off for lunch and dinner. He was trained to be a translator and interpreter in Japanese and shipped to the Philippines and, after V-J Day, to Occupied Japan, with only the rank of T-4. Caucasian counterparts received commissions, but no Nisei on graduation was commissioned. All during this period of three and a half years, George's parents and younger brother were imprisoned at the Minidoka Relocation Center in Idaho.

Esther Suzuki with her future husband, George Suzuki, then attending the Military Intelligence Service Language School at Fort Snelling, in front of Kirk Hall at Macalester College in St. Paul, Minnesota, 1944.

Upon his discharge from the Army, George and I were married in 1946. I had graduated from Macalester College by then. With me working as a secretary and the G.I. Bill, George graduated in March, 1949 with a B.B.A. from the University of Minnesota. He experienced great difficulty being hired and one frank employment agency employee said he put George's card in the back of the file because it was more lucrative to work with the employable. George took a civil service job with the United States Department of Agriculture and worked 28 and a half years as an accountant, auditor and supervisor, ending his career as a systems analyst.

Nami Jean and John were born in 1949 and 1950. Besides the nuclear family, there was the extended family of my father and mother, so our children grew up in a bilingual atmosphere and experienced the benefit of two cultures. We led a normal average life enhanced by these added dimensions.

Although George and I were baptized Methodist Episcopal, we joined Knox Presbyterian Church in 1949, where both children were baptized and active in Sunday School, Vacation Church School, church camp, Cherub Choir, Junior Choir and Youth Fellowship.

Esther and George Suzuki with their children, John and Nami Jean, in St. Paul, Minnesota, 1955.

Between George and me we held every office (elder, trustee, president of the Women's Association, etc.) except that of the minister.

Other group activities involving the children were Bluebirds, Campfire Girls, Cub Scouts, American Field Service, P.T.A., Y.W.C.A., Y.M.C.A. and the Festival of Nations.

Esther and George Suzuki with their children, John and Nami Jean, at the Festival of Nations in St. Paul, Minnesota, 1956. Attired in kimono, Nami Jean danced at the Festival.

Nami Jean and John earned their share of honors throughout their school years along with participation in athletics—swimming, baseball, golf, gymnastics, and skiing. Nami Jean graduated from Macalester College with a teaching degree and taught for several years before joining her husband, Steven Vizanko, in his commercial photography business. John has a Master's degree in Architecture from the University of Minnesota and is married to Kathleen Keenan, an art teacher. They have two children, Kae Tomae, eleven years old and John Keenan, seven years old.

For holidays, we continue to invite foreign students to our home. Especially on New Year's Day, we invite Japanese foreign students from Hamline University and Macalester College, as well as AFS (American Field Service) students, Japanese women who married U.S. servicemen, and their children.

Since 1942, I have been asked to give talks on my experience of the evacuation at various church groups, schools and women's groups. The topic expanded to include Japanese cooking, culture and dance, and I found myself giving programs on *sukiyaki* and *tempura* cooking. Once my sister, Lucy, and I drove to Chatsworth, Minnesota for a church group and had to travel home in a dense fog. It seems that everyone we knew became program chair of their club and there was no end to the demand for free speakers. My two sisters and I danced in the Festival of Nations from 1949 until our daughters, Nami Jean Suzuki and Jan Kirihara, replaced us. Now my granddaughter, Kae Tomae, continues the third generation of Japanese dancing at the Festival of Nations.

Esther Suzuki's granddaughter, Kae Tomae Suzuki, carries on the tradition of performing Japanese dances at the Festival of Nations in St. Paul, Minnesota, 1991.

In the early 1950's, there was a surge of interest in *origami*, the Japanese art of paper folding. In 1957, Nami Jean and I performed at the St. Paul Science Museum and our picture appeared in the St. Paul newspaper, calling us Japanese artists of *origami*. One week later, we were invited to give a demonstration for a children's fair at the Brooks Art Gallery in Memphis, Tennessee. We showed over 1,000 children how to fold in three appearances. The third was scheduled because of the overwhelming response. That evening Nami Jean and I were taken to the country club for dinner by the Tennessee State President of PEO, an international philanthropic educational organization which I had recently joined. Her guests were five couples whose husbands went to Japan regularly to look after their lumber and cotton interests. Nami Jean and I were the only ones who had not been there. Years later, as I was addressing a church couple's group about the customs of Japan, a happy thought came to me. Heretofore, when the audience found out during the question period that I had not been to Japan, they discredited my entire presentation. I now begin my talk: "Many ministers speak of heaven and hell, but I know they have never been there either."

One week I added up all the hours of volunteer work and the total was 37 and a half hours. Since college was looming in the future for Nami Jean and John, I decided I should use my degree, so I took Ramsey County's civil service test for social worker and passed. I worked the first 16 years in the Work Incentive Program getting AFDC mothers and fathers employed by assisting with childcare, health and other family problems precluding their employment. The last nine years, I worked with the frail elderly and the disabled (18 years of age or older) to help them maintain independent living, forestalling nursing home placement.

In 1975, the first wave of Southeast Asians settled in Minnesota. Since I was the only Asian social worker, most of these cases were added to my existing caseload. The need for bare necessities was so great that I enlisted the help of a group that I belonged to and knew would help—the Japanese American Citizens League. They came through with clothing, television sets, sewing machines, furni-

Esther Suzuki and her daughter, Nami Jean, demonstrated origami at the Brooks Art Gallery in Memphis, Tennessee, 1957.

ture and household equipment. I was glad that for once I was in the right place at the right time.

I also belong to professional organizations such as the Minnesota Social Service Association, Minnesota Mental Health Counselors Association, Minnesota Gerontological Society, and Senior Workers of St. Paul (social workers working with the elderly). I served for over five years on the St. Paul Community Education Advisory Council. In 1989, the WISE (Women in State Employment) presented me with a "Minnesota Treasure" award in recognition of my many years of community service. In October, 1989, I was awarded Lt. Governor Marlene Johnson's Outstanding Achievement Award.

During World War II, the National Japanese American Student Relocation Council assisted over 3,000 Nisei college-age internees in relocating to the Midwest and the East Coast to continue their education. In 1979, a group of Nisei who had benefited from the relocation program founded the Nisei Student Relocation Commemorative Fund to help Southeast Asian refugees acquire an American college education. Since 1982, the Commemorative Fund has annually been awarding scholarships to Vietnamese, Lao, Hmong and Cambodian students residing in states with significant numbers of Southeast Asians. Like the Nisei earlier, these students had their education disrupted by war. In 1987, I served on the Minnesota committee which awarded 14 scholarships to Southeast Asian high school graduates in our state.

In 1977, I met a social worker from Japan, Keiko Sakamoto, who was taking courses in Aging at the University of Minnesota preparatory to her job of the head social worker for *Yu Yu no Sato* which manages retirement communities for 2,000 people over the age of 55 in six different cities in Japan. In 1984, I received a letter from her requesting assistance in setting up tours of nursing homes, because she and her colleagues believed that Minnesota has one of the best social service systems.

Based on their studies in the United States, the planners and architects of *Yu Yu no Sato* built nursing home additions for the aging retirement community residents, and eventually an exchange program was established with Ramsey County Nursing Home and Presbyterian Homes. Later, *Yu Yu no Sato* developed an exchange program with Sweden. In 1990, *Yu Yu no Sato* staff, in appreciation, invited my husband and me to visit their various senior citizens' communities in Japan. It was a fascinating experience for us, and since then I have given many talks to social workers and others interested in working with the elderly population.

Throughout my career, I took courses at the University of Minnesota to keep current in my profession: Communicating with the Elderly, Sign Language, Spanish, Hmong, etc. I also received a 15-credit certificate in Foster Care.

I also took a 15-credit course on the History of Japan and became interested in learning the Japanese language in 1987 at the University of Minnesota. As youngsters, we three sisters did not attend the one-hour Japanese classes that most Nisei children attended after school. I used to think it was because our parents wanted us to be all American, but now I wonder if tuition was a concern. I do remember other Japanese Americans saying, "No wonder you three are so smart in school—you only have to learn one language." Our father tried to teach us at home and he bought the textbooks. Our youngest sister at age two from another room would recite out loud the Japanese "Dick and Jane" type rhymes which Eunice and I were trying to master. In time, Father found us not good candidates for home study. Two years of weekly extension classes at the University gave me enough knowledge to know that it was hopeless for me to continue, but at least I was able to communicate better during our 1990 Japan trip than on the 1972 trip when I had to use George as an interpreter.

It is back to volunteer work and writing memoirs. All the jobs that I could not do while working are beckoning. I agreed to be Class Agent for Macalester which is contacting former classmates annually for support. Then I am on a committee exploring ways that Macalester College can be helpful to its alumni who are senior citizens. We are named the "Great Scots." In June, 1992, I was elected to serve on the Alumni Board of Directors for three years.

I plan to continue my interest in Asian affairs, Continuing Education, family activities, travel, reading and writing. I serve on the Library Committee at the retirement condominium where I live.

My sister, Eunice, left Minidoka, Idaho, after two years of internment and enrolled in Macalester College in 1944 at 16 years of age, having finished high school in three years.

Eunice remembers the lack of medical facilities in Minidoka. Mother developed pyorrhea in the internment camp and had to have all her teeth extracted and dental plates made immediately after coming to St. Paul. Our father broke his ankle and as it was never set, the bone protruded and he walked with a limp for the rest of his life.

Eunice finished up at the University of Minnesota with a degree in Sociology at age 20. She married a graduate of the University and moved to Chicago, Illinois in 1950. Her older son is a lawyer in California, and her younger son with an MBA is employed in Tokyo, Japan.

My youngest sister, Lucy, came to St. Paul with our parents at the age of 14 when the Minidoka Relocation Center was closed in August, 1945. She enrolled in high school which she finished in three years. After reading Anne Frank's diary, Lucy asked me if I had saved the letters that she had sent me from the internment camp. I told her that I had returned them with spelling errors corrected in red ink when I wrote back to her. Her dreams of being another child author were dashed.

However, Lucy did find a letter dated June 20, 1945, in a book published by the Pilgrim Press in Boston, Massachusetts. When Lucy was 13 years old, Frances Maeda recommended that she write an essay on "Home is Where you Make it." It was published in Children's Religion and Lucy received $5 in remuneration. The accompanying letter went like this:

Dear Lucy,

Your story is very good and I think it will help our readers to understand the situation of the Japanese Americans. I don't know whether some of the rest of us who have always been on the outside could take an experience like that without expressing resentment. You have been wonderful through this and your story shows it. All good luck to you when you come outside into the world. I hope you will find it a good one with friends about you.

We shall send you a little check for your writing, which we are so happy to print. You did very well at this job. We appreciate your helpfulness so very much.

Lucy's grade school education for three and a half years was in the internment camp. Classes were held in barracks with wood-burning stoves not unlike the pioneer days of the one-room school-house. Teachers at first were Japanese Americans who had a few years of college (assistant teachers) or college degrees. They received the professional scale for Japanese Americans of $16 a month. The skilled labor scale was $12 a month, while unskilled laborers received $8 a month. This was a forty-hour week. Later recruitment brought in Caucasian teachers who were paid high salaries as inducement for "undesirable assignments."

Esther Suzuki (right) with her sisters,
Eunice (left) and Lucy, in Portland, Oregon, 1940.

There were two elementary schools, and Lucy attended Huntville Elementary School which was mostly for Portland people. There were 439 students with seven Caucasian teachers and four Japanese American teachers and assistant teachers. Stafford Elementary School, which was mainly for evacuees from Seattle, had a student population of 519 with 11 Caucasian teachers and six Japanese American teachers and assistant teachers.

The Minidoka yearbook has pictures of the 6th-grade children with a victory garden. Lucy says that she remembers there were no cooking facilities in the school but there were sewing machines. The Junior Safety Patrol was organized in December, 1942, and 150 boys and girls served since then on the patrol. A parent-teacher organization was started and hoped to affiliate with the state and national PTA.

On June 14, 1943, both schools had a flag dedication service. The flags were donated by the Minidoka Project volunteers, the Japanese Americans who had joined the combat unit at Camp Shelby, Mississippi.

There was only one junior high school which had 220 students in 1944 and 233 in 1945. The internment camp's senior high school had 634 students in 1944 and 297 in 1945. The faculty came from all over the United States—Minnesota, North Dakota, North Carolina, Illinois, etc.—but mostly from the Western States. A few teachers had Master's degrees.

Lucy recalls that her best friend came late in the school year and there was a big test the next day. Lucy loaned the newcomer her notes since they only had one book that the teacher lectured from. Lucy's friend got the highest grade in the class because she was extremely bright, but the teacher wondered how this happened. Lucy remembers her art teacher who taught them how to make paper-mâchè masks and wood block prints of scenes of the camp and cacti. She also remembers one Japanese American woman who volunteered to teach a tap dance class. Lucy and a friend became quite proficient and were allowed to leave the internment camp one day to dance for a Lions Club meeting in the nearby town. She ordered tap shoes on the meager clothing allowance vouchers issued seasonally. She recalls that if an item or items were out of stock, the items were never replaced nor credit given for future orders. She remembers tapping without tap shoes.

Lucy graduated from the University of Minnesota *with distinction* and was invited to join Phi Upsilon Omicron, the National Honor Society in Home Economics. Today she continues to work as a Home Economics teacher in St. Paul. Lucy and her husband, Mikio Kirihara, live in Bloomington, Minnesota. Her oldest son, Jay, is an engineer with an M.B.A. employed in Dallas, Texas. Her daughter, Jan, graduated from the University of Minnesota with a Math degree and married Mitchell Monson, a University of Minnesota graduate who owns a graphics business. The youngest, Peter, also graduated from the University of Minnesota and has recently opened up a coffee shop in the upcoming warehouse district in Minneapolis, Minnesota.

Reflections

My reflections at age 66 are kaleidoscopic, reflecting the colorful and ever changing world we live in.

The old guard (Issei) has passed but their pioneer spirit came to light during the evacuation, internment and relocation period, strengthening the second generation, the Nisei, who as displaced persons made their way to parts unknown. The move to Minnesota was part of a cosmic plan which gave birth to the third and fourth generations of our family.

The world has become our community and what occurs in "faraway" places affects our lives as though it were next-door. I recall that back in the 1930's, I had a Chinese friend, Rosie, who lived about six blocks away. On the way to school with my two younger sisters, we would stop to pick up Rosie and her younger

Tomae Torii (front row, center) with her three daughters and their families in Minneapolis, Minnesota, 1989.

siblings. One day she said they could no longer walk to school with us, because her mother had told them that we were Japanese and Japan had invaded China. That was hard to understand. In class I slipped her a note that we could meet one block beyond her house and go at least part of the way to school together. This arrangement was going along very nicely until her older brother saw our little group and told their mother. Rosie fearfully sent me a note that she was no longer allowed to even speak to me or she would be beaten up. The realization that our friendship could not continue made me very sad. Since I could not talk to Rosie, I never told her how I felt and could only guess that she too was saddened.

Before confinement, we experienced curfew in Portland, Oregon, which was declared shortly after Pearl Harbor. Japanese and Americans of Japanese ancestry could not be outside their homes from 8 p.m. until 6 a.m. This posed a problem for those who had to arrive at their jobs early. We could not travel more than five miles from our homes and could not be in the vicinity of any strategic places, such as the water tower.

Our look-alikes, the Chinese and Americans of Chinese ancestry, devised an ingenious plan to overcome the handicap of being mistaken for persons of Japanese heritage. Large buttons came out, "I am Chinese." The Star of David badges that the Nazis forced the Jewish people to wear marked them for the gas chambers, but the reverse of this was the Chinese button which gave them entrance *carte blanche* to restaurants, late night movies, and walks in "prohibited areas." I seem to recall that the King of Denmark, when ordered to force all Jews to wear the Star of David, appeared in public wearing it himself.

Thirty-four years later, I was working as a social worker in Minnesota. As Minnesota accepted many Southeast Asian refugees, racial hatred surfaced among a certain segment of society. Since I was easily mistaken for a Southeast Asian, one co-worker jokingly said that he would be my bodyguard, but later suggested I wear a T-shirt saying, "I am a Japanese American." However, he cautioned me against going near the Ford plant in that outfit.

Housing was scarce in 1945. The internment camps were closing one by one, and my sister Eunice and I had to drop out of college in order to find living quarters for our family of five. We went to about 90 places and were always asked, "Are you Japanese or Chinese?" After a while, I was tempted to answer, "Yes," an ambiguous answer at best. The ninety-first landlord said that his son had been wounded at Guadalcanal and nursed back to health by a Japanese American nurse in Hawaii, and he had been wondering how he could ever repay for his son's recovery. Here was his opportunity.

In my childhood I would fantasize: If I were a white person, if I were a movie star (it was usually Shirley Temple and not Anna May Wong), if I were rich. In 1938, when I was in the 8th grade in Portland, Oregon, the DAR (Daughters of the American Revolution) award was given to the most outstanding girl. This annual award was for the highest achievement in scholarship, citizenship, charac-

Esther Suzuki's family was reunited after World War II. Tokichi and Tomae Torii with their daughters, Lucy, Eunice and Esther (left to right), in St. Paul, Minnesota, 1946.

ter and leadership. Everyone whispered, "It's Esther," and the most astonished of all was the daughter of the PTA president who got the award. In growing up, what I thought was the bane of my life proved to be an enrichment and enhancement. Eleanor Roosevelt resigned from the DAR when Marian Anderson was barred from Constitution Hall.

A young Sansei in Cambridge, Massachusetts, on reading my account of how I came to Macalester, was struck and impressed with the number of persons who did step in to help, notably the Quakers, even though it was an unpopular and potentially dangerous thing to do. Dietrich Bonhoeffer who was hanged by the Nazis for resisting Hitler and helping the Jews said that for the first time he was seeing war from the underside—how the innocent and helpless suffered. Martin Niemoller hand-wrote the following in a personal letter to a person whose identity is unknown:

> "In Nazi Germany, first they put the Communists and the Jehovah's Witnesses in the concentration camps but I was not a Communist or a Jehovah's Witness so I did nothing. Then they came for the Social Democrats but I was not a Social Democrat and I did nothing. Then they arrested the trade unionists and I did nothing because I was not one of them. Then they arrested the Jews and again I did nothing because I was not a Jew. Then they came for the Catholics and I was not a Catholic so I did nothing. At last they came and arrested me but it was too late already."

One person can make a difference, and so whenever someone is trampling on another's rights, I speak up. I was encouraged by the words of Representatives Norman Y. Mineta and Robert Matsui to vote down anti-gay initiatives in Oregon and Colorado which would relegate the gay and lesbian residents of those states to second-class citizenship. The current military stance against the gays is another example of the military being above the justice system by trampling on individuals' civil rights, reminiscent of the military's role in the mass evacuation of 120,000 Japanese Americans in 1942.

As printed in the October 23, 1992 issue of the Pacific Citizen, "Our successful fight to redress the injustice of our evacuation and internment during the Second World War had two purposes: to gain official recognition that our rights as Americans were violated and, equally important, to ensure that such a gross violation of civil liberties should never happen again in this country."

Even though I am but one small voice, I write to Members of Congress, Senators, the President of the United States and editors of newspapers. Here in part is what appeared in the *Highland Villager* on February 27, 1991.

Dear Editor:

It makes me sad to have to write this letter to the editor regarding the use of the highly offensive and inflammatory so-called shortened form of Japanese. This harks back to 1941 when this derogatory term fanned the flames of racial hatred to the point of imprisoning 120,000 people (over two-thirds of whom were American citizens like me) in concentration camps.

In 1955 in St. Paul, a friend from church called to ask me to pick up my five-year-old son an hour later because all the boys playing war hadn't had their turn killing the "Jap." When I rushed over, she couldn't understand why, saying, "It's only like cowboys and Indians."

In the fall of 1942 when I was a freshman at Macalester, I received a letter with $10 enclosed from a teacher who had been a substitute in my high school during the evacuation process. She started a full-time job in a small town in Oregon where there was no

Quaker meeting. She decided to send her tithe for that school year to me. Her salary was $100 a month. I immediately wrote her a thank you note which she answered immediately. She asked that I not put my name on the return address as the inquisitive postmistress asked her whom she knew in St. Paul, Minnesota. My friend expressed concern that she might lose her job if the community discovered her friendship with a Japanese American since racial hatred was rampant there.

We had never been back to our birthplace in Oregon since we were evacuated. In August, 1990, there was a 48th-year reunion, which was the first reunion held, and George and I attended along with 950 people who came from Hawaii, the East Coast, California and Japan.

The Japan bashing prevailing these days is reminiscent of the atmosphere that pervaded the West Coast prior to Pearl Harbor. All the varied experiences of the past are valuable for the lessons they teach. Here are good words to live by: "All that's necessary for evil to triumph is for good men to do nothing" (Edmund Burke).

In the flurry of interest on the 50th anniversary of Pearl Harbor in December, 1991, many news articles, television shorts and radio interviews on evacuation were featured. Our two grandchildren were kept up way past their bedtime on a school night to listen to a radio account of my evacuation and imprisonment during World War II. The next day, then 10-year-old Kae said, "Grandma, I don't think it was right to put you in prison." (None of her classmates' grandparents had such an experience, and I hoped no one thought I was a criminal.)

A social worker colleague of mine who was born in Minnesota moved to Oregon and became a lawyer, then a Representative and a Senator for the Oregon State Legislature. She introduced the bill in Oregon, the state of my birth, for an apology for the violation in 1942 of the civil rights of the Japanese Americans.

A lawyer whom I recently met at the Minnesota Advocates for Human Rights said her membership in this organization was sparked by her childhood remembrance of the mass detention of Americans of Japanese ancestry.

This is why the educational component of the Civil Liberties Act of 1988 is by far the most important part of redress.

The American Association of University Women of the northern St. Paul suburbs, mainly White Bear Lake, is making 15-minute tapes of 12 women in U.S. history and I was asked to tell about my experiences of evacuation and detention. These tapes are on a Native American, Rachel Carson, Grandma Moses, a Cambodian refugee, Esther Suzuki, etc., and are being marketed primarily for schools.

Somewhere way back I learned the importance of taking pride in one's heritage and of knowing that one's course should be true rather than expedient. It hasn't been easy to maintain a feeling of

Esther Suzuki's grandchildren, John Keenan and Kae Tomae Suzuki, in Minneapolis, Minnesota, Christmas, 1989.

self-worth at all times, but the gift of life expects lifelong learning, adventuring, giving, resilience and affirmation. My parents, children and grandchildren have experienced the good life in Minnesota and express their appreciation continuously, for Minnesota is home. Our hope is in the future generation.

YOSHI UCHIYAMA TANI

I n telling the story of my life, I find that World War II (1941-1945) looms as a landmark event. This event marks, in some ways, my loss of innocence and my coming of age. What happened during the War that affected my life so drastically? What was my life like before the war? What has happened since? What about my parents' legacy? With these questions, my story unfolds.

My father, Hichiro Uchiyama, was born in Fukuoka, Japan, on May 18, 1888. He passed away on January 13, 1970, in Pasadena, California.

In 1905, he came to the United States via Mexico with his father who had lost some of his land in Japan due to poor business dealings. My grandfather returned to Japan after a couple of years, leaving my father on his own. Up to 1913, my father worked with the railroad gangs in Texas, New Mexico, and Arizona, and also harvested hops in Oregon.

My father returned to Japan in 1913 or 1914 to marry Sakae Shin, my mother. It was a marriage that had already been arranged by their families. Born in Fukuoka, Japan, on January 14, 1895, my mother died on October 19, 1984, in Pasadena, California. She came from a teacher's family. Although she had taken some exams with plans to become a teacher, she married instead.

Yoshi Tani's older brother, Hiroshi,
with her mother, Sakae Uchiyama, Fukuoka, Japan, 1916.

My older brother, Hiroshi, was born in 1915 in Fukuoka, Japan, while my father was still staying there following the wedding.

On December 14, 1916, my father departed Japan and arrived three weeks later in Seattle on January 7, 1917. Mother then left Kobe, Japan, on September 14, 1920, reaching Seattle on October 21, 1920, to join him. Since my older brother had started school, my parents decided that his schooling should not be interrupted and he was left behind in the care of his grandparents.

I was born in Seattle on July 19, 1921, and named Yoshiko. My younger brother, Aiji, was born on October 13, 1923. My father's occupation was listed on our birth certificates as a "cook."

My older brother continued to do so well in school that he remained in Japan. He received a scholarship to the National University of Fukuoka, then to Kyoto Imperial University and finally to

Tokyo Imperial University. During this time, we exchanged many photos and letters. My parents shared with us his letters written in Japanese. I wrote to him in English, and he wrote back in English saying what a good practice it was for him in learning English.

My parents' hopes to someday reunite as a complete family including my older brother never materialized. A photo, circa 1934, shows my older brother's photo inserted. Hiroshi had already received a diplomatic assignment to Manchuria by 1938, when my parents received a telegram that he was ill and wanted to see my mother. She left Seattle in September 1938, but received notice of his death en route to Japan. He died of pneumonia. My mother returned to the United States in November 1938. The sadness of his death remained for a long time with our family, especially Mother.

Yoshi Tani's parents, Hichiro and Sakae Uchiyama,
in Fukuoka, Japan, 1914. He initially immigrated to the United States
in 1905 and returned to Japan in 1913 or 1914 to marry Sakae Shin.

In 1917, Yoshi Tani's father, Hichiro Uchiyama,
returned alone to the United States. He settled in Seattle, Washington,
where he often thought about his wife and son left in Japan.

On November 3, 1926, my father's cousin wanted to return to Japan, and sold my father his shoe repair shop located in the University district for $1,000. My father operated this shop until the evacuation in 1942. He enjoyed fishing, clam digging, and gardening. I have fond memories of fishing with him from the docks, and of clam digging with my family along the beaches of Puget Sound.

My mother was primarily a homemaker. A photo taken in the 1920s shows that she attended an English school. Another photo, dated 1927, shows her holding a diploma with a group of graduates from Mrs. Sunohara's Sewing and Drafting School. She supplemented the family income in various ways. She was a skilled seamstress and sewed for other people when asked. I remember the times when we went to the end-of-the-month fabric clearance sales at the Bon Marche Department Store. I also remember some summers, when she helped out at the harvest time on berry farms and produce farms. She also learned to be a barber. At the time of the wartime evacuation, she was working in a place that produced *kamaboko* fish cakes. Thinking about my mother brings back other memories: helping her prepare delicious Japanese food for New Year's Day which was always an open house when friends dropped in all day; and the delicate aroma of *matsutake* (pine mushrooms) as she prepared them in various ways.

My younger brother and I were born at home with help from a midwife. At that time, our home was a fourplex in a residential area on the fringe of the Japanese business district which consisted of hotels, various shops, restaurants, banks, etc., all operated by the Japanese. There also were physicians, dentists, and pharmacists of Japanese ancestry, who were practicing nearby.

Yoshi Tani's mother, Sakae Uchiyama, arrived in Seattle, Washington, to join her husband. Their son, Hiroshi, had started school and was left in the care of his grandparents in Japan.

When I was about seven, my father decided to move because of the proximity of the red light district through which we had to walk to school. Of course, I didn't exactly know what was involved. But I saw enough to think that these women were not "nice" because they lured men inside, got them drunk and stole money from them. The neighborhood elementary school was Bailey Gatzert which had a large Asian student population. Miss Ada Mahon was the highly respected principal, a kind, caring, but strict teacher.

Yoshi Tani with her mother, Sakae Uchiyama,
in Seattle, Washington, circa 1922.

We moved into a three-bedroom house high up the concrete stairs from the street level. It had a big back yard where my father raised huge colorful dahlias, cultivated large single mums, and grew and experimented with all sorts of vegetables. He also enjoyed sharing all these flowers and vegetables with our neighbors and his shop customers. Our new neighborhood had a strong Jewish influence. A synagogue was located two lots away.

*Yoshi Tani with her younger brother,
Aiji, and mother, Sakae Uchiyama,
in Seattle, Washington, 1924.*

*Yoshi Tani with her parents, Sakae and Hichiro Uchiyama, and younger brother,
Aiji, in Seattle, Washington, circa 1934. A portrait of her older brother, Hiroshi,
who resided in Japan then, was superimposed in the background. Her parents'
hope to be reunited with their son to have a complete family never materialized.*

Yoshi Tani's mother, Sakae Uchiyama (third row, fourth from right), with her fellow students at Seattle English School in Seattle, Washington, early 1920's.

It was around this time that the first presidential election that I can recall was held. Although my father, as a non-citizen, could not vote, he always showed a strong interest in politics. He was for Al Smith that year. TV's weren't in existence, and he said that a plane would fly overhead and let us know who won by blinking either a red or green light. I stayed up with him to watch—Herbert Hoover won.

Herbert Hoover's term was marked by the Great Depression. I vividly remember that in those years, everyone was trying to be as economical as possible, cutting back on anything extravagant or frivolous.

Washington Elementary School, to which I transferred, had a large Jewish student population. When the Jewish students were excused for their special holidays, it was like a holiday for us, too, because the teachers lightened up on our classroom work. I remember Mr. Sears, the principal, as a friendly, caring educator who inspired us with the famous quotations and poems, such as "Today well lived makes every yesterday a dream of happiness, and every tomorrow a vision of hope."

From this elementary school, I attended Garfield High School and graduated in 1939, at which time I was asked to give the salutatory speech. The theme that year was the Golden Jubilee of the Washington Statehood, and my topic was "State of Washington in Review." Garfield was a large high school with a diverse student body from all walks of life and ethnic backgrounds.

During these childhood years, I was an active Camp Fire Girl. Our group was all of Japanese ancestry, but our leaders were of Japanese as well as non-Japanese background.

Although my parents were of modest means, they encouraged us to go on to college and I enrolled at the University of Washington in the fall of 1939.

Yoshi Tani's mother, Sakae Uchiyama (back row, center), at the commencement of Sunohara Sewing School in Seattle, Washington, 1927.

*Yoshi Tani attending the Western Washington Camp Fire Girls Conference
at Hotel Meany in Seattle, Washington, 1938.*

Besides closely knit family units, there was a network of extended support systems in the Japanese American community. For example, there were the Japanese ethnic churches of various faiths and denominations, where services were conducted both in English and Japanese. We attended the Buddhist Church, but had friends and neighbors in many of the churches most of which were within walking distance. Much of our social life revolved around these churches.

We also had various prefectural organizations composed of persons who came from the same prefectures in Japan. I have fond memories of annual New Year's parties where our family came together with other families that had ties with Fukuoka Prefecture in Japan.

Then, there was the Japanese language school (Nihongo Gakko) with its premises occupying close to a square block. One-hour classes were held after the regular school day with corresponding grade levels through high school. And some classes were at the postsecondary levels. Not all attended, but a majority of Japanese American children did, and the school was completely supported by fees paid by our parents. Many of the teachers were parents of our classmates. The language school's annual picnic at Jefferson Park and the graduation ceremony at Nippon Kan Hall were major community events for the Japanese American families. There was some grumbling among students about having to miss after-school activities such as sports, but I am glad that I was given the opportunity to grow up bilingual. The teachers and Mr. Nakagawa, the principal, worked hard at trying to inspire us with a vision of serving as a bridge between two cultures.

"Japan Town," with all its Japanese-operated stores, hotels, restaurants, banks, pharmacies, professional offices, was not too far from where we lived. So I grew up in a diverse urban setting. Through it all, there was a sense of being part of a broad, protected, supportive, self-contained, Japanese ethnic community.

Up to the outbreak of World War II and the subsequent evacuation, my life was a rather simple, secure, uncomplicated one: still a student living at home with my parents and younger brother.

On Sunday, December 7, 1941, I had just returned home from church when my father greeted me with news that the radio was announcing that Pearl Harbor had been bombed. We listened with shock and disbelief. As President Franklin Delano Roosevelt declared war against Japan, our dismay was heightened because my parents were Japanese immigrants. My brother and I were U.S. citizens by birth, but laws did not allow Japanese nationals like my parents to become naturalized, so they were not citizens.

I was 20 years old and a junior majoring in Dietetics at the University of Washington in Seattle. I worked part-time as a receptionist in the Dean of Men's Office on campus. Soon after the declaration of war, a number of students of Japanese ancestry started coming into the Dean's Office to withdraw from classes—the reason being that their fathers were taken from their homes by the FBI, and sent away for no apparent reason other than that they were leaders in the Japanese community organizations. At this point none of us had thoughts of mass evacuation even in our wildest dreams.

On February 19, 1942, President Roosevelt signed Executive Order 9066, authorizing the Secretary of War to prescribe military areas. On February 20, Secretary of War Henry L. Stimson appointed

General John L. DeWitt as military commander to carry out the duties and responsibilities under E.O. 9066. Soon thereafter, curfew went into effect and those of Japanese ancestry, both aliens and citizens, were not allowed out from 8 p.m. to 6 a.m. This curfew, while affecting alien Germans and Italians, did not apply to U.S. citizens of German and Italian descent. Few of us presaged that the curfew was merely a prelude to the mass evacuation of only persons of Japanese ancestry.

A total of 108 evacuation orders were issued affecting approximately 110,000 people of Japanese descent living in the prescribed military zones along the West Coast. Nearly two-thirds of these people were native-born U.S. citizens.

The April 22, 1942 issue of *The Seattle Times* reported that General DeWitt had issued 12 new civilian exclusion orders including No. 17 and No. 18 which directly affected us as they provided for removal of all Japanese from areas within the City of Seattle. A responsible member of each family was to report to the designated Civil Control Station for registration and processing on Saturday, April 25, and Sunday, April 26. We were ordered to move out of our secure and comfortable home. We were full of apprehension of our future and had to hurriedly sell, store, or give away all of our belongings that we could not carry with us in the two suitcases which each of us was allowed to take.

One of the items that I could not part with was a standard Underwood typewriter, a high school graduation gift from my parents. I left it with one of my college professors who later sent it on to me in camp. It traveled all over with me and I still have it. It gathers dust in our garage and I now use a word processor. But I don't think I will ever throw the old Underwood away.

During the evacuation, my gut feelings were those of powerlessness and injustice. Although our constitutional rights were violated, we, as a group, had so little political, economic, or media power. The Issei, my parents' generation, were non-citizens and spoke Japanese as their primary language. Even though the Nisei, my generation, were citizens, the majority of us were still under the voting age. However, I felt justice would prevail eventually. Fellow students, University faculty members, and co-workers in the Dean of Men's Office tried to be helpful. Gordon Hirabayashi, a senior at the University of Washington, challenged the constitutionality of the curfew and evacuation and initiated a test case. Many of us supported him with our hearts and minds. Although we were given the option to move elsewhere voluntarily, most of us had no place to go and were transported to the newly constructed Assembly Center at the Western Washington fairgrounds in Puyallup near Tacoma. The headquarters and barracks were built in the midst of the race track, grandstand, fun house, the dipper, and other concessions.

According to the journal I kept, we arrived at Camp Puyallup at about 10:10 a.m. on Thursday, May 14, 1942, and were assigned to Area D, Section 123, Room 31, a crude 20' x 20' room. Lunch was red Mexican beans and boiled cabbage, milk and bread with no butter. We had to fill our own mattresses with hay. Medical examinations were given by a staff of Japanese doctors and helpers. Dinner consisted of spaghetti with meat balls, mashed potatoes, vegetable salad, milk, plain cake, and bread. Curfew at 9:00 p.m., lights out at 10:00 p.m.

On June 6, 1942, I recorded that graduating Nisei students of Garfield High School had their graduation ceremony in the fairground's grandstand, presided by Vice Principal Hanselman. My brother, Aiji, was in this class of '42. We stayed at this Assembly Center for three and a half months, until the major relocation camps were ready.

During this time, I wrote lots of letters to those outside, read books, taught some classes, and worked at various jobs. Cooperation was essential as we sought to establish a semblance of normal life and community. This Assembly Center was named Camp Harmony.

On August 18, 1942, we left Camp Harmony by bus to board a train for Idaho via Portland and along the Columbia River. My journal notes: "Trying to sleep at night on the coaches was a nightmare."

My journal continues that on the morning of August 19, we found ourselves in a barren, desolate, sagebrush country. Never had I realized what dust was until we got there. Ironically, just before we entered the Minidoka Relocation Center in Hunt, Idaho, there was a sign reading "Democracy must win."

Though still an undergraduate student in Dietetics, by September 4, I started working as a camp hospital dietitian along with Shiz Higano. She already had a B.S. in Dietetics, but was doing graduate research work. Our nutrition professors from the University of Washington sent us books and information to help us. We were paid $19 per month.

It was at the camp hospital that I met my husband, George (also known as Tad for Tadashi) Tani. Born in Oakland, California, he was a graduate of the University of California School of Optometry and was a practicing optometrist before the War. He was sent to Minidoka from the Tanforan Assembly Center, with the understanding that he would work as a camp optometrist.

What was camp life like? The most significant aspect was that we had lost our freedom of movement; we couldn't go in and out of the barbed wire enclosure at will. Each family was assigned only one room in barrack-type buildings. Washroom facilities and meals were in separate community structures. In spite of these adverse conditions, a sense of community developed. School classes and church services of various denominations started. Social and cultural events were scheduled, and a weekly newspaper published. The hospital functioned to meet the internees' basic health needs.

In the meantime, the War Relocation Authority continued to implement their policy to resettle evacuees as expeditiously as possible. The WRA helped many Nisei leave the internment camps to continue their education, to accept job offers, or to enlist in the Army.

Minidoka Relocation Center in Hunt, Idaho,
where Yoshi Tani and her family were interned, 1942.

George left the Minidoka Relocation Center in the spring of 1943 for a job as an autopsy assistant at a hospital in Chicago. He had plans to apply to medical school or enlist in the Army. By the time he left, we had become engaged but marriage plans were indefinite because of the uncertainty of our future. I also wanted to complete my college education.

I left Minidoka in July of 1943, worked in Chicago doing secretarial work during the summer, and then registered in the fall at Milwaukee-Downer College in Milwaukee, Wisconsin. This institution was recommended by my University of Washington nutrition professor, Dr. Jennie Rowntree, who was an alumna of the college.

Yoshi Tani's friends, Yukio and Toshiko Nakayama, at a mess hall
in the Minidoka Relocation Center, circa December 1942.

141

In order to meet my college expenses, during the summer of 1944, I worked the midnight shift on an assembly line that produced tiny walkie-talkie batteries. I remember leaving work soiled with carbon dust. I completed my courses for a B.S. degree in Foods and Nutrition by January 1945.

In the meantime, George had enlisted in the Army. After basic training at Fort McClellan, Alabama, he was sent to the Military Intelligence Specialist Language School located here in Minnesota at Fort Snelling.

On February 10, 1945, George and I were married at the Fort Snelling Chapel. The reception was in the Army mess hall. My only attendant was Rose Sakemi, a friend from Milwaukee-Downer College, who was serving her dietetic internship year at the old Ancker Hospital in St. Paul. George's best man was his boyhood friend, Haruo Najima, who was stationed here. Our parents were unable to

George and Yoshi Tani were married at the Fort Snelling Chapel in Minnesota, on February 10, 1945.

George and Yoshi Tani at their wedding reception held in the mess hall at Fort Snelling in Minnesota, February 10, 1945. On George Tani's right is Captain Spark Matsunaga, the company commander, who later became a Congressman and U.S. Senator (Democrat-Hawaii).

come as they were still in the Minidoka Relocation Center. Takashi Matsui, my second cousin, who was a faculty member and chairman of an academic division at Fort Snelling, acted on behalf of my father. Guests were mostly from George's Army unit, Company I. Among the guests was the company commander, Captain Spark Matsunaga, who later served in the U.S. Senate and was instrumental in the passage of the redress bill aimed at providing compensation for all surviving internees.

We found housing in the upstairs apartment of a converted house in the St. Anthony Park neighborhood of St. Paul. Thus, my married life started as a soldier's wife. I started working at Dairy Products Laboratory nearby, doing quality control testing of dairy products. George came home only on weekends. He said a typical day for him on the base included 10 hours of classroom work and study. By August 1945, I was pregnant with our first child, George was scheduled to be shipped overseas, and then the atom bombs were dropped in Hiroshima and Nagasaki. Shortly after the nuclear bombing, George went to the Philippines and Japan, while I remained in St. Paul, working until the birth of our first son, Paul, in May 1946. George was finally discharged in the fall of 1946.

By January 1947, George was accepted to the University of Minnesota Medical School. He graduated with the class of 1950 and then served an internship at the old Ancker Hospital. Near the completion of his internship year, George was hospitalized at the V.A. hospital for resection of a tuberculous lesion. Those were stressful days.

By this time, we had two sons. In 1951, George's mother came to live with us to help with our children, for I had to work as the family bread winner, an economic necessity while George was in medical training.

While in St. Paul, I continued to work at Dairy Products Laboratory. When George became an ophthalmology resident as a Mayo Fellow in Rochester, I worked as a hospital dietitian there. My schedule was planned to fulfill three years of work experience approved by the American Dietetics Association in lieu of a one-year dietetics clinical internship.

George finished his ophthalmology residency in 1955. After looking over practice opportunities on the West Coast, he decided to practice in Minnesota. We returned to St. Paul, and he started practicing as an ophthalmologist with the Earl Clinic in October of 1955. He later established his own practice which is now known as Tani Eye Associates and Clinic. Along with his private practice, he also served on the clinical faculty in the Department of Ophthalmology, University of Minnesota Medical School. He retired as a Clinical Professor in 1985.

Our daughter, Kay, was born in 1956. In the 1950's and 1960's, as a parent now of three children of the baby boom generation, I made it a priority to keep involved with their activities. Those were the days of PTA meetings, serving as a cub scout den mother and Girl Scout Brownie leader, and of cheering at little league baseball games, high school gymnastics meets, and football games. With our daughter, there were about ten years of chasing around all over with figure skating involvement. As a family, we took up skiing as a way to enjoy the long Minnesota winters.

In those days, family vacation trips highlighted our schedules. We enjoyed the many natural wonders of our state and national parks. Camping out in tents was a big thing for a while. Walking across the Mississippi River in Itasca Park was a memorable event. We visited man-made wonders, too, such as the World Fairs in Seattle and New York, Disneyland, and Mount Rushmore.

My mother-in-law, Moto Tani, continued to live with us as a contributing integral part of our household. She lived with us for over 30 years and celebrated her 99th birthday with us. Her living with us, speaking Japanese, cooking Japanese foods, her talents with Japanese brush painting and *tanka* poetry contributed much toward our children's appreciation of their Japanese ethnic background. She passed away at the age of 102 in 1988.

Yoshi and George Tani with their children and their families at her house in St. Paul, Minnesota, 1984. Her mother-in-law (front row, center), age 99, lived with the Tani family for over 30 years.

Besides volunteer hours with our children's activities and organizations, other community involvement as a volunteer was and continues to be an important part of my life.

Six years on the St. Paul YWCA Board of Directors helped me better understand many issues including racism, "empty nest syndrome," effective communication, and leadership development.

Ongoing involvement with the Ramsey County Medical Society Auxiliary and serving as a Past President have given me an opportunity to learn, grow, and support health-related endeavors that improve the health and quality of life for all people.

Shortly after settling in St. Paul, we joined the Centennial United Methodist Church where I have enjoyed being involved in various ways over the years. Our children were all confirmed and married at Centennial. Both my Buddhist background and my present church commitment have been significant influences in my spiritual growth.

As I experienced the aging of my parents' generation, with my mother-in-law living with us, I became more interested in gerontology, and served for six years on the Metropolitan Council Advisory Committee on Aging. This committee works with the Metro Council Area Agency on Aging: (1) to identify and address major issues dealing with the elderly population in the seven-county area; (2) to develop Area Plans for programs on aging under Title III of the Older Americans Act; and (3) to make recommendations on funding. Now I am one of the Older Americans. It is a humbling thought to realize that stores carry not only infant diapers, but adult diapers as well.

Other areas of my community involvement have included: (1) serving as a Red Cross Certified Nutrition Instructor for three years; and (2) supporting activities of the St. Paul/Nagasaki Sister City Committee, the Twin Cities Chapter of the Japanese American Citizens League, and the Japan America Society of Minnesota.

As for my professional life, while I was a full-time homemaker raising our children, I kept up with the continuing education clock hours to remain qualified as a registered dietitian.

From 1977 through 1979, I worked as a nutritionist in the Ramsey Action Programs Senior Congregate Dining Project, a federally funded program under Title III of the Older Americans Act. The project provided low cost nutritious meals to those over 60 years old in a congregate setting.

Currently, I am still working as a Consultant Dietitian for a nursing home, a position I have held for ten years since 1981. Professional organizations that I belong to are: American Dietetics Association, Minnesota Dietetics Association, Twin Cities District Dietetics Association, and the Twin Cities Consulting Dietitians for which I have served as Secretary and Treasurer.

My husband, George, at age 75, continues to practice part-time as an ophthalmologist. Our two sons, Paul and Douglas, both graduates of the University of Minnesota Medical School, are ophthalmologists and practice in association with their father. Paul spent his undergraduate and eye residency years at the University of Minnesota, plus a year at the Mayo Clinic, whereas Doug's undergraduate years were at Yale and his specialty training at the Mayo Clinic.

Paul is married to Barb, who has experience as a kindergarten and first-grade teacher. They have three daughters. Doug's wife, Linnea, is a registered nurse, and they have two daughters. Our daughter, Kay, a St. Olaf graduate, has a Master's degree from the New York University in Dance Therapy and is working at the University of Minnesota. Her husband, Tom Winegarden, has a Master of Divinity degree from Luther/Northwestern Seminary, but shifted to medicine and is now a Psychiatry resident. They have one daughter.

The Tani family in St. Paul, Minnesota, Christmas Eve, 1991.

Along with their Japanese background, our six grandchildren (ages 2 to 13) can claim English, Irish, Danish, Swedish, Norwegian, Russian, and German ethnic heritage. They all live in Minnesota. Ongoing interaction with my family definitely adds many interesting and enriching facets to my life. My brother, Aiji, a retired chemist from the Jet Propulsion Laboratory at the California Institute of Technology, lives in Pasadena, California, with his wife, Mary. My parents worked in Sidney, Nebraska, and in Chicago after leaving the internment camp in June 1945. They retired in Pasadena,

California, where they lived the rest of their lives with my brother and his family.

As of now, I wear many hats—wife, mother, grandmother, dietitian, friend, sister, and community volunteer. Other interests that have occupied my time include golf (Past President of Mendakota Women 18 Holers), bridge, china painting, travel, *tanka* poetry writing. I am hoping we can continue skiing a few more years, since I have reached the age where I qualify for complimentary lift tickets at my favorite ski resort.

Within the last five years, I have had opportunities to celebrate three significant reunions. First, while I was a student at the University of Washington, I was a member of *Fuyo Kai*, a prewar University of Washington campus organization for women of Japanese ancestry. Its purposes were: (1) to bring together the Japanese women students into closer relationships; (2) to help us attain a better understanding of the highest ideals of Japan and America; and (3) to be an instrument for service to our alma mater. Not everyone eligible chose to join, but those of us who did developed warm, lifetime friendships that culminated in a reunion celebration in 1988. Ninety-five women gathered from all over the continental United States, Hawaii, and Japan. The sharing of postwar experiences indicated that "Just about everyone has done something positive with the negative experience."

Second, also in 1988, 16 people, consisting of the American descendants of my paternal great grandfather and their spouses, gathered in Seattle for another wonderful experience. They came from all over the country including Hawaii. For some, it was a first meeting of each other.

Third and last, I returned to Seattle in 1989 for the 50th reunion of Garfield High School's class of '39. It was an extremely memorable experience. With some of the classmates, we were even able to share our memories from elementary school days.

Throughout the postwar years, I continued to feel that eventually justice will prevail in regards to our forced evacuation and incarceration. I closely followed test cases such as those of Gordon Hirabayashi and Minoru Yasui, as well as other group efforts. Most of the information was from the *Pacific Citizen*, the weekly newspaper of the Japanese American Citizens League. Gordon Hirabayashi's case reached the U.S. Supreme Court. The Court, however, upheld the lower court's judgment, and Gordon served his time in prison. The wheels of justice moved slowly.

As information suppressed by the government became available to the public, the wheels of justice started to accelerate. In 1976, our bicentennial year, President Gerald Ford officially proclaimed that all authority conferred by Executive Order 9066 was terminated on December 13, 1946, with the proclamation ending World War II hostilities.

In 1980, Congress passed an act creating a Commission on Wartime Relocation and Internment of Civilians. In February 1983, the Commission reported that "military necessity did not exist in fact to justify the evacuation and exclusion of the Japanese-Americans from the West Coast," and that the exclusion was a result of "race prejudice, war hysteria and failure of political leadership."

On May 3, 1983, the Governor of the State of Washington signed into law a bill providing $5,000 compensation to Japanese Americans who were dismissed or resigned from state employment during World War II because of the evacuation. The bill recognized the "grave injustice done to American citizens and resident aliens of Japanese ancestry." I was included in this eligible list because of my part-time job in the Dean of Men's Office at the University of Washington.

In the meantime, I joined others in writing to our Senators and Member of Congress, regarding redress legislation. I thank Senator David Durenberger, then Senator Rudy Boschwitz, and Representative Bruce Vento of my district for their prompt replies and efforts in this legislative process.

Finally, on August 10, 1988, President Ronald Reagan signed the redress bill (Civil Liberties Act), acknowledging the injustice and providing for monetary reparations. The legislative process that led to the signing and the eventual distribution of the redress checks was a great educational experience. It is sad that so many people of my parents' generation did not live to see this day.

Reflections

I am pleased that the injustice arising from racism that the Japanese Americans endured during World War II has been addressed and redress is a reality. However, I am concerned that 50 years later, racism and hate crimes are still a big issue.

The July 8, 1991 issue of the *TIME* magazine posed the questions: "Who are We?" and "Whose America?" The lead statement was, "A growing emphasis on the nation's 'multicultural' heritage exalts racial and ethnic pride at the expense of social cohesion."

My hope is that there will be a continued dialogue promoting the understanding of the nature of racism and cultural diversity in America. By better understanding the many manifestations of racism, I hope that as Americans, we all can more effectively strive together in creating a sense of community in a sharing and caring way.

Along with a more "socially cohesive" America, I yearn for world peace. World War II was a war to end all wars, so I thought. But since then, Americans have been involved in the Korean, Vietnam, and the Persian Gulf Wars.

World War II gave impetus to immense and amazing new technological research and applications—nuclear power, TV in almost every home, computers, and fax machines. With these, it is possible now to be in touch with the world and beyond in an instant.

Thanksgiving Day 1991 was a few weeks away as I wrote this final chapter of my autobiography. It was with a sense of wonder and thanksgiving that I reflected on my life.

Just as I described my pre-World War II life, I am still living my life in a diverse urban setting with a sense of being part of a broader ethnic community. But what vast differences there are!

The Japanese ethnic community is no longer as parochial and dominant. However, this community is out there, stretching from coast to coast and beyond. How can we ever forget the many poignant moments, the tears and laughter, the common experiences that we have shared over the years?

The diverse urban setting is now almost global. It even touches the moon! The setting stretches from the urban into the rural areas, as far away as the dairy and sheep farms of New Zealand, where we had our home stays in 1990.

When Americans landed on the moon in 1969, I thought about my brother, a chemist, working in the space program. Buck Rogers of my childhood comic strip was no longer a fantasy figure.

When the Berlin Wall finally fell, I remembered with a shudder our visits there in 1966 and 1969.

When the Chinese students protested in 1989 in Tiananmen Square, I recalled the day when we stood in this same Square in 1984, and saw Mao's picture, the Mausoleum of Mao, and the Government Center.

When the Persian Gulf War broke out in early 1991, we found ourselves writing with concern to our nephew who was serving over there as a Marine pilot.

When news of the coup in the Soviet Union came in August, 1991, it really struck home. A few weeks prior to this, we had a house guest, an ophthalmologist from Moscow. We had met him over 20 years ago when we were on a medical people-to-people tour in 1969. At that time, we spent three days in Leningrad and three days in Moscow. Among the gifts that our guest left were a Russian language book and tapes with this note: "I'd like to give this learned book and tapes for your grandchildren who'll ... learn Russian in the future. Thank you, Boris."

Thus, so much of whatever happens, even in far away places, now seems to touch my life in a very personal way. Though we have traveled far and wide, Minnesota remains our home.

The best part of Minnesota, of course, is the people with whom we share our lives on a regular basis. Winters may seem long and harsh at times, but there is a sense of satisfaction and thanksgiving when we manage to cope with adverse conditions, embraced by the warmth of our family and friends. Some of the images that I have of Minnesota, I have described in *tanka*, a form of Japanese poetry composed of 31 syllables in five segments, respectively containing five, seven, five, seven, and seven syllables.

The forest's trees are
Dressed in fresh glistening snow —
How peaceful, it is —
Winter in Minnesota,
A "Theatre of Seasons."

Beauty of the snow
Is sometimes forgotten when —
One is on the road,
And traffic slows to a creep,
With skidding cars here and there.

Spring is in the air —
Blossoms blooming everywhere,
First the red tulips,
Then the purple irises,
Followed by pink peonies.

Summertime is here —
In the backyard swimming pool,
Sparkling in the sun,
Children splash and swim with joy,
On this hot and humid day.

       Leaves of brilliant red,
       Yellow, orange mixed with green —
       Deciduous trees,
       Along the Mississippi,
       Show off their autumn colors.

Minnesota Twins,
Wind-up, charge, from worst to first —
Hail, the Champions!
Homer hankies, "Home, Sweet Dome,"
Beat the great Atlanta Braves.

Need more be said?

KIMI
YAMADA
YANARI

When the Yanari family had a reunion in Denver in 1981, my husband Frank's brother in Japan, Masatomo, wrote down the Yanari family tree which he traced back to the Fujiwara Clan in 740 A.D. He sent it to the family to be included in a book published for the reunion. I realized then that after my parents passed away, I have had no contact with any of my relatives in Japan. I had no record of my side of the family except a few pictures, passports, and the files from the War Relocation Authority.

My father, Zengoro Yamada, was born on January 23, 1881, in Shinoda-mura, Aichi-ken, Japan, and immigrated to Stockton, California, around 1917 to seek his fortune in farming. In 1920, my mother, Kishi Uyeda, who was born on July 18, 1900, came from Saori, Aichi-ken, with a group of so-called "picture brides." Their marriage was arranged by their parents in Japan by exchanging pictures. Following her arrival in San Francisco, they were married on April 24, 1920. Father continued farming near Stockton in partnership with a couple of other Issei men.

Their first son, born in 1921, died a few days after birth. Next came myself on January 12, 1923, followed by my sister, Yoneko, on December 19, 1926. Then in 1927, Father decided to go back to Japan with his family. I am glad that I had this opportunity to meet at least both of my grandmothers; my grandfathers were gone by then.

*Kimi Yanari's father, Zengoro Yamada,
in Stockton, California,
circa 1917.*

*Kimi Yanari's mother,
Kishi Yamada, in Stockton,
California, circa 1940.*

We lived in Nagoya, but I can remember visiting the grandmothers out in the country. Mother had one brother named Kuwajiro Uyeda, who lived with Grandmother Ei Omiya Uyeda. I had the most fun at my maternal grandmother's place. There were grasshoppers and frogs to catch, but the beautiful lotus flowers which I wanted to bring home were just out of my reach in the ponds, and I remember I couldn't persuade my cousin to pick them for me. Fireflies were another thing that intrigued me. I remember my uncle fixing up a little cage for all the fireflies that I caught, so I could take them home and watch them twinkle their lights off and on. Another memory that stays with me about Grandmother's house is the huge family altar. We all sat in front of this *obutsudan* in the evenings and meditated while Uncle recited the *okyo* (Buddhist Scripture). I also can remember celebrating various festivals while in Japan. One particular festival which stands out in my mind was *Tanabata*. My uncle had cut down a big bamboo tree from his yard and brought it all the way into Nagoya. I have no idea how far he had to walk pulling the cart with the bamboo tree. We decorated it with *origami* and other hangings. Ours was the biggest bamboo tree standing outside in the neighborhood.

Kimi Yanari with her mother, Kishi Yamada,
in Stockton, California, 1924.

We lived in Japan for three years until I was seven years old, which gave me an opportunity to attend the first grade in Nagoya. I remember one thing I really wanted to do was to learn to play the piano, but no one took me seriously. There was an older, childless couple renting our upstairs rooms, who treated me like their own grandchild. When they heard me constantly talking about a piano, they half jokingly told me they would get me one if I finished first in my class. When I did finish at the top of my class, they didn't know what to do because they really didn't think I would try that hard. Getting a piano was out of the question. As a consolation, however, when we left Japan shortly afterward, they presented me with a *Taisho koto*, a small string instrument as a going away present. I could play any tune I wanted on it by just pressing on the right keys, and it was

Kimi Yanari's maternal grandparents, Ei Omiya Uyeda (center) and Kurakichi Uyeda (right), with their granddaughter.

a source of great fun and pleasure for many years until some keys eventually broke off and could not be repaired.

Father decided to return to America, back to Stockton, to start over when the money ran out. Unfortunately, this was about the time of the Great Depression (1930), and one misfortune after another followed. We lived in town, but Father worked on a farm some distance away and could come home only once a month to bring home his meager paycheck. Two years later, as a result of a knee injury sustained while at work, Father could not work for a while. Mother then had to take a job as a cook for the Zuckerman potato farm on McDonald Island, which necessitated all of us—my parents and four children—to move out to the country in 1933. The following two years were precious to me as it was the only time I really had to get to know my dad and enjoy having him home. Up to that time, he was gone most of the time working.

In 1935, Father died from some more injuries sustained in a truck accident while at work. There was no insurance or social secu-

Kimi Yanari (second row, third from right) with her first-grade classmates in Nagoya, Japan, 1929.

rity benefits or worker's compensation in those days, and Mother was left destitute with us two girls and two younger boys. Family friends urged her to go on government welfare at this time, but she refused as she felt that would bring disgrace and shame to the family. She continued to work hard as a camp cook as cooking was the only way she knew to support her family. Within the next two years, my two little brothers died—Toshio, four years old, with pneumonia, and Hideo, age seven, following a tonsillectomy operation. Looking back, I don't know how Mother ever managed. She kept on going determined to see that we got educated.

After completing the eighth grade in a one-room school house on McDonald Island, I had to move into town to attend high school. Through some friends, Mother found an American family who hired me as a domestic while attending high school. The McAndrews family consisted of a mother and four adult daughters. I couldn't have had a finer, kinder family to live with. They treated me like a member of their family throughout the years that I lived with them while attending high school and business college. The oldest daughter was a school teacher, and the three younger sisters worked in offices as secretaries. I guess the paths I took to learn to become a secretary were formulated while living with them. From Mrs. McAndrews I learned how to cook and how important good nutrition was for one's health. The daughters became my role models. Although I did not have any time for extracurricular activities, I did manage to attend the Stockton Buddhist Church frequently and kept in touch with some Japanese friends.

After graduating from high school in three and a half years, I enrolled in a secretarial course at the Humphreys Business College. Other Nisei girls told me I would never be able to get a job with a private firm and that the only chance of getting a job was through Civil Service. I was fortunate. The College sent me out for an interview to Gumpert & Mazzera, a prominent and prestigious law firm in Stockton, and they hired me. I can still remember Mother's tears of joy when I handed her my first paycheck. The only thing that had kept her going was her hope and trust that as soon as I finished school, I could get a job and would be able to help her.

I had worked for Gumpert & Mazzera for exactly one year when the evacuation order came in May of 1942. Mr. Gumpert and Mr. Mazzera called me into their office and told me that this evacuation order was unconstitutional, and that if I wanted to stay, I could keep the job. They also offered to fight for me even if they had to go clear up to the President of the United States. However, my big concern was for Mother; all her hopes and dreams were completely shattered just when I was starting to be of help to her. Thanking Mr. Mazzera and Mr. Gumpert for their warm support and concern for me, I told them that I would have to leave with my family. They presented me with a watch when I left and told me to contact them if they could be of help to me in any way. I knew also that I could count on the McAndrews for any assistance we might need. My mother, sister, and I were living at the time in a two-room upstairs apartment of a home owned by a Japanese family. We had hardly any furniture, but what a frantic situation it was for Mother to have to decide how and what to pack and what to do with all the household items we couldn't take. I remember she had some special Japanese records which she hated to part with. She decided to break them up and dump them in the garbage can. We were able to cram a few boxes of kitchen articles and clothing in the garage. The rest of our property was stored in the Japanese Christian Church. Only two trunks and her old treadle sewing machine were later shipped to her after she came out to St. Paul, but the disposition of the rest of her property was unknown.

We were first checked into the temporary Stockton Assembly Center on the San Joaquin County Fairgrounds. From then on, it seemed like we had to wait in one line after another for everything. When I saw the horse stables where some people were housed, we considered ourselves lucky for getting one of the units in the barracks. However, there were no partitions dividing the units for each family. We had to put a rope across and hang sheets for privacy. For the young people, it was just a new experience in meeting and getting acquainted with other young people, but for Mother it was a bewildering experience full of anxiety and apprehension. As soon as I got settled down, I applied and got a job as secretary to the Community Activity Director. Because I had to help my boss in the process of closing the Center, I stayed behind and left Stockton with the last group for the Rohwer Relocation Center in Arkansas. The Stockton Assembly Center closed officially on October 17, 1942.

We were sent by train to the Rohwer Relocation Center, just outside of McGehee, Arkansas. When we saw the unit assigned to us in the Rohwer Relocation Center, 40-7-C, I could not accept the fact that we would have to stay here for we didn't know how long. The room was bare with one pot-bellied stove and three cots—no curtains, no closets, no shelves, nothing. We had no stores to buy what we needed. However, Sears and Montgomery Ward catalogs were made available to us. According to official records, a total of 8,475 people were sent from Santa Anita and Stockton to this camp, making it the sixth largest city in Arkansas. The volume of business Sears and Montgomery Ward received from the internees must have been enormous.

No one stayed idle. They all got right to work to improve their living quarters, and some even put in landscaped gardens and walkways. I couldn't do any carpentry, but I found out where some men were getting lumber. I enlisted the help of a girl next-door and went out one night to the lumber yard and pulled out two 1' x 12's

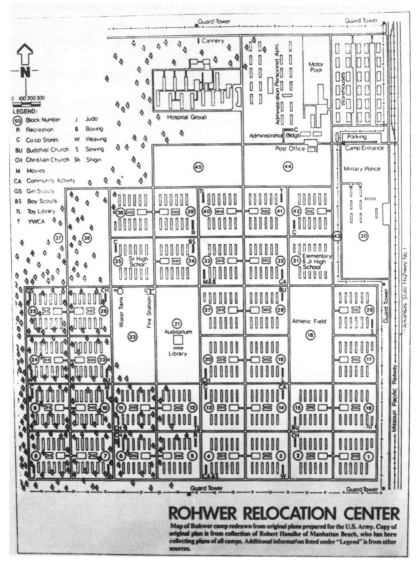

A diagram of the Rohwer Relocation Center in Arkansas
where Kimi Yanari and her family were interned during World War II.
Reprinted from "The First Rohwer Reunion" with the permission of the editor.

and ran back to our unit with them, eluding the mounted MP. That was the only time I ever stole anything. With this lumber some boys built shelves and a bench for us.

At the Rohwer Relocation Center, I worked as secretary to the Project Attorney, Jack Curtis, for $16 a month. The administrative staff members were all good, kind men, and I was treated very well. They allowed me to take a trip to Little Rock to attend a YWCA function, and to visit the Jerome Relocation Center 25 miles away. On another occasion, a busload of girls including myself were permitted to visit Nisei soldiers at Camp Shelby, Mississippi, where the 442nd Regimental Combat Team, the all Japanese American volunteer unit, was getting its basic training. There, I ran into one young soldier from Stockton. A few months later I heard that he had been killed in action.

Kimi Yanari (first row, far right) with other members of the Spinster Club in navy blue uniform sweaters knit by each member, in the Rohwer Relocation Center, Arkansas, 1943.

Mother, with all the free time now, enrolled in sewing and flower arrangement classes offered and taught by internees. She also participated in other activities and kept busy, even making *sake* on the side. The uncertainties of the future were forgotten for a time. As soon as the school system was established, my sister continued her high school education. Many clubs and social and athletic activities were organized to keep us busy. The biggest social event, I think, was the queen contest held in February 1943, in which I was a runner-up. It was indeed one of the highlights of my life.

Kimi Yanari (far left) was a runner-up in the queen contest held in February 1943, in the Rohwer Relocation Center, Arkansas.

As the internees started to apply for leave to find jobs, I realized it was up to me to go out first and find a job and place to live. I was not a bit concerned, feeling quite confident. But I can imagine how Mother was worried when I told her I wanted to go to Chicago and find a job. I had a nice letter of reference from Mr. Gumpert to the Chicago Bar Association and didn't think I would run into any problems. About that time, Frank Yanari, who was stationed at Fort Snelling, came to Rohwer on his furlough to visit his friends and I was introduced to him. Family friends and Mother then persuaded me to take a 30-day leave to St. Paul and have Frank help me find a place to live. Never had I been so scared as when I was on that train traveling alone from Arkansas to a place I had never been to before. It was good to have someone I knew meet me at the station. Frank told me later that he had a difficult time finding a place for me to stay until the following article written by Paul Light of the *St. Paul Pioneer Press* appeared in the newspaper.

> ... This boy happens to be of Japanese parentage. But he was born in the United States, attended American schools, joined the Army soon after Pearl Harbor. His loyalty to the United States can't be questioned. His superior officers thought enough of him to make him a sergeant.
>
> He came to Fort Snelling some months ago with his young wife, also American born. Both are well educated, cultured, pleasant.
>
> His duties permit him to leave the post at night. But he has had to remain separated from his wife because St. Paulites won't rent them living quarters. Even apartment buildings with "Vacancy" signs have turned them down.
>
> The point I'm trying to make is that a convicted traitor is given consideration. A loyal American soldier is not.
>
> Mrs. Mary Gates of the Office of Civilian Defense gives me the facts about the young American-Japanese couple. The Civilian Defense Volunteer Office

maintains a room and apartment registry for service men and their families.

She hopes some apartment owner will
read this and right the injustice by no-
tifying her that quarters are available.

The sergeant apparently isn't dependent on his Army income. He's willing to pay from $50 a month upward.

In response to this article, a Czechoslovakian lady living near
Seven Corners in St. Paul had offered to rent him two rooms in her
home. I was fortunate Frank was able to get this place for me. I also
got a job right away as a stenographer at Colonial Felt Mills, the first
place I went to apply.

Having found a job, I was then eligible to apply for a permanent leave. I then accepted Frank's proposal of marriage. Mother
could not leave camp yet, but my sister applied and was accepted
into the Cadet Nurse Corps at St. Joseph's Hospital. She then received her permanent leave and came to St. Paul. She eventually
finished her nurse's training at the University of Minnesota and
worked as Dr. Owen Wangensteen's scrub nurse in the University's
Main Operating Room. She and her husband, Dr. SePuan Yu, later
moved to Schenectady, New York, where he took a job with General
Electric Research Lab.

With the help of Mr. and Mrs. Willie Akamatsu, who had a
gift shop in St. Paul, we got married in the Fort Snelling Chapel on
November 27, 1943. In spite of the sugar rationing in effect at that
time, a cook at the Fort Snelling Hospital where Frank was stationed
managed to bake us a beautiful wedding cake. My sister was the
maid of honor. I walked down the aisle on the arm of Colonel Guthrie
of the Station Hospital, who stood up for me in place of my father.
My only regret was that Mother could not be there. Having volun-

tarily left Stockton before the evacuation order, Frank's family was in Denver, Colorado, but no one in his family could come.

Willie and Ruth Akamatsu had a gift shop in St. Paul, Minnesota, 1944.

By the summer of 1944, all internees were preparing to leave as the War Relocation Authority announced that the Rohwer Relocation Center would be closed in 1945. My sister finally received permission to return to the Center on January 8, 1945, to bring Mother out to St. Paul. Although the thought of a grandchild expected in March of that year lifted her spirits somewhat, I don't think Mother ever recovered from her feelings of hopelessness and depression. Emi, our first daughter, was born on March 4, 1945. Since Mother was more than willing to take care of Emi, I decided to go back to work.

After being transferred to the Military Intelligence Service Language School for a short while, Frank got discharged from the Army on November 10, 1945. The discriminatory treatment he had received in California just before the war was so unpleasant that it

*Kimi and Frank Yanari were married in the Fort Snelling Chapel
on November 27, 1943. Left to right, Frank, Kimi, bridesmaid
Yoneko Yamada (Kimi's sister), and best man James Kurata.*

did not take him long to decide to settle in St. Paul. This was fine
with me. The people we met here were really kind and warm-hearted.
While looking for a more adequate place to live than the two rooms
we were renting, we heard about the Resettlement Hostel at Seven
Corners, formerly a small hotel. It was not exactly what we wanted,
but the cost was reasonable and we moved in. Miss Evans was the
Director, and Mrs. Tomiko Ogata did all the cooking for the residents. We really enjoyed the feeling of camaraderie and communal
living at the hostel. We lost contact with those that moved away, but
we formed a lasting friendship with those who remained.

*Kimi Yanari (center, on the floor) with her daughter, Emi,
at a Christmas party held in the Resettlement Hostel in St. Paul, Minnesota,
1946. Seated in the back from left to right are Aiko Ogata, Yoneko Yamada
(Kimi's sister), Tomiko Ogata, Miss Evans (hostel director), and Hiroko Ogata.*

Frank decided to become a watchmaker and enrolled at the
St. Paul Vocational School. Mother left for Denver, where we felt
she would be happier around more Japanese people and where there
was a Buddhist Church she could attend. I had to quit work then, but
as soon as Emi was two and a half years old and was accepted at the
Wilder Nursery School, I applied at the law firm of Otis, Faricy, Burger
& Moore. Mr. Warren Burger interviewed and hired me. I was mainly
assigned to Mr. Richard Moore but did work for all the other attorneys in the office when needed. The experience I gained was invaluable.

Several attorneys, after leaving the firm, moved up into very
high positions in the private sector, as well as in the public sector.
Mr. Burger was one of them, having been appointed Chief Justice of
the U.S. Supreme Court in 1969. Later, in 1984 when I went to
Washington, D.C. to attend a computer seminar, I visited Chief Justice Burger in his chambers and received a most cordial welcome.

Kimi Yanari paid a visit to Chief Justice Warren E. Burger in his chambers
at the U.S. Supreme Court in Washington, D.C., March 23, 1984.
In the postwar period, she worked as a legal secretary for his law firm,
Otis, Faricy, Burger & Moore, in St. Paul, Minnesota.

Since my husband's and my families were both Buddhist and we grew up in Buddhist communities, Frank felt the need to organize a Buddhist group here. After 1945, most of the approximately 4,000 Nisei soldiers stationed at Fort Snelling and their relatives had moved out of Minnesota. However, Frank was able to contact a small remaining group of Japanese Americans, including Mrs. Flora Terakawa, the widow of the Rev. Tansai Terakawa, and we held our first Buddhist service on May 5, 1946, at the Unitarian Church located at 1526 Harmon Place in Minneapolis.

The membership in the Twin Cities Buddhist Association has never been big enough to have a full-time minister. But the group has stayed actively together all these years thanks to Father Daisuke Kitagawa's help at the incipient stage, and owing to the spiritual leadership provided us not only by ministers from the Chicago Midwest Buddhist Temple, but several ministers who came for graduate studies at the University of Minnesota. The Rev. Yurii Kyogoku stayed from 1960 through 1963. I am truly grateful for all she taught me. We are also indebted to the Rev. John Cummins of the First Universalist Church for letting us use his church for our services.

In 1948, with borrowed money as down payment, Frank and I finally bought a modest house in West St. Paul. Mother came back to live with us, but on April 26, 1950, she died from a massive cerebral hemorrhage at age 50. This was four months before our son, Dean, was born. I so wish I could have done more to make her happy. I'm sorry she did not live long enough to be able to enjoy the same wonderful relationship with all her grandchildren as I am experiencing now with ours.

After Dean was born, I quit my job, and we sold our house in St. Paul and moved to our present home in St. Louis Park to be closer to Minneapolis, where Frank had opened a watch repair and jewelry store. I stayed home until our children were all in school. Toyo was born on February 28, 1953, and Gail, on August 25, 1954. For the next 14 years, I kept busy with our children's activities serving as Den Mother, Room Mother; working in our vegetable and flower gardens; sewing most of our clothes; and getting involved in Japanese American community and Buddhist Church activities.

Emi now lives in San Jose, California, with her husband Naoya Nobuhiro and two children—Jonathan and Annie. Emi works as an administrative operations analyst in the School of Social Sciences at San Jose State University. Her husband manages a Japanese restaurant in Menlo Park.

Dean lives in St. Louis Park with his wife Maxine and three children—Sara, John, and Jason. Dean served four years in the Navy and now works for the Post Office. His wife runs a day care center.

Toyo, her husband Bill Lang, and their son Martin, eight years old, are all musicians. Bill plays and teaches saxophone, and Martin plays the cello. A music graduate of Gustavus College, Toyo teaches the Suzuki violin method privately. She also plays with the Metropolitan Symphony Orchestra.

Our youngest daughter, Gail, and her husband, Ben Wong, live in Eden Prairie with their children, Jason and Alissa. Gail is the production manager with Colorgraphics in St. Louis Park. Ben works as a computer programmer for Hennepin County.

Our children have experienced some ups and downs in life, but they have all proved capable of coping with whatever may come their way. They are extremely hard-working and managing well. They are my great pride and joy. The grandchildren, too, seem all happy and well-adjusted. In a column recently written by Pat Gardner in the *Star Tribune*, Alissa, in a discussion of nationality, was quoted as saying, "I'm half Chinese, half Japanese and all American!"

In 1964, after the children were all in school, I got a job as secretary to the Chief of Police of the St. Louis Park Police Department. Twenty-four years later in 1988, at my retirement party, Chief Clyde Sorensen, my first boss, said he couldn't see at the time he hired me how "a gentle, petite girl" like me could handle the big, rough, and hardened officers of the Department and the kind of work dealing with all elements of the seamy side of society. Although my previous legal secretarial experience was mostly in civil law and did not involve much criminal law, I was confident that I could handle any office work in a police department.

However, there was much to learn because the cases were quite different from anything that I had worked on before. Occasionally, I even had to search women suspects when they were arrested and brought in. I did find the Chief and his men, in spite of their hard exterior appearance, very kind-hearted, supportive and always ready to help. The succeeding Chiefs I worked for—Richard W. Setter and Mancel T. Mitchell—were also men whom I highly respected and learned a lot from. I retired from the Police Department on June 30, 1988.

Kimi Yanari at her retirement party on June 30, 1988,
with three police chiefs she worked for, (left to right)
Clyde A. Sorensen, Richard W. Setter, and Mancel Mitchell.

In 1977, to increase my skills, I studied for and passed a two-day examination given by the International Institute for Certifying Secretaries, receiving my Certified Professional Secretary (CPS) rating. My responsibilities and authority were then gradually increased from supervising one clerk when I started, to supervising a clerical staff of seven by the time I retired. I also performed duties as secretary and treasurer of the Hennepin County Chiefs of Police Association. Not only did I learn about my Chief's responsibilities, but also the issues that all the police chiefs in Hennepin County had to deal with.

In 1972, the Bloomington Affiliated Garden Clubs decided to build a Japanese garden at Normandale Community College and asked for help from the Japanese American community. Frank remembered that a group of Nisei soldiers had expressed a wish to leave something to the people of Minnesota for the wonderful reception and friendship they had experienced while stationed here. He felt this would be a great project for them to contribute to. He organized a small committee of local Military Intelligence Service (MIS)

173

veterans and launched the huge task of compiling a list of former Nisei MIS'ers who were by then scattered all over the world.

The Nisei veterans' group was successful in raising sufficient funds to build the *bentendo* (shrine for a goddess) and the curved bridge in the Normandale Japanese Garden. We have been involved with the Garden ever since. Our daughter Toyo was the first to get married there in 1980. The Garden Committee now schedules 40 to 50 weddings a year in the Garden. In May of 1992, the MIS veterans' group from Los Angeles held their 50th reunion in the Garden. Approximately 350 people attended not only from Los Angeles, but from all over the country including Hawaii.

The Nisei veterans of the Military Intelligence Service were instrumental in creating a Japanese garden at Normandale Community College in Bloomington, Minnesota, in 1976.

Reflections

As I look back over the past 50 years in Minnesota, I often wonder where I would be now if World War II hadn't broken out. I probably would still be living in the small Japanese community in Stockton, California. The forced relocation certainly broadened my horizon and provided me a wonderful opportunity for personal growth and development. I am truly grateful to all people who have touched my life—teachers, all my wonderful bosses, friends, neighbors, members of the Japanese American community and various social and professional organizations.

174

Contrary to my initial fear that our cultural heritage would be lost to our children living in Minnesota, I am delighted to learn that they can learn just as much or even more here due largely to the continued efforts of open-minded Minnesotans to promote better understanding of other nationalities and cultures in the state. One example is the Festival of Nations in which the Japanese American community participates. For years, the folk dancing presented at the Festival was taught by Michi Hirota, a member of our Buddhist Church. We have been involved with the Festival ever since our oldest daughter Emi was five years old. I had to learn how to dress our daughters in *kimonos* and tie the *obis*. As they grew up, I had to learn to sew *yukatas* (summer *kimonos* made of cotton). Four years ago, our granddaughter Sara, eight years old at the time, danced in the Festival. She wore the *kimono* my sister had worn when she came back from Japan 62 years ago. My mother had it packed away in her trunk.

*Kimi Yanari's daughter, Emi, at the Festival of Nations
in St. Paul, Minnesota, 1964.*

Kimi Yanari flanked by her daughters, Toyo (left) and Gail (right), at the Festival of Nations in St. Paul, Minnesota, 1968.

Kimi Yanari's granddaughter (right), Sara Yanari, at the Festival of Nations in St. Paul, Minnesota, 1988. Sara is wearing a 62-year-old kimono which belonged to Kimi's sister, Yoneko Yu, nee Yamada.

There were many other events our family participated in—Aquatennial, Minnihon Center, a ball sponsored by the Women's Association of the Minnesota Symphony Orchestra, the annual *sukiyaki* dinners by the Japanese American Citizens League and the Normandale Japanese Garden, the openings of the Japanese Garden at the University Arboretum and the Ordway Japanese Garden at Como Park, Dayton's Flower Show in the 8th-floor Auditorium, the Walker Art Center events, and most recently, the Special Olympics in 1991.

Kimi Yanari's son, Dean, dancing at the Aquatennial in Minneapolis, Minnesota, 1970.

I also appreciate the wonderful opportunity I have for learning, without even going to Japan, the old traditional crafts of making silk flowers, *kata tsumami, maru tsumami* (silk folding), and *bon seki* (sand painting on tray). I am a student of Mrs. Chizuko Ando, who came to St. Paul from Tokyo in the early 1970's. She has been teaching and demonstrating her exquisite art craft in the Twin Cities area for many, many years. I am also taking up *sumie* (Japanese brush painting) from Reiko Shellum, another Japanese teacher and artist in the Twin Cities.

Following my retirement in 1988, I have been quite involved at the St. Louis Park Lenox Senior Center, not only as a volunteer teacher of Macintosh computer courses, but working with senior citizens and helping them wherever I can. Both Frank and I find our retirement days busy, happy, and rewarding. I intend to continue to learn from old friends, new friends, and new experiences as long as I live, and I live my days in gratitude for all that I have received.

Kimi Yanari teaching a computer class to senior citizens at the Lenox Senior Center in St. Louis Park, Minnesota, 1991.

MARY
TAKAO
YOSHIDA

Dedicated to my grandchildren:
Kyle, Patrick, Matthew, Holly, Jenna, Jennifer and Ryan

My life as a child was a simple one, to put it mildly, but many, many thoughts are locked inside my head which periodically surface to remind me of where I've been. Many of the dates and events may not be exact, but they are as best as I can recall. I felt for all these years that these "private thoughts" were too insignificant and even silly to be recalling.

But as I began to recollect, I realized that my "private thoughts" weren't silly and insignificant as I had felt, but rather they were my guideposts to bring me to where I am today. The recollection also made me realize that I wanted to share with you, my grandchildren, my thoughts so you can better understand who I am and why I am what I am. I now feel that I am a much stronger and hopefully a better person because of it all. When we are children, our feelings are very true and straightforward, but as we get older, they become clouded and confused. As we search out our real feelings, we begin to see pieces fitting together and we develop a sense of purpose. I'm sure those hurdles are put there for a purpose and we overcome and move on as stronger persons.

179

I was born on June 6, 1923, in a small town called Central Point in the southern part of the State of Oregon. In those days, there were very few hospitals and they were far away. It was common practice for doctors to make house calls with their black lunch-bucket type medical bags, especially for the delivery of a baby. In fact, most babies were delivered by midwives and I'm quite sure that was how I came into this world.

My father, Kakuji Takao, was born in 1891 in Takamatsu City on the Island of Shikoku in southern Japan. In 1908, he was sent to America to study at the age of 17. He attended the University of

Mary Yoshida's father, Kakuji Takao, in front of his house in Takamatsu City, Kagawa Prefecture, Japan, 1949. He moved back to Japan in 1948.

Oregon and became fluent in English. He studied Agriculture and wanted to experiment to see how he could grow larger tomatoes. He went back to Japan to marry his arranged "picture" bride, which was the custom of that time.

Father married Yaeno Tomida and returned to America with his bride. I was next to the last child of eight children. An older brother and an older sister were taken back to Japan to live. Hiroshi and Haruko passed away in Japan without our ever knowing them. Henry was two years older than I, but died in infancy. So, the only real family that I knew consisted of my older sister, Toshiko, who is eight years older; George and Joe who have both passed away; and my sister, Mona, who is two years younger. Joe was four years older and passed away at age 16 due to complications from measles. George was older than Joe, but contracted polio when he was two years old, spending much of the time in a hospital in Portland, Oregon. Therefore, I didn't really know him other than the fact that he was my brother. I became acquainted with him after moving into the barrack in the Tule Lake Relocation Center which was shared by my father and George. We continued to keep in touch and he came to live with my father and me in Minneapolis, Minnesota. George passed away in Minneapolis at age 64 from liver failure.

Mona is the only member of my family who is like a sister as we grew up together and stayed together. Our mother passed away at the age of 40 when I was quite young. Consequently, I remember very little about her. My only clear recollection was getting very ill at the graveside services when my mother was buried. Mona and I were the youngest, around six and eight years of age, respectively, at the time of our mother's death. Since we needed care, Father sent us to live with a childless Issei couple on a farm in Medford, Oregon. Our older sister, Toshiko, thought this was a temporary arrangement made by our father until he could get things in order following Mother's death. She later found out this was a permanent arrangement and was very angry, for Father had not consulted her. She had pretty much assumed the mother's role in taking care of us during Mother's illness.

As I recall, we lived in a big white house sitting on top of a hill. There was a road which we called a highway, because it was asphalt and had a white line down the middle. This road ran in front of our house at the bottom of the hill, so we couldn't see cars as they came by. It was a rare treat to see or hear cars coming as they were few and far between. Cars then were of a standard black boxy type without much variety. They were so noisy that we could hear them coming down the road at some distance. Since we couldn't see the road from the house, we would climb on top of the porch rail just to get a glimpse of the "miracle machine!"

At the time I started school, I was living in Tolo with my mother, father, two sisters and two brothers. We didn't have kindergartens, pre-schools, or any of the many opportunities that are available today. I don't remember my first day of school, but I do remember the schoolhouse. It was a typical storybook schoolhouse sitting out on a farm with the familiar bell tower. We walked to school, cutting through all the neighbors' backyards or fields. We always found interesting things to occupy us on our trek. For instance, one day we got too close to the bee hives which one of the neighbors had. It must have been close to honey gathering time, as before we knew it, we had a swarm of bees coming straight toward us. My brother Joe yelled "run" and he passed me up and told me to hurry. I ran as fast as I could, but my short legs just couldn't outrun the wall of bees—they came in like dive bombers! I kept running and must have passed their territorial boundary, if they had such, because I survived with only a few stings. The swarm turned around and disappeared just as fast as they appeared. Surprisingly, we always seemed to make it to school on time in spite of our dawdling along the way.

This schoolhouse had grades 1 through 6 in one big open room, almost like a barn. There was a long hallway near the back which was lined with hooks to hang our wraps. We left our galoshes, on rainy days, and our lunchboxes on the floor under our coats. This old schoolhouse had a huge pot-bellied stove in the middle of the room for heat on chilly days. We had one teacher who went from one grade to the next, checking homework and evenly dividing her teaching time between grades—each grade had, at the most, four or five students. Joe was the only student in the 6th grade. I remember how embarrassed I was when I had to sit with a boy in the same desk as we were the only two students in that grade that year. I would guess that must have been 2nd or 3rd grade. The desks were the large, wooden, old-fashioned kind with the seats attached. It was wide enough for two kids, but I sat as close to the edge as I could so that we wouldn't touch each other. The top of the desk had a groove for pencils and a hole on the upper right hand corner for our bottle of ink. Ball-point pens were not available then, so all our penmanship lessons were done with the dipping pen.

Of course, being out in the country, we had an "outhouse" in the back of our schoolhouse. It was a "one seater!" The school yard also had a metal slide which was characteristic of school yards of that time. During the recess and after lunch, we all played dodgeball and other group games which I can't recall, but a day didn't go by that we didn't start with dodgeball. With only one teacher, I realize

A grade school which Mary Yoshida attended in the early 1930's while living in Tolo, Oregon. This photograph was taken in 1990.

now how hard it must have been for her to control the whole school and to select activities that would include every student at every age level.

Our house in Tolo had huge pillars on the corners of the open porch which ran across the front of the house and around the side. The rooms inside were big and empty with only a large table in the dining room and double beds in the bedrooms. The back room was a converted porch with a large wooden trough-like sink under the pump and the walls were lined with make-shift shelves to store canned foods, pots and pans, soap, etc. Outside of the house I remember a shed which stored farm equipment. I remember a huge mulberry tree next to the shed and the overhanging branches almost covered the roof. Mona and I climbed onto the roof and picked and ate mulberries until our mouths were blue and our clothes were all stained. We must have been a sight!

Our new living arrangement with Mr. and Mrs. Hyosaburo Yokota, whom we called *ojisan* and *obasan*, was not a legally binding agreement, but rather a mutual understanding between friends. *Ojisan* is a Japanese term for a man who is like an uncle and *obasan* is a similar term for a woman. Mona and I told all our friends at school that they were our aunt and uncle as we didn't know what else to call them. That label remains even today when I correspond with my high school friends in Medford.

Ojisan was a very small man, but I distinctly remember him with his crew cut hair and a mustache. He always wore pants that flared out at the thigh, but were skin tight below the knees and were tucked inside the boots which were laced up to his knees. They were always khaki colored and reminded me of an army general. My mental image of him is one of a very stern authoritarian figure, and Mona and I were always afraid to talk to him. I don't recall him ever trying to carry on a conversation with us—only giving orders of what to do around the farm. The Yokotas also did truck farming.

Our "new" home was a small two-bedroom house—more like a lake cottage without a sewer system and a hand pump for water. The house had a small entryway porch on the front, but we never used the front door. There was a long screened porch on the back of the house, plus an area which was enclosed with makeshift walls, but the ground was the floor in this part of the house. This area was used as a work area. One section had a milk separator and an old brown wooden ice box with a hinged top which was opened and filled with large blocks of ice. The other section had a well, pump, and a large sink which was used for everything that needed water, e.g., cooking, washing, etc. This area was the most used with makeshift shelves lining the walls; mostly made from wooden crates which were used to take melons and other larger items to market. The sink was very crudely sitting precariously on cement blocks and bricks or whatever was around to hold it as steadily as it could for the various chores that needed to be done at the pump.

The bedrooms were so small that there was only room for one double bed and no closets. Therefore, the small room located between the two bedrooms was used for a closet. This room, I assume, was originally meant to be the bathroom. We had a small chamber pot which we could use during the night and then empty it the next morning in the "outhouse." The "outhouse" we had was a two-seater! I used to think it was about a block away, but in reality, I guess it was less than 200 feet away. It seemed like a long way to go on a chilly winter night!

The house was approximately five miles from the city of Medford, Oregon, and was considered a rural area as we did not have any utilities except for electricity. Medford did have a small airport and our property bordered the airport runway. The weather in Oregon stayed pretty mild. We occasionally got snow, but not enough to even make snowballs. The houses did not have storm windows or storm doors, and the only heat we had was from a black pot-bellied stove in the living room and an old-fashioned wood stove in the kitchen. These stoves were the only means we had to get hot water. We used the sink on the porch for brushing our teeth and washing up and oh, that well water was cold, especially in the winter time! Since there was no bathtub or shower which is essential when you get so dirty working on a farm, *ojisan* built an old-fashioned *ofuro* (deep bathtub) which is what they have in the country of Japan.

Mary Yoshida's foster mother, Kimi Yokota, who raised her and her sister, Mona, after their mother passed away. This photograph was taken in the garden of Kimi's house near Medford, Oregon, in the postwar period.

This *ofuro* was a deep rectangular wooden box which had a metal bottom and sat on top of a grate. The grate was supported by two brick walls to leave the center open for firewood to be burned to heat the water. Inside the *ofuro* room, there were slats of wood approximately three or four inches wide on the floor with low benches to sit on. Mona and I would wash up together, even scrubbing each other's back. We would take some warm water from the *ofuro* and soap and rinse ourselves off before stepping down into the warm soaking water. The tub also had slats on the bottom so we wouldn't burn our feet on the metal bottom. Low benches were also inside the tub on each side so we could sit and the water came up to our necks. Our *ofuro* probably could seat three small persons, but it would have been a little cramped as I recall. I can still remember that wonderful feeling of soaking up to our neck in this warm, almost hot water. I would get so sleepy sitting there until *obasan* said we had to get out. I'm sure she was worried that we would really fall asleep and might even drown in the water. It was the most relaxing, enjoyable time that I can recall. We all used the same water over and over until it got a little dirty and then we would have to drain it out and refill it again, hauling the water from the pump with a bucket.

Outside of the house, the farm had a large barn which housed two horses and approximately six to eight milking cows. The horses were harnessed up and used to pull the plow, the manure spreader and the wagon for hauling hay in from the fields. *Ojisan* was always getting angry at the horses because they wouldn't go where he wanted them to and he would hit them often with the strap of the reigns. I used to feel sorry for them and would brush them extra special and feed them the green leafy parts of the alfalfa hay when I could find some. It was fun to have the horses take food from my hands with their big thick lips and push it between their teeth—they were careful not to bite my hand with their teeth. When they finished what I gave them, they would nudge me with their nose, asking for more. Those horses became very special to me; I would talk to them and they seemed to sense our companionship as they would come running to the fence when they saw me coming. Of course, they were looking for the treats of carrots, cabbage, etc., which I always had for them, but still I felt they understood me.

The barn was also used to milk the cows in the morning and evening. The milking machine wasn't invented at that time; I had to help with the milking every morning before going to school. The cows were always waiting when we opened up the big sliding barn doors which were splattered with dried manure. It was dried on so hard after years of splattering that it almost looked like a coating of stucco, but I don't think the smell ever went away! The cows marched in a single file to their own stalls to eat their hay—their heads were clamped between the slats, and milking proceeded by washing down the udders to keep the milk clean. We sat on low three-legged round stools and placed a bucket on the floor between our knees and proceeded to push and pull—two nipples at time to rhythm—until all four nipples were empty and no more milk could be squeezed out. Cows are like pets, they get used to one person's milking and know the feel, but if someone else tries to milk them, they may not like the way it feels and decide to kick the bucket over, milk and all! When all the cows had been milked, their neck harness was released and they filed out of the barn and walked contentedly in a single file down the path out to the pasture. They were content to be relieved of the pressure from the milk which got large and heavy. Cows too had a certain look of contentment as they lay under a shade tree chewing on their cud, their tails swishing back and forth to keep the flies away.

Besides the barn was a large screened-in area with a shed where turkeys were fed and raised to sell for Thanksgiving. This was a small venture with maybe a dozen turkeys, but they were so noisy gobbling that it sounded more like 50. Next to the turkey shed was a fenced-in mud hole where we had a few pigs for our own food supply. They also served to take care of all our garbage. Across the way was a chicken coop and a hen house where we gathered eggs, using some for eating, some for selling, the others for hatching baby chicks to keep the cycle going.

In the front of our little house was about an acre of land which was our vegetable garden, where we grew carrots, green peppers, onions, string beans, corn and a variety of melons. It was a small truck farm by today's standards, but everything was done by hand, which required tedious hours of seeding and hoeing after school. When the harvest time came around, we worked late into the night washing the carrots and turnips and tying them into bundles to take to the market in the morning. In the fall, it began to get dark early and we used kerosene lanterns. I can still feel that freezing cold water from the well which was used to scrub the vegetables. My fingertips were in pain from the cold. After the vegetables came the melons—cantaloupe, honeydew, casaba, and watermelon. The melons were so heavy that it was back-breaking work to harvest them, but I guess I preferred them to the vegetables, as we didn't have to wash the melons, we just wiped off the dirt. Finally came the squash and pumpkins just before Halloween! Mona and I were so relieved when we could finally carve our pumpkins because we knew then that the field work was done.

The summer of 1940 brought many changes to my life. I graduated from Medford High School in June and moved into the city to work as a salad girl at the Medford Hotel. I worked for a year to save money to go to college in the fall of 1941. Toward the end of the summer of 1941, my sister, Toshiko, came down from Seattle, where she was working as a nurse at a tuberculosis sanitarium, and helped me enroll at Oregon State College in Corvallis, Oregon. She also helped me find a home where I could work as a schoolgirl (a student working as a live-in maid to pay her way through college), since I couldn't afford any more than the tuition and books for college. Things went well at Oregon State College in spite of the loneliness which I felt at night. I made friends among other Niseis who were working in homes as I was and we began to meet regularly for support from each other. I was determined to work hard and get good grades in college. Can you imagine my shock when I later sent for my credits to enroll at Texas Wesleyan College? I had forgotten that incompletes automatically turned into "F's." I received my orders for evacuation just at the time we were all preparing for final exams.

I can still see that morning as if it were just yesterday—it was about 8:00 a.m. on Sunday, December 7, 1941. I was living with Mrs. Buxton in Corvallis, Oregon, as a schoolgirl and was a student at Oregon State College. Mrs. Buxton was a rather large woman with silver-gray hair; a staunch, civic-minded "native daughter" who was left a widow with means. She had a large house near the Oregon State College campus and needed someone to help her.

On that particular morning, I made breakfast as usual before going to school and took Mrs. Buxton her breakfast tray in bed, a ritual I repeated daily. But as I entered her bedroom, she wasn't herself; she appeared flushed and irritated and very uneasy. I thought she was ill, but she immediately said in a louder, harsher voice than I was accustomed to, "Mary, listen to this bulletin on the radio!" We both listened in silence as it was repeated over and over again, "Japs bomb Pearl Harbor." I wasn't exactly sure where Pearl Harbor was, but I had heard of it and had a sinking feeling that it was part of the United States.

I stood there and we both looked at each other. I'm sure all sorts of thoughts were going through her head as through mine. The only thought I can recall coming to me immediately was, "I hope they won't ship us all to Japan." Neither one of us said a word for what seemed timeless, continuing to listen to the radio and finding out in the process that Pearl Harbor was in Hawaii. I tried to ease the tension by telling Mrs. Buxton her breakfast was getting cold, and that I had other chores to do before going to the library to study. But then the tears came—the shock, the confusion, the uncertainty were all too much. Mrs. Buxton reached over and hugged me from her bed and said, "I won't let them take you!" We both cried, and I was rather surprised as I had not seen this warm and compassionate side of this woman. I don't know what happened the rest of that day—it's all a blank! I don't even recall going to the campus as I had planned.

There were many Nisei students on the Oregon State College campus and they had a Nisei Student Organization. I was too busy between studies and taking care of duties as a schoolgirl to be involved, but I did enjoy the friendship of the other working girls until Pearl Harbor. Then we all joined the student group and the topic was always Pearl Harbor. It was a wonderful support group to share our feelings and concerns. If anyone received news from home, good or bad, it was shared. I felt at loose ends and couldn't put myself into my studies—constantly wondering what was going to happen next.

As days passed, talk among the friends continued to be about the war and all the speculations as to what was going to happen to us. We tried to think positive to keep our spirits up, and all agreed that because we were native-born citizens of the United States, we were in no danger, in spite of the fact that our parents came from Japan

Mary Yoshida (front row, far right) with her fellow Nisei students at Oregon State College at a party in Corvallis, Oregon, 1942. Seated in the front row, center is Carl Somekawa who subsequently relocated to Minnesota.

and weren't allowed to become citizens. With this faith as our shepherd, we proceeded as best we could with our studies. I continued to serve Mrs. Buxton her breakfast in bed, ever mindful and always with one ear tuned to any radio we could get close to. In those days, radio was our only link to the outside world besides the daily newspaper, but radios were expensive and very few students had them.

Being on a college campus gave us some protection, but still, all Japanese and Japanese Americans were put under a curfew—not to be outside after dark and to always carry our birth certificate with us at all times. I did not have a birth certificate and had to begin the process of locating it by writing to several county court houses as I had never been told, nor had I bothered to find out, exactly where I was born. Until this all happened, there was never a need for a birth certificate. I finally did get my certificate, but discovered in the process that I was born a year later and a few days earlier than I had always assumed.

Many of the Niseis left the college to go home to be with their families as word began arriving that the FBI was taking some Isseis to prison. Those of us who remained bonded together and waited—time was eternity. Rumors were flying and it was difficult to know exactly what was taking place outside the campus. By January of 1942, our worst fears began to turn into a grim reality. The grapevine told us that some Isseis, especially those who had been leaders in our respective communities, were being rounded up and taken to some prison camp in Texas. Soon others, Isseis and Niseis alike, began receiving letters about the impending mass evacuation of all persons of Japanese ancestry into relocation centers for the duration of the war.

Then the inevitable occurred in May 1942. I received my notice to report within 48 hours to a train station in Portland, Oregon, which was approximately 60 miles north of Corvallis. From there we were to be taken to a relocation center called Tule Lake in Northern California. We were instructed to take only what we could carry, but no cameras or firearms as we would be searched thoroughly.

As I recall, we traveled day and night in this noisy, overcrowded coach train. A few college mates from the Portland area were also aboard the train, so I didn't feel totally abandoned. We huddled together and talked all night, all feeling despair, uncertainty, hopelessness, interspersed with periods of depression. However, we made the best of the situation and tried to bolster each other's spirits.

The Tule Lake Relocation Center was the largest of the 10 camps and housed approximately 10,000 internees. I never realized until much later the extent of the planning that must have been going on for some time prior to our internment. How did the U.S. Government sort out the different Asian nationalities? How did they know how many camps they would need? And how did they figure out the whole process of feeding, housing, and transporting the internees? It's rather mind-boggling!

As we arrived the following day, we came to a halt outside the barbed-wire fence. All we could see for miles were rows upon rows of black tarpapered barracks lined up in orderly fashion on the barren desert land which at one time was a lake bottom. I could see from the train the cloud of dust which was to be our daily environment until who knows when! I later found out that all the camps were built identical to ours. At intervals around the barbed-wire fence stood tall guard towers, each manned by military police standing guard with a bayonet. It was a chilling sight but this was our reception!

Mass confusion followed, but as I glanced over the crowd from inside the train and as we were being herded out, I thought I saw some waving arms and smiling faces which looked vaguely familiar; or was my imagination playing tricks to lift my spirits? As the last wave of bodies was finally secured inside the locked gate, it was true, I could see now that those faces were ones belonging to college friends whom we had earlier bid tearful farewells to, thinking they were to be our final farewells. The sight of those faces was like a bright ray of sunlight after weeks of gray dark clouds. Only this time, for some reason, it was different. Those rays penetrated deeper and with such force that I felt a glow inside which was to be instrumental in changing my value system. Later I began to realize that what we left behind wasn't that important or even where we were then. But it was the people, family, friends, and neighbors that life was all about!

Our friends helped usher us through the registration process to get our barrack assignment and meager supplies which consisted of an army cot and one blanket per person. As fate would have it, *obasan* and *ojisan*, whom my sister Mona and I had lived with in Medford, were already at Tule Lake, so it was like a joyful homecoming. Since I had been living with them on the outside, I was assigned to live with them. I was thus fortunate not to have to face the initial shock of entering an empty, dusty barrack which was a depressing sight for most incoming internees.

Obasan had begun the process of trying to make the place as livable as possible. Bed sheets were hung on wires stretched across the room to separate the living from the sleeping quarter. *Ojisan* had scouted the area and picked up empty orange crates and other boxes which had been used to ship fruits and vegetables to the internment camp to feed the personnel and the internees. These boxes were used for tables and chairs. *Obasan* stood an orange crate on its end, draped a cloth over the top, and put a few pictures and other small cherished items on display to give the room a little homey atmosphere.

The camp was divided into a block system—so many barracks to a block—and each block had one mess hall in the middle as well as central laundry and shower facilities and latrines. Persons living in each block were hired for the various tasks that needed to be done to operate the camp—jobs such as cooks, dishwashers, cleaning crews, etc. There were other jobs outside one's own block, e.g., hospital workers, teachers, truck drivers, etc.

All camps had the same universal pay scale which was divided into three categories: (1) $19 per month for professionals, (2) $16 per month for semi-professionals, and (3) $12 per month for laborers. These wages certainly didn't do justice, but served in a small way to support morale. It was enough to sustain us, for there really wasn't anything to spend money on. We did have a canteen but all they sold were candy, gum and small items that one could buy to dress up one's "home." We could buy candy and gum for a penny! If I remember correctly, gum was 5¢ a pack. Of course, I should have had foresight to save every penny I could for the time when I would be out and needed it, but under the circumstances, I guess we couldn't look ahead.

The total camp was operated and governed by the internees— each block elected a representative to handle complaints and to try and make necessary changes for the comfort of the internees. These complaints ranged from "lousy" food to a need for better mattresses. Most of us had to fill our own mattresses with the coarse straw which

Mary Yoshida's brother, George Takao, harvesting beets in Idaho on a furlough from the Tule Lake Relocation Center, 1942.

George Takao, seated, with two other Nisei beet harvesters in Idaho, 1942.

George Takao in front of his living quarters on a beet farm in Idaho, 1942.

was piled high at a central warehouse—again I was reminded of younger days when I had to pitch hay from the fields onto open wagons. A conveyor was used to move the hay into the barn. This was the winter food supply for our cows and horses. Mona and I had fun rolling around and lying on the hay. We also had straw which was much coarser and was used for bedding for the chickens and turkeys. The straw was fun to play in for short periods of time, but to sleep on it night after night brought many complaints especially from the frail elderly persons who were having problems with arthritis and other physical ailments due to advancing age.

As weeks passed, time began to hang heavy—the novelty of the internment experience, coupled with the adjustments which were necessary, occupied our time and thoughts to make the days go by just a little faster. With that subsiding, there was little left to do. Isseis were especially at loose ends since most of them were unaccustomed to being idle.

It must have been January or February of 1943—a time when the winter blues were beginning to hang heavy over all the internees and work began to seem useless under the makeshift living conditions. I felt the hopelessness and despair and needed to try somehow to get out and go on with my life as I had heard others had done. I went to the Administration Building which was located near the main entrance to the camp. This building housed the offices of the Caucasian administrators and was approximately a mile from our barracks. We were almost centrally located, whereas others were many miles away. In fact, the northernmost group of barracks was labeled "Alaska" as they were so isolated.

In the front part of the Administration Building, there was a reception area where notices and messages were posted. I scanned the board faithfully and almost daily, hoping to find something or some place where I could go. Persistence finally paid off as I saw a notice for someone interested in working in a home in St. Paul, Minnesota. I took the ad and wrote to Mrs. Butler. In the meantime, I tried to find out where St. Paul, Minnesota, was, since I had never been outside the State of Oregon, and was curious to know what was on the other side of the Rocky Mountains.

Our correspondence finally led to the day when I could walk out of the barbed-wire gates to a new beginning. Things that followed are rather hazy. I don't recall the process of leaving—the packing, the farewells, etc. But they must have happened as I recently scanned a book entitled *Tule Lake Directory and Camp News*, which was published in 1988 by Harry Inukai from Hood River, Oregon. Harry was the managing editor of the *Tulean Dispatch*, a camp newsletter at the time. This book is a large hardcover book similar to the older high school and college yearbooks. In it, I found news items of my farewell party with the names of all my friends who were present.

I feel sad that I have little recollection of the one year of my incarceration. Although only a few scattered incidents bring back memories, on the whole, the year was lost. I wish I could remember my feelings, for example, when a third-grade boy who developed a crush on me carved a beautiful lapel pin out of pine wood. He took pains to sand and varnish the wood. He did a beautiful job, and all I can recall are his farewell tears as he brought the pin to my barrack before I left. I was assisting the Caucasian teacher who was called out of retirement to teach the third grade. The WRA (War Relocation Authority) made many retired teachers an offer they couldn't refuse, so many came out of retirement to take advantage of the situation. Because this third-grade teacher had been retired for some time, she was having difficulty relating to the students. Not only did her age interfere, but also she was not familiar with Japanese culture where education was primary in our lives. The students were bored with what she was trying to teach. Even though I was only a college freshman, I felt I was able to challenge the students much more. I became frustrated and couldn't wait to get away from the whole situation.

Before my teaching assistant position, I worked at the hospital setting up diet kitchens. I happened to be majoring in Home Economics at Oregon State College—how I picked that major is still a puzzle! I did the best I could with available supplies and guidance from the professionals. All I can say about that experience was that I learned a lot about diabetes and baby formula!

My exit from the Tule Lake Relocation Center in April 1943 should have been an exciting moment, similar to the emotional reaction displayed when the Berlin Wall was removed and East Germans were free to travel to West Berlin in November 1989. However, my mind was a blank. I guess the blanks could be attributed to the fact that for one year I was uprooted and really didn't feel that I belonged anywhere.

My earliest recollection of that time period was my trip after boarding the train en route to St. Paul. It was a comfortable coach and certainly an improvement from the one on which I entered the camp almost one year previous. The scenery looking out from the train window was breathtaking. I couldn't believe what I was seeing—a fairyland with green grass and trees! The farm lands were beautiful! I was so absorbed in the scenery that time flew by. I don't think I ate anything but must have fallen asleep only to be awakened the next morning to find myself in Omaha, Nebraska, where I was to change trains for St. Paul. I felt refreshed and even a sense of relief in spite of the fact that I didn't know what was ahead.

I couldn't get over the size of the station in Omaha; the pillars seemed to reach the sky—I can still remember that sight, I felt so small. I don't recall how long my total trip took, but I finally arrived in St. Paul on April 30, 1943. Mrs. Butler was there with her son, David, who was probably nine or ten years old, and I was glad to have someone there to meet me. Strangely enough, I had no fears or apprehension about coming to a totally strange place with maybe a dime in my pocket—I guess you would call that "blind faith!"

Mrs. Butler drove me to her home on St. Clair Avenue in St. Paul. Again, it was like walking into a storybook castle. The living room alone was larger than any home I had ever lived in during my childhood. It had a winding stairway to the second floor, and my room was on the third floor. It was large and lovely with my very own bed and bathroom! But as I recall, in spite of its loveliness, it was lonely. I settled in to do the best I could under Mrs. Butler's supervision. She was very patient with me as I was not familiar with foods and customs of formal entertaining but was willing to learn. My first embarrassing situation occurred when Mrs. Butler whispered to me that I had forgotten to put on the 'finger bowls.' I had never heard of such and had to confess I didn't know what they were.

David was a big help to me and became a constant companion. He was always alone, and when his mother entertained, he was not included so he spent a good deal of time with me in the kitchen. He even ate with me, which in those circles was a taboo, but it didn't bother David. I never met Mr. Butler in the three years I spent with the family off and on. He was only mentioned in passing, and David would only say that he worked in Washington and didn't get home very much. I grew very fond of David and enjoyed his company. He had a sister going to Smith College.

David was instrumental in introducing tennis into my life for which I am still grateful. He was willing to teach me as he had no tennis companion other than his mother, and she was too busy volunteering for the war effort.

As I got better acquainted with Minnesota, I began working to get Mona out of the Tule Lake Relocation Center to join me. As luck would have it, Mrs. Butler's brother, Mr. Bigelow, wanted Mona in their home. The Bigelow and Butler families were very supportive and wonderful in helping Mona and me make the transition from camp life to a new life in a totally unfamiliar environment.

Toshiko went to the Minidoka Relocation Center near Twin Falls, Idaho, since she was working in Seattle, Washington, at the time of evacuation. She was able to find a nursing job at St. Mary's Hospital in Rochester, Minnesota. With the three of us here in Min-

Mary Yoshida (far right) with her Nisei friends, (left to right) Sachiko Okano, Mary Ann Yoshida, Charles Mizota, and Cosmo Sakamoto, at a Camp Savage open house, 1943.

*Mary Yoshida (front row, center) with the "Maids Day Off" gang
at a Chinese restaurant in Minneapolis, Minnesota, 1944.
Many Nisei women worked as maids to pay their way through college.*

nesota, we were able to get together again after such a long time. We had wonderful get-togethers on weekends when Tosh could come to St. Paul.

As things became routine, I began searching for a college or university where I could pick up where I left off. Due to the quota system imposed by all colleges, the local schools were filled, but I did find an opening for two Niseis at Texas Wesleyan College in Fort Worth, Texas.

The summer of 1943 went quickly and soon I was on my way by bus to Fort Worth, Texas, to attend Texas Wesleyan College (TWC). TWC is a four-year church-affiliated college with a strong emphasis on religion. It was quite a revelation to me, because I had been influenced by Buddhism and Shintoism before the war.

*Mary Yoshida (left) with her sisters, Toshiko (center) and Mona Takao,
in St. Paul, Minnesota, 1943.*

My reception at the college was overwhelming. A counselor
was assigned to Tomi, the other Nisei, and myself prior to our coming on campus. She had arranged for babysitting jobs for both of us
to earn some spending money. She had also arranged for me to be an
assistant to the dormitory "mother" to help pay for my room and
board. I don't recall what assignment Tomi had. To our amazement,
we had both been assigned a senior student to be our "bodyguard,"
which we found a little uncomfortable until we became better acquainted and realized the responsibility the school felt for our safety.
It was a unique experience for the school to accept responsibility for

two minorities, especially Japanese Americans who had recently been interned in an American concentration camp, and whose ancestral country was the enemy with whom we were still at war.

It took me a while to convince my counselor that I could safely go downtown without being escorted. It also took time to ease the tension—no one knew what to expect—they had never been in such a situation before. This tension was quickly revealed when I was to be interviewed by a reporter from the Fort Worth newspaper. I came down to the lobby of Ann Waggoner Hall—the dorm I was assigned to—and as I entered, everyone stood up! I was frightened for a minute, wondering if I shouldn't have granted the interview. I glanced at the "dorm mother" who was also standing. She was old enough to be my grandmother! I was reassured by her smile and we sat down. The reporter was very kind and made it clear from the outset that I didn't have to answer any questions about the internment camp if it was not comfortable for me to do so. I don't remember what he asked me during the interview.

As we adjusted to class routine, the barriers began coming down and Tomi and I were beginning to feel more comfortable on campus. I engrossed myself into campus life, joining many clubs and organizations.

Since our future was still filled with feelings of apprehension and uncertainty, I felt that the church or church-related work might be an accepting field of work. I knew I wanted to work with people, which seemed to be in the genes of our family. Our mother was a nurse, and both Toshiko and Mona are nurses. With the strong influence of religion on the campus, I was led to major in Religious Education. However, I enjoyed my Psychology minor even more, hoping someday to pursue that fascinating field.

The three and a half years I spent at TWC were filled with many new experiences. During that time, I was fortunate to be among the eight students selected by a faculty committee for inclusion in "Who's Who in American Colleges and Universities." I also received the "Golden Shears" pin for the outstanding "student of the week." This pin was a revolving pin, but having worn the pin was the only way one could become a "Guardian of the Golden Shears" which was a prestigious title on campus. These are but a few of the many wonderful memories that I shall cherish.

Mary Yoshida (far left) at the crowning of the Campus Sweetheart at Texas Wesleyan College in Fort Worth, Texas, 1945.

Although I experienced true "Southern hospitality" on the confines of the campus, I also saw firsthand the racial discrimination and segregation in the South which was taken for granted. For the first time, I saw public restrooms with labels, one labeled "whites" and the other "blacks." Thankfully those labels are no longer allowed, but the feelings were still much alive then. I recall an incident where I got on a Fort Worth city bus with some friends from the college. It was my first experience away from the campus. As I entered the bus, I was confused as to where I should sit, for all the blacks were in the rear and the whites were up front. Being an obvious minority, I felt more comfortable sitting with other minorities, so I went to the back and sat down. The driver caught my eye and motioned to me to come up. Once again fear came over me as I walked to the front wondering what I had done or what he was planning to do. He was very kind and just explained that I was sitting in the wrong seats—those were for blacks!

For two summers I went back to Mrs. Butler's in St. Paul, which was like a homecoming. Mona had enrolled in the nursing program at the St. Joseph's Hospital in St. Paul which was affiliated with the College of St. Catherine. She received further training at the Minneapolis General Hospital, Glen Lake Tuberculosis Sanitarium, and Women's Mental Institution in Fergus Falls, Minnesota. Toward the end of my third year in college, I chose to remain at school during that last summer since I found I would have enough credits to graduate by the end of August. It was a hectic time, trying to finish my classes, at the same time trying to prepare for graduation. I wrote to my father about the graduation and I don't recall where he was at that time, but he came! It was a wonderful feeling, a sense of accomplishment on that blistering hot August day in 1946 when I walked across the stage in cap and gown to receive my diploma. It even had a gold star on the outside corner of the cover which meant that I was graduating with honors. At long last, I had my Bachelor of Arts degree which I worked so hard to get! I was just glad to get it all over with and go on with my life. It was a small class, as I recall, so it wasn't hard to spot my father in the audience. I had never seen him so radiant! Life wasn't easy for him, so I was happy that I could make him proud.

Father and I left Fort Worth together by bus and came to Minneapolis, which was just across the river from St. Paul. Father immediately contacted a real estate agent to look at houses. My memory fails me as to where we lived in the interim of house hunting and job hunting. I do recall, however, going with Father and a real estate agent and driving by a small comfortable-looking house in North Minneapolis near Patrick Henry High School. The agent was hesitant to even show us the house, but we insisted and he finally admitted that the family next door made it clear that they didn't want minorities living next door. I became both angry and confused and told the agent, "If they don't want us, we don't want them either!"

We saw several other houses within the price range that my father had in mind. I never gave much thought as to how he planned to pay for a house; I assumed he had plans and I never questioned.

He finally settled for a large two-story older house on the corner of Fifth Avenue and Penn Avenue in North Minneapolis. It was a depressing sight at first—terribly run-down, but as we looked it over, I became excited about the possibilities. It was well built with hardwood throughout the house plus a brick fireplace. I dreamed of sitting in front of a glowing fire in the fireplace! As we waited for the final papers to be drawn up and knew when we could take possession, we went out and made our first purchase, two beds—one double and one single—from the Salvation Army store. We made arrangements for the beds to be delivered as soon as we had the keys to the house. So much was happening that it was hard to separate the different emotions which began to surface. On the one hand, I was excited about having a house which we could call our own, and on the other, I was uncertain about how to go about looking for a job and frustrated that I didn't have money to fix up the house, etc.

I decided I had no choice but to search the newspaper and go out "door knocking" for a job. We had no telephone to make contacts, so I took a chance and felt confident when I saw an advertisement for a Religious Education Director for a large downtown Minneapolis church. I tried to find something appropriate to wear for such a job, but my wardrobe was pretty meager. All I had were "hand-me-downs" collected by my counselor at TWC.

Our house was just two blocks from the Glenwood Avenue streetcar line. I was very self-conscious and shy about venturing out, wishing I had something better to wear. I knew I had to go out and knew, too, that the longer I delayed it, the harder it would get. I took the newspaper and went out the door. I walked the two blocks to the streetcar line and waited and waited. Just as I had given up and started home, I heard the streetcar coming. I couldn't turn back now! I entered and sat down. Now, my thoughts turned to what I would do and say when I got to the church, getting more nervous as the streetcar approached downtown.

I entered the church office and was greeted by the secretary who introduced me to the minister. The minister was very cordial and made me feel at ease. I showed him the newspaper advertisement to explain my presence and to share my recent graduation from Texas Wesleyan College. I also took along my college yearbook called "Txweco" to point out my activities and involvement in college life. He seemed very impressed. He asked how I happened to pick Minneapolis to live, which opened the doors of my concentration camp experience. Somehow this triggered a change and our conversation ended rather abruptly. He said, under the circumstances, he would have to get approval from the congregation and that he would get in touch with me as soon as possible. At the time, I didn't give it much thought as I was pretty naive about applying for a job. But as time went on, I began to realize what was happening, and that this was a pure case of discrimination. My image of the church became tarnished.

I had the mistaken idea that I could begin working as soon as the interview was over and I would go home with a job. I did have a backup advertisement, just in case, and since I was already downtown, I thought I might as well keep going. This was a receptionist's job at the YWCA. It was a clerical position but I didn't mind—it was a job! Armed with the newspaper again, I left the church and found my way to the YWCA on 12th Street and Nicollet Avenue in downtown Minneapolis. Again, I entered hesitatingly, wondering if I was doing the right thing—I knew absolutely nothing about the YWCA! I inquired at the desk and was sent to the third floor Physical Education Department. The director was a stern-looking person, but that all faded when we began talking and I left very much impressed. She said I could start work on the following Monday.

The job hunting ordeal had drained me emotionally; I was glad to be on my way home. I was anxious to tell my father that I had a job, but instead, when I entered our house, all I could do was cry. I threw myself on my bed and cried and cried until I couldn't cry any more. It was a wonderful release for all the pent-up frustrations! Even the empty, dirty house didn't look as impossible as I had thought. While I was job-hunting, Father had found an old discarded table with two chairs, a few pots and pans. He had also picked up a few groceries and was trying to fix a meal for us.

The house remained empty for a long time as there were many priority items that needed immediate attention, such as a new furnace with winter closing in on us. The furnace was an old coal-burning furnace with a coal chute on the outside of the house. On the inside, we had to feed the furnace by shoveling coal on the flames, and gravity carried the heat upward. Coal was becoming a "thing of the past" and Father thought we should convert to oil as soon as we could. We had to replace broken windows, and the outside siding would never pass any kind of inspection, not to mention what an eyesore it was. Slowly repairs were made, and I was able to buy a few pieces of furniture from the Salvation Army to hold us over. That first winter we did have a beautiful fire in the fireplace and enjoyed it sitting on the floor!

My job at the YWCA went well. In fact, Eleanor Kiley, Director of the Physical Education Department, who gave me my first job, had put in a recommendation for me as Assistant Teen-Age Program Director, as that position was soon to open.

There were four or five Assistant Teen-Age Program Directors at the Minneapolis YWCA, each assigned to a different area of the city. The work involved social group work with senior high school girls. I was responsible for organizing "Y-Teen" groups at North and Patrick Henry High Schools, and later at West High School, all in the Minneapolis School District. I spent the summers at Lyman Lodge, a YWCA camp on Lake Minnetonka, as a Camp Counselor. My work at the YWCA opened many doors of opportunity for learning and serving. I'm sure I was learning more than serving and wished at times that I could turn back the clock and be able to talk to some of those troubled girls who had big problems.

Times were different, but those teen years were just as difficult then as they are today. Many a night I would get a late night call from a sobbing teenager who had just broken up with her boyfriend and didn't know what to do or where to turn. Most just needed a shoulder to cry on, but there was always one or two who needed more than a shoulder. The job carried with it a great deal of responsibility—I'm not sure if I could handle it in our present society! For example, I took a busload of Y-Teens to a Y-Teen Conference at Moorhead, Minnesota. The week-long conference was held on the Moorhead State College campus and we were housed in the dormitory. On the second night of the conference, I made the rounds for bed check and found one of my students had stuffed her bed to make it appear as if she were sleeping. Fortunately, I had heard by the grapevine that this girl had met a guy when a few of the girls went into town the day before, and that she was planning to sneak out. I waited for her to return through the ground floor window and we talked. She begged and pleaded for another chance as she was "learning so much from the conference," but rules were rules. I felt terrible having to call her parents to come and get her.

For a long time, that decision which I had to make bothered me as I wondered if I was too harsh and should have given her another chance. That burden of guilt was finally lifted when that same girl sought me out years later and said she appreciated what I had done—she claimed that was a turning point for her. I thanked her for putting my anguish to rest.

Father Daisuke Kitagawa, an Episcopal minister, was assigned to assist with the resettlement of Issei and Nisei in Minnesota. I had known Father Dai (a name we all knew him by) from my Tule Lake days and felt fortunate to be able to assist him in organizing groups. He had already organized several groups before I arrived in Minnesota. One of those groups was forming a Christian church for Issei and other Japanese-speaking people under the auspices of the Episcopal Church. He was also instrumental in organizing the "Married Couples Club," with the thought of bringing together people of all nationalities and backgrounds to mingle socially to get to know people as people. This group emerged from the larger body of the Episcopal Church to try to assist those coming out of the internment camps in resettling and adjusting to life on the outside.

Mary Yoshida and Father Daisuke Kitagawa at the Cass Lake Interracial Camp in northern Minnesota, 1949.

Out of this "Married Couples Club" emerged the present "Rainbow Club." With the new name, the group was able to reach out, encompass and put into practice other goals originally established. One of those goals was to have children of different backgrounds play together socially, in the hope that they would grow up realizing that people are people regardless of race, creed, color, etc. In May of 1991, we celebrated the 90th birthday of a charter member, Robert "Bob" Mitchell, who has been the backbone of the "Rainbow Club" since its inception as the "Married Couples Club." He is still very much a part of the club as he steers the club back to its original goals. The name, "Rainbow Club," was submitted by Harold Wilson, a charter member, who has since passed away, but the name and the club go on.

A "Fellowship" group was organized at the YWCA for Nisei to create a gathering place. This group became a focal point for many activities and was valuable in facilitating a transition from camp life to new life in a strange place. This group was a very loosely knit group open to anyone who wanted to join, whether out of curiosity

Father Daisuke Kitagawa with charter member Robert Mitchell (far right) at the 20th anniversary of the Rainbow Club in Minneapolis, Minnesota, 1965.

or for any other reason. All were welcome. We planned social activities, e.g., dances, picnics and whatever else the group felt the need for.

The "Fellowship" group became involved in the U.S.O. for entertaining the G.I.'s from Camp Savage and Fort Snelling. Members of this group also made up the nucleus for the J.U.G.'s (Just Us Girls) softball team with the Minneapolis Park System. We were coached by Frank Ishikawa and Frank Tanaka, and went on to win the City Championship in 1947. Phyllis (Matsushita) Takekawa was our pitcher and I played second base. We had a great time practicing and playing together, finally reaching a point where most of us could say our "roots" were taking hold in Minnesota.

The "Fellowship" group became a place where we could meet members of the opposite sex and romances began to blossom. It was

Mary Yoshida (second row, center) with other members of the J.U.G.s (Just Us Girls) softball team in Minneapolis, Minnesota, 1947. Coached by Frank Ishikawa (back row, right) and Frank Tanaka, the team won the City Championship in 1947.

through this group that I, too, met my husband. Minoru Yoshida was enrolled in the Military Intelligence Service Language School at Fort Snelling after being drafted from Dakota Wesleyan University in Mitchell, South Dakota. Min's younger brother, Mako, was a "regular" at the "Fellowship" group meetings and brought Min to the meetings after he was discharged from the service in 1946. Mako had resettled with a job in Minneapolis and brought his parents to join him from the Topaz Relocation Center. Min had an older brother, Masao, who went back to Japan after the internment, as well as an older sister, Kuwa, who passed away in California in 1981. He also has a younger sister, Etsu Date, living in Alameda, California.

In the meantime, during the 1947-48 period, my father worked at a Chinese restaurant in downtown Minneapolis, with plans, then unknown to me, to return to his "homeland." He felt the responsibility of seeing that his children were taken care of. Since we bought the house and Mona and I were able to make the payments, he must have felt his mission was accomplished. George was working in

Mary Yoshida's father, Kakuji Takao, with his second wife, Toshie, in the yard of their house in Takamatsu City, Kagawa Prefecture, Japan, 1950.

Chicago, Illinois, but joined us when we bought the house. It was in the fall of 1948, if my memory serves me, that my father left for "home." It was both a sad and a happy time for all of us. I guess we all silently felt that we would never see him again.

I was happy for my father to be able to live out his dream of seeing his own brothers and sisters while they were still around. He had an older brother, two younger sisters and a younger brother. Fortunately, they were all still living and were able to see my father again. We were also very happy to hear later that my father had remarried and built a comfortable home. He passed away on May 21, 1972, at the age of 81.

On Easter Sunday of 1950, Min and I announced our engagement to be married on August 5th. It was a busy summer following our engagement. I sold our house on Penn Avenue and moved with two co-workers into an apartment near the YWCA. I spent most of the summer at Lyman Lodge as Acting Camp Director. I was frantically pushing for a new Camp Director, which they promised to hire in time for me to plan for our wedding. Although weddings then were on a much smaller scale than they are now, we still had to do all the work and time was running out! As the song goes, "we made it to the church on time!"

We were married at Calvary Methodist Church in North Minneapolis by Father Daisuke Kitagawa. We borrowed Mako's car for our honeymoon and drove to Milwaukee to see Min's sister, Etsu Date, and her family. We then took the ferry, the *Milwaukee Clipper*, across Lake Michigan to Niagara Falls in New York.

After our trip, we settled into a small rear three-room converted apartment with a shared bath. It wasn't much, but I guess we were living on dreams. Our bedroom was a converted, windowless storage room with space for only a double bed which we had to crawl over to get in and out.

Mary and Min Yoshida were married on August 5, 1950, at Calvary Methodist Church in Minneapolis, Minnesota.

I continued to work at the YWCA for two more years. Min worked for the City of Minneapolis doing accounting work. He first worked at the "old" Auditorium and later transferred to the Minneapolis Park Board Finance Department until his retirement in 1983. We both took the bus to work for the first year and had saved enough to buy our first car. We were so proud. We bought a basic black Chevrolet sedan with no frills, but it was ours and it was new! As I didn't know how to drive, I continued to depend on Min. But our weekend shopping trips became less hectic. It was a relief not to have to juggle bags of groceries on the bus.

As time went on, we began to think and plan for more permanent living quarters and felt we could squeeze out a down payment on a house. By then, I was expecting our first child and that small bedroom just wouldn't do!

I received an unexpected send-off from the YWCA when I announced my resignation. It was a combination of baby shower and farewell. It was an emotional event for me, as so many former Y-Teens had come back to wish me well. The staff had become a family, which made leaving that much more difficult.

It was the summer of 1952 when we began in earnest to look for a house. Debra Jean was born in September and we moved into our present house on Halloween night. I remember it well, since we were totally unprepared for the onslaught of over 100 children coming for "trick or treat!" We plunged in with the excitement of turning an empty house into a home. My working at Henry High School gave me a feeling for the neighborhood. Our house was in the last block before the city limits. Beyond the city limits were corn fields as far as we could see. We had to live within the city limits at that time, if we worked for the city. That ruling has since been changed. Being a small town country girl, the corn fields were a wonderful sight to see.

Distance posed a problem, and I decided it was time that I learned to drive so as not to feel so isolated. A friend was willing to teach me, so with Debbie in the car seat, we went out. Hindsight makes me shudder as to what could have happened to our two-year old daughter! One incident occurred during that adventure, when my girlfriend yelled "STOP!" as I was turning into our alley which makes a sharp turn. I stopped just inches from the telephone pole! Needless to say, she was relieved when I finally finished and passed the exam on the first try.

Living became routine. Min's parents moved back to California to get away from Minnesota's winters. Our roots were solidly planted in Minnesota. Our time and efforts were centered around the family, school, and community activities in which our children were involved.

Min Yoshida's parents, Yutaro and Tome Yoshida, at the Japanese American Community Center in Minneapolis, Minnesota, 1954.

Debbie went on to graduate from Brainerd Community College in Brainerd, Minnesota, where she met and married Fred Schwanke from Pilager, Minnesota. They have three children, Kyle, Patrick, and Holly. Our second daughter, Marlys Marie, was born in 1955. She graduated from Anoka Ramsey Community College in Anoka, Minnesota. She married Stephen Walters, whom she knew from high school days. They have a son, Matthew, and a daughter, Jenna. Our son, Mark Minoru, was born in 1962. He graduated from Minneapolis Technical Institute's Aviation Mechanics Program. He married his high school classmate, Joan Arborgast. They have a daughter, Jennifer, and a son, Ryan. Our three children, respectively, live in Coon Rapids, Maple Grove, and Brooklyn Park, Minnesota.

As the children were growing, we felt an obligation to expose them to their "roots." We had an active Japanese American community and a Japanese American Community Center. Debbie, Marlys and I participated in the annual *Bon Odori* festival dances at Minnehaha Park in Minneapolis for several years. As was to be expected, neighborhood friends and school activities eventually took over with little time left for our daughters to participate in the activities of the Japanese American community. This was also the case for many of the Nisei, and eventually integration took place to the extent that the need for the Japanese American Community Center no longer existed.

As the children became less and less dependent, I began to feel the need to move on. About that same time, the Principal of Olson Junior High School, Roger Olson, called to inquire if I would be interested in a part-time job as a "home visitor." He was looking for someone to check on and work with students who were chronically tardy or absent from school. I took on the challenge and quickly received a jolt into reality. The deplorable conditions that existed in some homes were the reasons why they couldn't make it to school.

Mary and Min Yoshida with their children and their families in Minneapolis, Minnesota, circa 1975. Front row, left to right: Min, grandson Kyle Schwanke, Mary, and son Mark. Back row, left to right: Fred and Debbie Schwanke and Marlys and Stephen Walters.

It was quite an education for me, but a sad one, as I felt the hopelessness and helplessness that existed.

From this "home visitor" job, I moved on to a newly created part-time position as a health service assistant. This was a Civil Service position also created by Roger Olson to take care of the daily health care needs of students while at school. I enjoyed the student contact and hopefully touched a few students who were in dire need of a "mother figure," even for a short period of time each day. A few students routinely came in for their morning hugs before going on to their classroom.

I made several moves within the Minneapolis School System, but remained in their employ until my retirement in 1988 after 20 years of service.

Reflections

As I reflect back over the last 50 years since my internment, I feel that the struggles we endured made me stronger and certainly more compassionate toward others in their struggles. Hindsight is important, but living in the past can't change what has been done. It has made me very much aware that learning is never ending. Somehow, *obasan* instilled in Mona and me a burning desire to learn. We both have been able to fulfill one phase of that desire in tribute to her.

I have been able to pick up that yen for learning again after my retirement and have attended three Elderhostels and hope for many more. The Elderhostels are a very affordable way to keep on learning. Depending on the program selection, one can be stimulated physically, mentally, and emotionally. There is something for everyone. There is something about a college campus that thrills me, and most Elderhostels are held on college campuses.

Recently, I went on a pilgrimage to the Tule Lake campsite, hoping it would jog my memory to fill in some of the gaps that I hadn't been able to fill. It was hard to imagine that during World

War II we had been confined behind barbed wire in that desolate place! The barracks were all torn down, as were the guard towers and the fence, except for the bits and pieces that connected to the gate through which we entered. I was glad to know that I wasn't imagining that the railroad tracks were just outside the gate—those tracks are still there! The framework of the stockade was partially destroyed, but the potbellied stove and the bolts holding bunk beds were mangled but very visible.

When I was inside that barbed-wire fence, I used to think that I would someday like to climb on top of Castle Rock and sit with my legs hanging over the side and view all the barracks down below. Castle Rock is still there as well as Abalone Hill—two of our well known landmarks. The name "Abalone Hill" comes from the fact that the hill looks like an abalone shell. I took the tour to Castle Rock hoping to make that climb, but I only went up to the base of the rock. Since the rock was slippery and went straight up, I gave up the attempt. After all, that was 50 years ago! I was close enough that I could see the cross that had been put up there and it was still standing.

I have always thought positive about things working out, and coming to Minnesota was no exception. I have always tried hard to earn the respect of the people with whom I have come in contact. I have also tried hard to help our children understand that their actions would never be theirs alone. Our minority features make it impossible for us to act on our own—we are always viewed as members of a certain minority. This is hard to understand and even harder to take as you grow up in a society which is in a measure controlled by peer pressure.

Minnesotans have accepted us for what we are and not for what we represent. We were welcomed and made to feel that we belonged. This was important in those early days, as many of us had bad experiences which put us on guard. Most of those barriers are gone, and I would like to think that the benefits derived from our settling here in Minnesota have been mutual.

My recent pilgrimage to California made me appreciate Minnesota even more. I was saddened to discover that many Nisei were still somewhat bitter over their internment experiences. After the war, many Japanese Americans returned to the West Coast where they had lived before, and were naturally drawn together again. In Minnesota, on the other hand, we are so dispersed. Our contacts with other Nisei are few and far between. I think the advantages outweigh the disadvantages as we have been able to put the past behind and move on.

After 50 years, we can close one chapter of history, since we have received a formal letter of apology from President George Bush on behalf of the United States, as well as a token restitution for each survivor of the American concentration camps. Our continued vigilance must be maintained, however, until that chapter of American history is written and taught in all schools across the country.

You grandchildren, who are Yonsei (fourth-generation Japanese Americans), will pioneer for us a new generation of integration. My sincere hope is that the best of all cultures will shine forth, but not at the expense of losing our "roots."

Hopefully, some future generation will reap the benefits of a peaceful, integrated world and may even see that "pot o' gold" at the end of the "rainbow!"

HARUKO KURAMOTO HASHIMOTO

Linda van Dooijeweert

Haruko Kuramoto was born on January 2, 1922, in Sacramento, California, a daughter of Sukeichi and Nobu Kuramoto. Since Haruko passed away on November 12, 1980, this essay was written in her memory by her eldest daughter, Linda van Dooijeweert.

Sukeichi Kuramoto, Haruko's father, left Yamaguchi Prefecture in 1889 for Seattle, Washington, at the ripe age of 16 years. He found living quarters with a Caucasian family of the same Christian faith. Since it was time for Sukeichi to seek a wife, his family in Japan sent him Nobu Kuhara's picture. She was the daughter of one of the families in the neighborhood. He in turn sent his picture to his family to present to Nobu. She agreed to marry Sukeichi and left Japan for San Francisco's Angel Island around 1910 to meet her future husband for the first time.

Sukeichi and Nobu Kuramoto settled in as farmers at the Bailey ranch in Walnut Grove, California. He soon became the foreman of their vegetable farm and pear orchard. Around the year 1921, the Kuramotos moved from Walnut Grove to nearby Locke, California. The Locke rooming house became their home until the onset of World War II. There they raised five children, three girls and two boys. The eldest is Matsue (Tao) born in Walnut Grove, followed by Kikue (Okamoto) born in Sacramento and Eimi Kuramoto born in

Japan. Haruko (Hashimoto) and the youngest child, Setsuo Kuramoto, were both born in Sacramento.

Haruko Hashimoto with her mother, Nobu Kuramoto,
in Locke, California, circa 1928.

Sukeichi and Nobu, along with their two eldest daughters, took a trip to Japan in 1918, and it was on this trip that Eimi was born. Many years after World War II, Eimi Kuramoto resided in Richfield, Minnesota. He is still remembered by many Niseis in the Japanese American community here. He now lives in Kensington, California, near Berkeley.

Haruko attended the Walnut Grove Oriental School through the eighth grade. The entire student body was comprised of Chinese, Japanese and Filipinos. The Caucasian children attended their own elementary school located one mile away. They were bused daily to their school, but the students of the Oriental School had to walk to class. As the Walnut Grove Asian population grew, the Oriental

School near Chinatown became a firetrap, and a new school was built in 1937.

Walnut Grove had a Chinatown and Japantown, as well as a white section of town. The Chinese and Japanese lived on the east side of Walnut Grove, while the Caucasians lived on the west side of the Sacramento River.

Courtland, California, a nearby city of Walnut Grove, also had segregated grammar schools for whites and Asians. The students remained segregated until reaching high school age, and then they were permitted to attend the same school. And that was only because the city could not afford two separate high schools.

Haruko and her brothers, Eimi and Setsuo, also attended Japanese language school to learn to speak and write their parents' mother tongue. The school offered one-hour classes after grammar school. Dr. Terami was the instructor who later moved to Minnesota with his wife and taught Mathematics at Macalester College. Haruko went on to Courtland High School and graduated in 1941.

Walnut Grove is known as a farming community near the Sacramento River. It was the heart of the asparagus growing district, and Bartlett pears were the principal product of the region. Haruko's mother and eldest sister, Matsue, worked in a nearby packing house in Locke during the harvest seasons for pears, apricots, cherries and plums.

The Kuramoto family attended the Walnut Grove Japanese United Methodist Church which was founded in 1915 by Isseis. Other future Minnesotans that belonged to the church then were Dr. Terami, Louise Taketa (Nomura) and Jim Murakami. Jim's mother and Haruko's mother were good friends and belonged to the church's *fujinkai* (women's association). They were all members of the church until the evacuation of May 1942. Just recently, the church closed due to the dwindling *Nikkei* (Japanese American) population in this farming community.

Haruko Hashimoto (second row, third from left) with her brother, Eimi (second row, second from right), and other members of the Walnut Grove Epworth League in Walnut Grove, California, 1938.

Haruko was evacuated from her home in May 1942 along with her mother, brothers and sisters. Her father had died in June 1936 before the outbreak of the war. The Kuramoto family was detained in a temporary evacuation camp called Turlock Assembly Center in Turlock, California. It was located on the fairgrounds where evacuees lived for over a month in small barracks of black tar paper. In July 1942, the Kuramoto family and other Japanese detainees were transported aboard trains with covered windows to the Gila River Relocation Center in Arizona. The military police were everywhere. The evacuees could not go anywhere; they became prisoners in boxcars. Their freedom was taken away from them.

Life in the relocation camp was a major hardship for all families. The weather was inclement and the living conditions were extremely uncomfortable. The air in Arizona was hot and dry and the camp quarters were small and overcrowded. The Kuramoto family lived in 77D barrack. Meals were prepared by Japanese cooks and

The Gila River Relocation Center in Arizona where Haruko Hashimoto and her family were interned during World War II, circa 1942.

served in the mess hall. Haruko worked as a waitress on the crew of Mess Hall No. 9, earning $16 a month. Army cots and blankets were provided by the government in the rudimentary sleeping quarters. Communal bathrooms with showers and laundry rooms were also shared. No sporting activities outdoors were allowed. Women embroidered, knitted, crocheted and conversed with each other to pass the time. Haruko attended a sewing school where the government paid the teacher $17 a month. Nobu and Haruko also taught others how to make chrysanthemum flowers with paper. The Kuramotos were members of the Christian church in camp.

After the war, the Kuramoto family went their separate ways. Matsue (Tao) and Kikue (Okamoto) returned to Walnut Grove, California. Eimi, the eldest son, left for Kansas City, while Haruko, Setsuo, and their mother Nobu, decided to make Minnesota their home. Other Niseis and Isseis who ventured to Minneapolis and St. Paul from Walnut Grove were Dr. Terami and his wife, Jim Murakami, Louise Taketa (Nomura) and her father. Louise Taketa was a close friend and classmate of Haruko's. They attended Walnut Grove Oriental School together and graduated from Courtland High School in 1941.

Haruko Hashimoto and other members of the Kuramoto family belonged to the Canal Christian Church at the Gila River Relocation Center in Arizona, 1943.

226

Haruko Hashimoto (far left) with her mother, Nobu Kuramoto (front, second from left), and Dr. and Mrs. Terami (far right and second from right), at Minnehaha Park in Minneapolis, Minnesota, circa 1952.

Haruko Hashimoto with her mother, Nobu Kuramoto, and brother Setsuo, in St. Paul, Minnesota, circa 1948.

The three members of the Kuramoto family left for Minnesota on April 24, 1944, and took up residence at 1605 Third Avenue, Minneapolis by December of 1944. They gave up their West Coast home, family and friends and started anew in Minnesota. Here they felt that there was an atmosphere of friendliness, and that perhaps they would encounter less discrimination and prejudice. Setsuo attended and graduated from North High School in Minneapolis. Since Haruko had attended sewing school full-time after her high school classes in Walnut Grove, she possessed sufficient pattern/dressmaking and tailoring skills to get a job around 1945 at Winget-Kickernick's in downtown Minneapolis. Her mother, Nobu, also worked at Kickernick's which was a manufacturer of rayon-nylon undergarments.

Haruko married Tsuyoshi Hashimoto on August 22, 1948. Tsuyoshi was the third of six sons of Nami Hashimoto in Watsonville, California. During World War II, he was interned at the Poston Relocation Center in Arizona and later drafted to attend the Military Intelligence Service Language School at Fort Snelling in Minnesota. After the war, he worked for the Seeger Co. which later became the Whirlpool Corp. Haruko and Tsuyoshi were married at St. Mark's Cathedral in Minneapolis by the Rev. Daisuke Kitagawa. Frank Yanari was the best man; he had initially introduced them to each other. The usher was George Ono, and Dr. Terami (Walnut Grove) gave Haruko away at the wedding.

Haruko spent her time volunteering for the Japanese American community. She assisted with the Nisei Girls Club events, such as the Girls Day Tea and Dinner on September 25, 1946, and the *Hina-Matsuri* Tea on March 2, 1947, for the purpose of raising money for the Reconstruction Finance Fund of the YWCA. She donned a *kimono* for the unveiling of the statue of Leif Erickson at the State Capitol. Haruko participated in the Festival of Nations sponsored by the International Institute. She helped organize booth exhibits and *odori* (Japanese dancing), represented Japan in the procession, and assisted with the Japanese food booth.

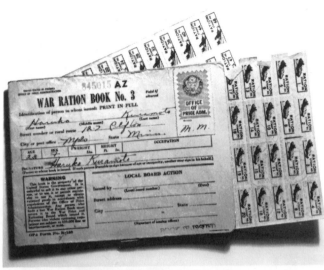

War ration book No. 3 issued to
Haruko Kuramoto (Hashimoto), 1945.

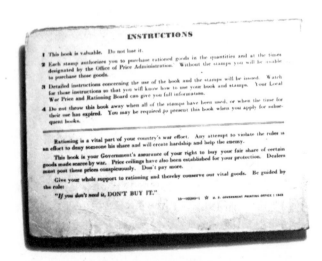

Instructions on the back of war ration book No. 3 issued to
Haruko Kuramoto (Hashimoto), 1945.

*Haruko and Tsuyoshi Hashimoto were married
in Minneapolis, Minnesota, on August 22, 1948.*

Haruko worked as a clerk at the St. Paul YWCA located at
123 West 5th Street in downtown St. Paul. As the original YWCA
building was sold to St. Paul Fire and Marine Insurance Company,
the YWCA moved to a new site on Kellogg Blvd. She started working there around 1946. The YWCA site is now occupied by the Sat-
urn School which President George Bush visited in 1991.

In the postwar period, Haruko served as a staff person and
volunteered her time for the St. Paul Resettlement Committee. This
group was comprised of volunteers from the YWCA, YMCA, interfaith church groups, and the International Institute of Minnesota. They
assisted with the operation of the second hostel which opened on
Kellogg Boulevard in St. Paul. Since the Minneapolis hostel could
not keep up with the demand of resettlers needing assistance, another hostel was needed. Warren Burger was the first chairman of
the St. Paul Resettlement Committee, who later became the Chief

Haruko Hashimoto (second from right) at a Nisei Girls get-together dinner in Minneapolis, Minnesota, 1946. Seated from left to right are Mae Nakayama, Julia Sakai, Thelma Kawakami, Minnie Matsuura, Haruko, and Miss Marshall.

Haruko Hashimoto assisted with the Girls Day Tea sponsored by the Nisei Girls Club at the Minneapolis YWCA in Minnesota, 1948.

Haruko Hashimoto helped set up and staff the Japanese exhibit booth at the Festival of Nations in St. Paul, Minnesota, circa 1949.

Justice of the U.S. Supreme Court. Mrs. Hiroko Ogata was hired by the committee to meet the new Japanese American relocatees, assist with lodging at the hotel, and cook meals. The Resettlement Committee also tried to teach the new arrivals what it was like to live here in Minnesota.

Haruko volunteered to solicit blankets for the hostel. She and Ruth Tanbara, who was on the YWCA staff and a close friend of hers, would prepare Japanese dishes for the newly arriving Japanese Americans. Ruth and Haruko served Warren Burger his first taste of a Japanese dinner. Haruko also would assist at Nisei get-togethers and provide any stenographic services needed.

Ruth and Haruko would greet new Nisei girls who arrived at the YWCA to stay. The maximum the girls could stay there was two weeks. Many of them came to Minnesota because their Nisei boy-

Haruko Hashimoto (back row, second from right)
worked as a clerk at the St. Paul YWCA in Minnesota, 1949.
Ruth Tanbara (third row, far right) was also on the YWCA staff.

friends were stationed at Fort Snelling. Ruth and Haruko would introduce the Nisei girls around and try to secure for them employment mainly in domestic service.

Haruko took time off from her job at the YWCA when I was born in 1951. She would often times bring me to the YWCA to see her co-workers, since there were not many young mothers working at the Y. I was delivered by Dr. Hodgson who was the original author of the abortion law.

Bruce, the youngest and only boy in our family, was born in 1954. He attended the University of Minnesota and currently works in the audio-visual department of a Roseville junior high school. He often coaches tennis or hockey and remains a bachelor. Bruce resides at our parents' home at 878 Fremont Avenue on the east side of St. Paul.

Haruko Hashimoto worked as a volunteer for the St. Paul Resettlement Committee which operated this hostel on Kellogg Boulevard in St. Paul, Minnesota, to provide temporary housing for Japanese American relocatees from the internment camps, circa 1945.

My younger sister, Barbara, is now married to Bob Selstedt and has one daughter, Miyuki. She attended St. Mary's College and presently works at Medtronic. Her husband, Bob, works at the Star Tribune, and they live in Woodbury.

I, Linda, am the eldest of the Hashimoto family. I attended the University of Minnesota, St. Paul campus, majoring in Fashion Design and Illustration. I worked at Dayton's Department Store through college and later married Willy van Dooijeweert who was a former luggage buyer for Dayton's. Willy is from the Netherlands. We reside in Arden Hills, a suburb of St. Paul. We have a chain of five local stores called URBAN Traveler for which we do extensive traveling to markets to keep up with the trends. In his spare time, Willy is a national soccer referee.

I am a fanatic volunteer. I am on the Friends of the St. Paul Chamber Orchestra Board working as vice-president for ways and means. I have been on the board for over ten years, mainly develop-

Haruko Hashimoto (back row, second from left) holding her daughter, Barbara, with her husband, Tsuyoshi (front row, far left), holding his son, Bruce, and sitting with his daughter, Linda, at the 80th birthday of Mr. Y. Taketa (front row, third from right) held at the University YMCA in Minneapolis, Minnesota, 1955.

ing and selling products with the chamber orchestra logo on it. I have volunteered for several years for the Robbinsdale Whiz Bang Days as a junior royalty judge. I interview five- and six-year-old girls and boys, two of whom will later represent the City of Robbinsdale and go on to compete for the Minneapolis Aquatennial commodore and princess titles. I also serve on the Board of the St. Paul-Nagasaki Sister City Committee, and am active in the Japan America Society's 5:01 Club and the Japanese American Citizens League. I coordinate adult and children dance groups for the Festival of Nations, and teach new dances to be performed each year. I have been doing this for the Festival of Nations for about 20 years.

I also spend a day or two each January at the Los Angeles Gift Show, working on orders of Japanese gifts for the bazaar/gift booth at the Festival of Nations. The proceeds from the booth go to the Japanese American Citizens League. The volunteer group of dancers qualifies the bazaar and Japan food booth to participate in the Festival of Nations each year. The proceeds of the food booth go to the St. Paul-Nagasaki Sister City Committee.

I serve on the Board of the Nikkei Project which provides outing and activities for our elderly Issei. The Multiple Sclerosis Society is another group that I try to donate some of my time to, since my mother, Haruko, died of MS in 1980. I'm also the resource person for the St. Paul and Minneapolis Public Schools. I have done many classes and assemblies on Japanese culture and dance for pupils of all ages.

Haruko Hashimoto with her children, Linda (left), Bruce, and Barbara, at the Festival of Nations in St. Paul, Minnesota, 1958.

Acknowledgments

I wish to thank Matsue Tao, Ruth Tanbara and Jim Murakami for assisting me with this anthology project. It was extremely difficult for me to piece together the facts, since my mother and father passed away in 1980 and 1990, respectively. Furthermore, as a third-generation Japanese American, I had no direct knowledge of what my parents experienced before and during World War II. However, my mother's thorough record-keeping of scrapbooks and photo albums provided me with additional inspiration. This project gave me the gift of knowing more about my heritage and the hardships that the Nisei, the second-generation of Japanese Americans, had to endure.

TOSHIKO
BABA
YONEJI

ecause of the great flu epidemic in 1918, I was destined to be born in the port city of Seattle, Washington. My father and mother, Goroku and Mika Baba, had landed in Seattle on October 10, 1918. They were planning to go to Wyoming where he was to join his brother and nephew to work in the coal mines. However, my father came down with the flu and was unable to travel. Consequently, all plans to move inland were canceled and they made Seattle their home.

My parents were born in Okayama, Japan: my father on July 4, 1884, and my mother on May 2, 1885. They were married there on November 22, 1905. My parents had started their married life in a small house on the family farm. Their first son, Seiji, was born on February 14, 1907. Shortly thereafter, my father left for the United States, leaving his wife and newborn baby behind.

After my father left, my mother continued living in the house. She helped with the family business which, along with growing rice, was weaving mats (*goza*). In 1973 when I visited Okayama, Japan, the old homestead where my parents had first lived was still on the property. It was being used as a warehouse.

My father arrived in Seattle on March 26, 1907. He got a job as a cook on the railroad in Nampa, Idaho, and worked for ten years.

In 1917, he went back to Japan and brought his wife to the United States. However, my parents left their son with their relatives.

I was born in Seattle on February 23, 1921. It was less than three years after the Armistice was signed ending World War I. Woodrow Wilson was the President of the United States, and a one-pound loaf of bread cost ten cents. If it hadn't been for the flu epidemic and if my father had started working in the coal mines, I might have been born in Wyoming. I might also have lost my father when I was a baby. My cousin, Kataichi Baba, was killed in a mine disaster in Frontier, Wyoming, on August 14, 1923. Ninety-nine men were killed in that accident. My cousin was 30 years old at the time. My father, having stayed in Seattle, got a job as a short-order cook in a small coffee shop.

My brother, Seiji, came to the United States in July 1921. My parents had sent for him when it became evident that Congress

Toshiko Yoneji's parents, Goroku and Mika Baba,
in Seattle, Washington, 1918.

Toshiko Yoneji's father, Goroku Baba (center, with a hat on), working as a cook at Coffee Cup Restaurant in Seattle, Washington, circa 1919.

Toshiko Yoneji (left) with her sister, Margaret, in Seattle, Washington, 1924.

would prohibit Japanese immigration to this country in the near future. The Japanese Exclusion Act of 1924 was indeed passed, and this restriction continued for 28 years. My sister, Margaret, was born on August 7, 1923, and our family was complete.

My father worked as a cook for most of his lifetime, whereas my mother worked at a variety of jobs. At first, she was a chambermaid in a Japanese hotel in downtown Seattle. My sister and I were sent to a Japanese Baptist Church day care center at that time. During some summers, my mother went to neighboring farms in Auburn and Kent to pick berries. She took my sister and me along. The children played in the fields and babies slept in their buggies while the mothers worked. I remember one day at the lunch table. My mother had finished eating and started to go out to the fields taking my baby sister along. I got up to go, too, and was severely reprimanded by the farmer for not finishing my lunch. I cried so hard that my mother had to come and get me. I was probably four years old at the time.

Later my mother worked at a Japanese language newspaper, the *Great Northern Daily News*, as a *kanagaeshi* to return Linotype Japanese characters to their original boxes.

There was a Japanese lady in our neighborhood who was the backbone of the Japanese community, and upon whom we depended for many things. She was Mrs. Ichiyo Uyeno, a midwife who delivered both my sister and me in our home. She was also the *"baishakunin"* who arranged my brother's marriage. When I was five years old, she was the one that took me to the doctor's office (not to a hospital) to have my tonsils removed. It was a one-day, in-and-out surgery. I remember the doctor giving me ether as an anesthetic before the surgery and then Mrs. Uyeno taking me home. She gave me 50 cents for being a good girl and I felt so rich.

Until I was nine years old, we lived at 1026 Washington Street in the heart of the red-light district. We were too young to know what the ladies in the neighborhood houses did. We just knew that they sat by their windows and beckoned the men in by tapping on the window. Therefore, we used to call them "window tappers." I asked my mother what they did and she just said the men were invited in for a drink. Here are words to a song we children used to sing, without an inkling as to what it was about:

Oh, I wish I were a fascinating lady
My past would be dark and my future would be shady
I'd live in a house with a little red light
I'd sleep all day and I'd work all night
And once a month I'd take a short vacation
And drive all my customers wild
Oh, I wish I were a fascinating lady
Instead of a legitimate child.

The Baba family in Seattle, Washington, circa 1926.
From left to right, Toshiko, Goroku, Mika, Seiji and Margaret.

While I lived in this house, I attended Pacific School. One of my most vivid memories of that period pertains to what happened one winter. There was a lot of snow on the ground in the morning, and my mother carried me piggyback all the way to school. I was five years old then.

We moved to 1510 Yesler Way in 1930 and this was where we lived until evacuation. It was a predominantly Jewish neighborhood. My classmates at Washington School, which I now attended, were mostly Jewish. We liked to go to school on Jewish holidays because only a few students in our class attended school. The Jewish students went to synagogue and we had a holiday in school. Speaking of holidays, it is interesting to me that during my years in elementary school, all of us learned Christmas carols every year in spite of the fact that most of the students were Jewish. Such is not the case today. Many public schools do not permit the singing of Christmas carols.

Toshiko Yoneji (second from right) at a piano recital in Seattle, Washington, 1931.

242

There were two synagogues in our neighborhood. A rabbi lived next-door. On holidays he butchered chickens for his congregation to make it kosher. Whenever we heard chickens clucking in the back yard, we went out to watch. The rabbi would tie the chicken's legs and hang it upside down from the branch of a cherry tree. He would slit its throat and immediately pull off all its feathers. We were told that feathers were easy to pull while the fowl was warm. The feathers fell into a galvanized wash tub he had under the chicken.

During the formative years of my life, Japanese was the language spoken at home and among my friends. When I first started Washington School, I spoke to an Asian girl in Japanese thinking she was Japanese. She gave me a blank look. It turned out she was Chinese. We became very good friends.

Japanese Language School was an integral part of my life during these years. Everyday after public school we attended Japanese School from 4:00 to 5:00 p.m. Occasionally we would play hooky especially during the football season. Garfield High School often had a championship team, and one day after school we went to a football game instead of to Japanese School. We sat in the rain all during the game. When I came home, I discovered the green color in my coat had run on to my white blouse, completely ruining it. I decided that was punishment for skipping Japanese School.

Speaking of rain, it is true that Seattle does have a lot of rain in the winter. But even more than the rain, I remember the fog. We would wake up in the morning to the sound of fog horns coming from Puget Sound. It would be zero visibility outside and extremely humid. By the time we walked all the way to school, our hair, which we had carefully curled, was limp and damp. In spite of this, I still feel nostalgic and think of my growing-up days when I hear fog horns.

Another thing that kept me busy while I was growing up was a weekly piano lesson. I took lessons for six years, but I never became very good at piano playing because I didn't like to practice. Nevertheless, I was asked to play the organ at church occasionally to accompany the congregation singing hymns. My sister told me that she was too embarrassed to come to church when I was scheduled to play the organ because I made too many mistakes.

As for recreational activities, my parents took us fishing or clam digging to the area beaches. We went on the streetcar because we did not own a car. My father also enjoyed playing *shogi*, the Japanese version of chess, and would stop every evening after work to play *shogi* with some friends. Occasionally this was a sore point with my mother who felt that her husband should come straight home from work, instead of stopping to play *shogi*.

During summer vacations, we would go on the cable car that ran in front of our house to Lake Washington for swimming. I remember the fare was three cents. But before we were old enough to go to Lake Washington by cable car, it was at Collins Playfield where

Toshiko Yoneji (front row, fifth from right) at the commencement with her teachers and fellow graduates at the Japanese Language School in Seattle, Washington, March 31, 1940. This school had over 1,500 students in 1937.

I first learned how to swim underwater and float. Collins Playfield was just a block from our house and we would walk there and use the shallow (and probably very dirty) wading pool. Collins Playfield was also where a giant bonfire was built every spring. The children in the neighborhood would bring potatoes from home to roast in the fire. Usually the potatoes were burned to a crisp, but it was an exciting event nonetheless. Roller skating was another pastime much enjoyed. Our skates were the metal ones that were clamped on to our shoes. Many a Saturday we skated along 15th Avenue all the way to Volunteer Park. There we would wander through the cemetery looking for the headstone of a 16-year-old Nisei girl who had been murdered by a spurned lover.

An annual event was our Japanese School picnic at Jefferson Park. One summer, when I was 13 years old, I got up early Sunday morning, the day of the picnic, to make *maki zushi* for our picnic lunch. My mother and sister were in Japan that summer, so I had to make the lunch for my father and myself. In my family, *maki zushi* is made by first laying out a sheet of *nori* (dried seaweed) and then sprinkling vinegar on it. This I proceeded to do by first dipping my hands in a bowl of vinegar. As I did so, I screamed with pain. I had forgotten that the previous day I had done our family laundry. This was done in a galvanized wash tub with a wash board. My knuckles had been scrubbed raw in the process of scrubbing the week's wash of sheets, towels, underwear, etc. The vinegar was worse than salt in my wounds. I managed to finish making the *maki zushi*, but to this day I still remember the vinegar on my raw knuckles.

When I was attending the University of Washington, I was elected into Sigma Epsilon Sigma, a business honor society for women. On the day I received my pin, my boyfriend was waiting for me in front of our house when I came home from school. He immediately took the pin, saying he was going to keep it. I said absolutely not and chased him all around the block but was not able to retrieve the pin. I never saw the pin again. It was a beautiful pin incrusted with tiny pearls embossed with the Greek letters "SES" on it. I wanted to at least take it into the house to show my parents because I knew they would be so proud. But no such luck. Later that year I did have something to show my parents. At an awards banquet for business students, I was honored with a silver trophy with my name added to the names already engraved on the trophy. I knew the trophy was on permanent display at school and not for me to keep. However, I wanted to show this to my parents, so I took the trophy home with me after the banquet. Of course, my parents were proud as I knew they would be. I took the trophy back to the office the next morning and found everybody in an uproar wondering who had stolen the silver trophy. I told them the reason I took it home and was not punished. When I graduated from the college, I was elected into Phi Kappa Phi. I was able to keep the pin I received from this honor society.

News of Pearl Harbor hit us when we came out of church that Sunday, December 7, 1941. Although my parents belonged to the Nichiren Buddhist Church, I had been attending the Shinshu Buddhist Church. This church was close to my home and had many activities for young people. I was a member of the Camp Fire Girls group sponsored by the church. This group consisted of Japanese American girls. However, we participated in the city-wide activities of the Camp Fire Girls.

*Toshiko Yoneji (center, seated) with Camp Fire Girls
in Seattle, Washington, 1936.*

When the war came, I was a junior at the University of Washington. December 8, Monday, was a tense day for us at school. At our first class in the morning, we all listened to the radio as President Franklin Roosevelt solemnly asked Congress to declare war against Japan, because of the "Day of Infamy" at Pearl Harbor the day before.

At the University of Washington, I was active in the *Fuyokai*, a Japanese American women's organization. The Japanese American men also had their organization called the Japanese Students Club (JSC). The JSC always sponsored a homecoming dance in October. In December, the *Fuyokai* sponsored a dance and usually asked the homecoming date to this dance.

After the 1941 homecoming dance in October, I was dreading the day when I would have to ask my date to the *Fuyokai* dance. What a relief it was when the war came and the dance was canceled.

Dating was a new experience for me and I was naive and unsure of myself. In those days, I did not believe in interracial dating. There was a Caucasian young man who was a teaching assistant in my Economics class. He asked me many times for a date and I always refused. He even came several times to the Guggenheim Engineering Library where I worked part-time to ask me for a date. How my attitudes and opinions have changed over the years! Today, all three of our children are married to Caucasians and I heartily approve of it.

Because of the war, the *Fuyokai* was disbanded and all the money in our treasury was donated to the Society of Friends (Quakers). It is interesting to note that the final records of the Treasurer of the *Fuyokai* can be found at the University of Washington archives. In 1988, almost 50 years after my *Fuyokai* days, a reunion of the group was held in Seattle. Almost 100 women attended and it was a memorable occasion.

When the war broke out, confusion and uncertainty reigned. Fifty-one Japanese nationals were arrested by the FBI in Seattle the day after Pearl Harbor. By December 10, over 100 Japanese had been arrested. Most of these men were ordinary people but leaders in the community. In Seattle, there was a blackout from 11:00 p.m. to a half hour after dawn the following day. After March 27, 1942, there was a curfew after 8:00 p.m. for all Japanese.

My parents systematically destroyed all Japanese-language magazines, books, and records. My father's guns and cameras were confiscated. When evacuation orders were posted, my parents stored a few personal things in a nearby church. All the rest of the household goods, my parents' lifelong accumulation of furniture, books, dishes, etc., were carted away by a used furniture dealer who paid us next to nothing. I remember specifically getting $5 for a beautiful Victrola phonograph and $25 for our piano.

We were saddened to have to leave a cherry tree that my father had planted and nurtured over the years. It had blossomed for the first time in the spring of 1942, but, of course, we were evacuated before we could harvest any fruits.

The Buddhist Church that I had been attending was closed by government authorities, and our minister, the Rev. Ichikawa, was arrested by the FBI. There was much anti-Japanese sentiment at this time. Even a Christian minister was prone to exhibiting racial hostility toward Japanese Americans. In *America's Concentration Camps*, Allan R. Bosworth wrote about such a misguided clergyman:

> The executive director of the Pacific Coast Japanese Problem League, Dr. John Carruthers, was a graduate of Princeton and a Presbyterian minister. Before the California State Senate on October 19, 1943, he said: "It is our Christian duty to keep the Japanese out of this western world of Christian civilization." As the result of prayer, he said, he would urge "the deportation, if possible, by every means possible, of all the Japanese from the American continent."

Since I am now a Presbyterian, it hurts me to think that a Presbyterian minister would make such remarks.

Evacuation orders were posted in April of 1942. During the first week of May, I went to Washington Hall to help register the people who were to be evacuated. On May 14, 1942, a caravan of ten buses with a police escort left Seattle and arrived at Puyallup Assembly Center about 10:00 a.m. In normal times, Puyallup was the site of the annual King County Fair in the State of Washington. My brother and his family were left behind in Seattle because their two-year-old daughter, Jo Anne, had chicken pox. They had to arrange their own transportation to the Assembly Center. My brother, his wife, and two daughters finally arrived on May 22.

When we arrived at Puyallup Assembly Center, we were assigned a family number and handed mattress bags which we then filled with straw. We were sent to Area D which had the grandstand and animal stalls. I remember noticing that the people already there in Area D looked like caged animals in a zoo. The curfew started at 9:00 p.m., lights went out at 10:00 p.m., and reveille was at 6:00 a.m. We had to go to Area B for showers because there were none in Area D.

While I was at Puyallup, I volunteered to teach school in the morning and worked at night in the administration offices doing clerical work. The schools were makeshift facilities with volunteers staffing the classrooms. I taught a class of 15 third-graders, all girls, I noticed. I don't know where the boys were. School, of course, was not compulsory and I suppose the boys were not interested.

I had visitors just once while I was at the Assembly Center. They were four teaching assistants and friends from the School of Business at the University of Washington. We were able to visit at the high wire fence, I on the inside like a prisoner and they on the outside. I think they came strictly out of curiosity since they did not bring me any of my belongings, nor did they have any business to transact.

On August 18, 1942, we boarded a train for the Minidoka Relocation Center in Hunt, Idaho. There were M.P.'s all over, the train was filthy, and all the window shades were drawn. When we got to Idaho, there was dust everywhere. It got into our eyes, hair, noses, and clothes. It seeped into the barracks through the cracks in the walls. Sometimes I even missed all the rain we had in Puyallup despite the leaky roof we had. Mosquitoes were bad. I once measured a bite which had swollen to three and a half inches in diameter.

The barracks in Minidoka were 120 feet long and 20 feet wide. They were divided into six units. The two end units measuring 16' x 20' were for families of two or three people. The next two units were 24' x 20' for families of five to seven members. The two center units were 20' x 20' for four people.

The only bathroom facilities we had were outhouses. Here, too, dust came through the cracks in the summer and snow in the winter. A laundry room, showers, and toilets were being built, and on January 31, 1943, the ladies' flush toilets were ready for use finally. However, there were no individual stalls for privacy.

At Minidoka, I got a job as clerk accountant in the War Relocation Authority office. I started out getting $16 a month and got a raise to $19 a month in March of 1943.

In January, 1943, I also volunteered to teach a beginning bookkeeping class for adults once a week in the evening. Forty-seven people showed up for the first class, so we divided the class in two and got another teacher.

My sister, Margaret, was in her senior year at high school at the time of evacuation. For her graduation, a number of Garfield High School teachers came to Puyallup Assembly Center from Seattle on June 6, 1942, with their diplomas and *Arrows*, the school yearbook. In June of 1943, Margaret left Minidoka Relocation Center to attend the Seton School of Nursing in Colorado Springs, Colorado. As for me, I left the camp for a temporary job in Ann Arbor,

Michigan. I worked as a clerk in the records department of the University of Michigan Hospital.

I had heard previously from the Student Relocation Council that I had been accepted as a student at the University of New Hampshire in Durham, New Hampshire. I learned later that I had been admitted there with some reluctance. The Student Christian Movement (SCM) on campus had heard that Japanese Americans detained in the internment camps were looking for schools to continue their education. SCM contacted the university administration. They were told that a Japanese American would be a security risk, because there was an ASTP (Army Specialized Training Program) unit on campus. After some discussion, the administration relented and agreed to accept two Japanese American women, but not any Japanese American men. Nisei men were still considered security risks.

On October 4, 1943, I boarded a train at Ann Arbor headed for Durham, New Hampshire. As the train approached Detroit, the conductor came to me and said I would have to get off, because the train was going through Canada (Windsor, Ontario) and Japanese Americans were not permitted in Canada. I was petrified. What was I going to do all alone in a strange city? Fortunately, a kind Caucasian lady, who sat beside me, said she would vouch for me, so I was able to stay on.

My year at the University of New Hampshire was uneventful except for one small incident. One day a Caucasian student named Mike called and asked for a blind date for the following Saturday night. I was still a little reluctant about interracial dating. However, being the only Japanese American on campus, I decided to accept since obviously there were no Japanese American men to date. I was excited when Saturday came and was ready and waiting for him. About the time Mike was to pick me up, I was called to the phone. A voice said it was Mike calling to say he couldn't go on the date because he had broken a leg. I momentarily felt sorry for this poor guy until it dawned on me that the whole thing was a big hoax. As it turned out, I never met Mike.

My part-time job on campus was in the library. At Christmas, the head librarian, Thelma Brackett, gave a pencil to each student working at the library. My pencil turned out to be special. Knowing that I was short of funds, Thelma had carefully washed and ironed a 5-dollar bill and wrapped it around the pencil just for me. Her kindness brought tears to my eyes.

It was in New Hampshire that I had my first experience with snow skis. When visiting at the home of Jan Winn, she found some old wooden skis in the barn and let me use them. She also let me use an old sled which had belonged to her mother years ago. Warm clothes were also borrowed. It was also in New Hampshire where I learned to climb up high on a birch tree and swing to the ground hanging on to one of its branches. Bungee jumping, it was not, but to me, it was a big thrill.

Toshiko Yoneji skiing and sledding with her friend, Jan Winn,
while visiting her in New Hampshire, 1943.

After I got my degree in Accounting in August 1944, I moved to New York City. There I got a job in the accounting office of Russian War Relief, an agency shipping relief supplies to Russia, a U.S. ally at the time.

This was during World War II, and New York City was the port of embarkation for servicemen from all over the country going overseas. Every Saturday night, there was a dance at the Japanese Buddhist Church where we met many Nisei servicemen. We also went to dances sponsored by the USO (United Service Organizations) and JACD (Japanese American Citizens for Democracy). In November of 1944, we went to a JACD dance given for "Boys from Snelling." My roommate and I invited several of these boys over for Thanksgiving dinner consisting of a roast leg of lamb among other things. Whatever possessed us to have lamb for Nisei boys, I'll never know. I have never again had lamb for Thanksgiving.

One of the boys who came to dinner that Thanksgiving was in the Army Signal Corps Military Intelligence at Fort Monmouth, New Jersey. In March of 1945, he came into town with a fellow from his outfit named Mits Yoneji. After a whirlwind courtship, Mits and I were married on May 5, 1945, at the Japanese Methodist Church in Manhattan. When I wrote to my parents about my marriage, my mother was pleased to find out that Mits was born in the year of the monkey. She had a lot of faith in the Japanese zodiac. Since my father was born in the year of the monkey and both my mother and I were born in the year of the rooster, she said we would have a good marriage because theirs had been successful for over 50 years.

For our honeymoon, we went to Niagara Falls and to Minneapolis. Minneapolis was included in our itinerary because Mits' older brother, Takeo, was stationed at Fort Snelling. This was my chance to meet him and to prove to him that I was not some loose woman that Mits had picked up off the streets of New York City.

In Minneapolis, we were staying at the Dyckman Hotel. On May 8, 1945, sirens woke us up about 8 a.m. proclaiming the end of the European War. It was V-E Day! Everybody was celebrating. There was a ticker tape parade on Park Avenue. Stores and restaurants were closed. We were able to get breakfast at the hotel, but nothing was open by supper time. After wandering around, Mits finally came back to the hotel with a dish of spaghetti for us to eat.

Toshiko and Mits Yoneji were married in New York City, 1945.

In June of 1945, Mits and his outfit were shipped overseas to Okinawa and Korea. World War II came to an end on August 15, 1945. It was V-J Day and we went down to Times Square to see the mob celebrating. Times Square which had been dark during the war was ablaze with lights. The next day I went to work and found nobody there. Everybody was still celebrating, so a friend and I went row-boating in Central Park.

Mits returned home to New York City in February of 1946. He immediately joined the "52/20 Club." This was a U.S. government program granting all returning servicemen $20 a week for 52 weeks.

His next goal in life was to finish his college education. While he applied to various schools around the country, he worked as a lapidary in Harlem and we continued living in Manhattan. Our apartment building was on the corner of 112th Street and Broadway. Our living space was extremely cramped. It consisted of one small room just big enough for a bed, a dresser and a chair. We shared kitchen facilities and a bathroom with three other tenant families.

Life was pleasant, however. For a nickel we could ride the subway to the amusement park at Coney Island for a roller coaster ride. We went for long walks along Broadway, through Central Park and Riverside Drive to Grant's Tomb and Riverside Church. In the summer we went to Rockaway Beach and Jones Beach. On Easter of 1946, I put on my Easter bonnet and we joined the famous Easter parade along Fifth Avenue. We then went to the Easter Show at Radio City Music Hall, home of the Rockettes. There were also many Broadway shows we could attend.

In the fall of 1946, we moved to Des Moines, Iowa, where Mits was accepted as a Pharmacy student at Drake University. I got a job at the Iowa Farm Bureau Federation. In 1948, Mits and I went to Kauai, Hawaii, to spend the summer with Mits' parents. While there, I got a job as a secretary to the manager of Kauai Inn. At lunch time on my first day of work, I was directed to the kitchen to eat. There I found other Japanese American employees eating lunch. Afterwards, I found out that the secretary I had replaced had always been served lunch in the dining room. She was Caucasian. At that point, I probably should have been assertive and complained to the management. I didn't, however, and continued to eat lunch in the kitchen all during my days of employment there.

Veterans' housing for Drake students was at Fort Des Moines. These were apartments converted from barracks used by the WAAC (Women's Army Auxiliary Corps) during the war. We were in a two-bedroom apartment until September of 1949. By then there were so many veterans requesting housing that our two-bedroom apartment was designated for families with two or more children. Having no children, we had no choice but to move to much smaller quarters. I was pregnant at this time, and on May 31, 1950, our twin daughters, Sheryl and Carol, were born. Mits immediately applied for a two-bedroom apartment and moved into it before I left the hospital. We thought it was quite an achievement to have two children right away so that we could go back to a larger apartment.

One of the things I remember about the apartment at Fort Des Moines was the ice box. We had to remember to empty the pan under the ice box before it started to overflow. Many a time, our neighbors downstairs would come knocking on the door asking us to empty the pan because the water was seeping through their ceiling.

A memorable event while we lived at Fort Des Moines was the 1948 presidential election, Thomas Dewey versus Harry Truman. Mits and some friends sat by the radio all night listening to the election results. All the polls had said that Thomas Dewey would be elected president. Newspapers were already on the streets that night proclaiming that Dewey had been elected. It was not until the next morning that the final results were in, and surprise, surprise, Harry Truman was our new President.

Our third child, Jerry, arrived on February 27, 1953. By this time, Mits had graduated from Drake and was working as a pharmacist, and we had moved from Fort Des Moines into a small house in Des Moines.

After living in Des Moines for a few years, we decided that Des Moines was not where we wanted to raise our children. Mits had been stationed at Fort Snelling and had been favorably impressed with Minnesota. The people were friendly. A wonderful farm family in Wisconsin had also befriended him. Contrast this to what happened to me when I lived in New York City. I was on the subway coming home from work when I suddenly felt faint and didn't think I could make it any further. I got off at the next station and lay down on the floor right there, being too sick to move. All kinds of people came by me, stepped over me and walked around me, but not one person stopped to help me or ask what was the matter. After about ten minutes, I felt a little better, got back on the subway and went home. Compared to this impersonal city, Minnesota was paradise. So we moved lock, stock and barrel from Des Moines to Bloomington in October of 1954.

From 1963 to 1973, Mits operated Oxboro Pharmacy in Bloomington. Two hold-ups marred our years there. The first was on October 2, 1968, when two men with nylon stockings over their heads came in with their guns drawn. At first I thought it was a Halloween prank, but I immediately knew better when we were ordered to lie down on the floor. One of the gunmen struck Mits in the forehead with a gun butt and forced him to open his safe and give them money and drugs. When the gunmen left, I got up off the floor to see Mits with his face covered with blood. Six stitches were required to close the gash in his forehead. The other hold-up occurred on January 3, 1972. Cash and drugs were taken but no one was hurt.

The Yoneji family in Bloomington, Minnesota, 1989.
From left to right, Sheryl , Mits, Jerry, Toshiko, and Carol.

Our three children grew up in Bloomington where the population was 10,000 in 1954 and is now over 80,000. Sheryl graduated from the University of Colorado cum laude and is now working at Martin Marietta in Denver after attaining her Master's degree in Computer Science. She is married to David Davidson and they have two children: Jennifer, born on October 12, 1978, and James, born on the Fourth of July in 1980. Carol graduated from Denver University, Phi Beta Kappa and is working at the Federal District Court in Denver. She is married to Don Henderson and they have one daughter, Kimberly, born on April 7, 1978. Jerry went to Bemidji State University in Minnesota and graduated from the University of Minnesota Dental School. He is now practicing dentistry in Great Falls, Montana. He is married to Jennifer Compson and they have two children: Heather, born on March 21, 1980, and Julie, born on November 5, 1981.

Toshiko and Mits Yoneji (center, seated) with their children and their families in Bloomington, Minnesota, Christmas, 1989.

There were two unpleasant episodes in my son Jerry's life in Minnesota. Jerry was about ten years old when the first episode occurred. We had just arrived home from Wisconsin when the phone rang. It was a neighbor woman who ranted that a Jap boy had been harassing her all day by ringing the door bell and running away. She said she was sure it was our son. We, of course, knew for sure it was not our son because we had been gone all day. Nevertheless, it was a very upsetting incident.

The other episode occurred when he was a teenager. He was walking out of Hoigaard's Ski Shop with his own skis which he had just had repaired. He was apprehended for shoplifting but was released immediately because he had the receipt in his pocket. It is my feeling that he was picked up because he is a minority.

A memorable event in Carol and Sheryl's lives was their participation in the St. Paul Civic Opera's production of "The King and I" in 1959. They played the twin daughters of the King of Siam.

Toshiko Yoneji's twin daughters, Carol and Sheryl, played the twin daughters of the King of Siam in the St. Paul Civic Opera's production of "The King and I" in St. Paul, Minnesota, 1959.

While the children were growing up, I was a leader of a Camp Fire Girls group, worked with PTA, and was a volunteer for the school lunch program. In 1957 and 1959, I was the chairperson of the Easter Seal Drive for Bloomington.

Chairwoman Toshiko Yoneji planning the Easter Seal Drive for the City of Bloomington, Minnesota, 1957.

After the children left home, I worked in the Finance Department at Bloomington City Hall. In 1978, I passed the Certified Public Accountant's test and became a CPA. This had been my dream since college graduation.

My years working for the City of Bloomington were enjoyable and uneventful except for one incident. One day while I was walking home from City Hall after work, a car came charging out of Harrison Park and blocked the sidewalk in front of me. Out stepped a tall man who approached me. I was scared to death. He turned out to be a co-worker who had recently been fired. He had learned that I walked that route home everyday and was watching for me in the parking lot. For some reason he thought I was responsible for his being fired and demanded to know what was going on. I managed to convince him that I had nothing to do with his dismissal, so he let me go. It was a most traumatic encounter, nonetheless. A short time later I developed a painful case of shingles. This is an inflammatory skin disease often caused by stress. I am sure that this incident triggered my shingles. How well I remember the day I woke up with the first symptoms of shingles! Of course, I didn't know what the problem was until my doctor diagnosed it later, but I knew something was wrong. It was on a Monday morning, August 3, 1981. Ronald Reagan was the President and the air traffic controllers had just gone on strike. Isn't it funny the sort of things one remembers in our lives? Shingles is something that stays with a person for a long time. When Mits and I started round dance lessons in September, I was still experiencing a pain from the shingles.

Reflections

After World War II, my parents relocated to Vancouver, Washington, and later to Seattle. My father died in 1963 at the age of 79, and my mother passed away in 1968 when she was 83 years old.

World War II did bring many painful experiences such as having to leave our home in Seattle and go to an internment camp. In June of 1945, I also lost my maternal grandmother, Riki Yamagawa, and my cousin, Akiko, because of this war. Their home in Okayama City, Japan, was bombed with American incendiary bombs and totally demolished, killing my grandmother instantly. Akiko died a short time later.

Overall, however, life has been good to us. We are now both retired. We continue to live in Minnesota because we like it here. There is no Japanese community as such in Minnesota. The Japanese culture is more diluted here. We do not get many Japanese movies, plays or performers. However, these things are not necessary ingredients in our lives. I keep busy with many activities. I volunteer as treasurer of the Oak Grove Presbyterian Church which has 1,400 members, Mits and I being the only Japanese Americans in the congregation. I also volunteer as treasurer for the Bloomington Nursery School, and I am recording secretary for my PEO chapter.

PEO is a philanthropic educational organization of women all over the world. The sisterhood supports and maintains Cottey College in Nevada, Missouri. Our leisure activities include playing bridge, square dancing, and travel.

Toshiko and Mits Yoneji at a square dance convention in Seattle, Washington, 1981.

Most of the time our being Japanese American makes no difference in our daily living. Only occasionally does someone come up to me and ask what country I came from and where I learned to speak English. Just recently, someone asked me, "Do you get back to the old country very often?"

The people have been friendly here as we knew they would be. Variety is the spice of life. The weather in Minnesota certainly adds spice to our lives. There's skiing in winter, canoeing and fishing in the summer. In the fall there are beautiful colors that we can view as we take long walks along the many park trails. In the spring there are wild flowers that come up in the woods everywhere.

Minnesota is our home and we feel fortunate.

TAI
SHIGAKI

W hat an irony it is that it takes a couple of generations before curiosity about one's heritage surfaces! Even at the
age of 70, I do not ever remember being particularly curious about my ancestry. In 1990-91, one of my grandnieces went to
Japan to teach English and was assigned to the prefecture from which
both my mother and father immigrated in the first decade of the twentieth century. It was through her that I was able to get a translation of
the family genealogy. I dwell a little more in detail on this, because
it reflects a great deal of culture and the practices of rural Japan of
that period.

According to the records, the Shigakis have owned land in
the Town of Kosa, Kamimashi County in the Prefecture of Kumamoto,
for at least 200 years, which is the extent of the documentation.

The keeping of the family registry of the common people
was apparently started in the nineteenth century. Some of the dates
are questionable, because it was only through oral tradition that this
data was available. Compulsory education did not go into effect
until the nineteenth century, and so the commoners were illiterate
and did not know how to write. Information preserved in these early
years was passed down by word-of-mouth only. Dates of birth and
death are not recorded but are presumed when a son takes over the
farm.

In the family of my father there were eight sons, my father being the youngest. Two male names disappeared from the registry when they took on their wives' surnames. This was not an uncommon practice in families with many sons who married into families with daughters but no male heirs. The family record follows only the male line, so there is nothing known about the female members.

Tai Shigaki's parents, Zempei and Toku Shigaki, with their eldest daughter, Chiye, in Huntington Beach, California, circa 1918.

My mother was a Yoshimura and came from the Town of Mifune which is in the same county and prefecture as my father. She was the first of ten children. Her family was in the merchant class and lived in town. Like many Japanese women in the early 1900's, she came to the United States as a picture bride. She joined her husband as a farmer's wife, and I was born in 1921 on a farm in Huntington Beach, California. Shortly after my birth, the family moved to Los Angeles and then to Venice where my father died in 1927.

Tai Shigaki's mother, Toku Shigaki, in Los Angeles, circa 1923.

I was the youngest of four children; I had two sisters and one brother. My oldest sister died before I was five years old. Since I was so young and she was sickly and confined much of her life, my memory of her is very vague. My remembrance of my father is only what people have told me rather than any personal memory.

I enjoyed a carefree, happy childhood with just the four of us—my sister Toshi, my brother Yoshio, and my mother. My mother was always available because she was a dressmaker and did her sewing at home. In 1928, we moved to Gardena where my mother was employed as a seamstress in a department store owned and operated by a Japanese family. We moved into a neighborhood where I had many Japanese playmates nearby for the first time.

This happy existence lasted for a few years until my mother remarried and we moved to an all-white neighborhood a few miles away. Our harmonious family of four was intruded upon by this strange man. But it wasn't too bad because he was a deep sea fisherman who went out to sea for weeks on end. When he was home my

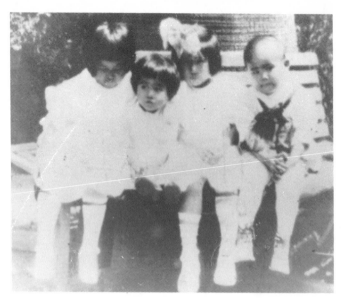

*Tai Shigaki flanked by her sisters, Toshi (left) and Chiye (right),
and brother, Yoshio, in Los Angeles, circa 1923.*

*Tai Shigaki with her brother, Yoshio, and sister, Toshi (left),
in Los Angeles, circa 1924.*

mother catered to his desires, which meant eating an unfamiliar Japanese diet. We were used to an Americanized Japanese menu and a much more relaxed environment. This dual cultural existence lasted until the United States Immigration Service removed our stepfather for a brief period for illegal fishing in foreign waters and reentry into the United States. By this time, my mother had developed a dressmaking business of her own where she taught sewing to young Japanese women. She produced dresses for farmers' wives which my father sold. He would be on the road weeks at a time making the rounds of the farms all over Southern California to take orders and make deliveries.

Tai Shigaki (left) with her new playmates in Gardena, California, 1929.

In 1937, my sister got married and established her own household. My brother went to a trade school to learn the dry cleaning business. And I commuted to Los Angeles City College.

The event of greatest significance in my life took place in my junior year in high school. It was my conversion to the Christian faith and the commitment I had made to full-time Christian service.

I had been attending the Baptist Church since moving to Gardena at age seven, but it was ten years later that public acknowledgment was made of my intent and dedication to go into professional church work.

So, on December 7, 1941, I was on my way to a Baptist Church in Los Angeles to attend the regional World-Wide Guild Girls rally. I had heard the news of the invasion of Pearl Harbor but didn't sense the impact of its significance at that time. I was surrounded by caring people who did not display any animosity, so I was protected from the general public reaction. For me, it was the end of the semester, and term papers and final exams were looming ahead. Getting through them was more consuming than what was going on in Hawaii, Europe or Asia.

It was my fortune that I had a number of very loving mentors at this stage in my life. Gale Seaman was the Baptist Student Worker at Los Angeles City College where I was active in his programs. And Amy Acock, a retired missionary from Japan, was my Bible teacher from the Gardena Japanese Baptist Church where I had been attending since a child. Both, on their own, realized the necessity for me to get out of the Pacific coastal area. They used their influence to get me transferred to the University of Redlands in January 1942. At this time, it was thought that inland California was safe. So, I went to Redlands, rather oblivious of all the rumors of evacuation that were flying around. I was just thinking about how to get through my school work, while being preoccupied at being a co-ed living on campus for the first time.

Then letters started coming from home that my parents were moving to Salt Lake City. My brother had gotten married so as not to be separated from his girlfriend. My only regret was that it was not possible for me to attend his wedding due to travel restrictions. Then, the most disturbing word came that both my sister and brother were to go to the Santa Anita Assembly Center. I still lived in an unreal world, oblivious that I would also be affected. There were several other Japanese students at Redlands, who were all from Hawaii except three of us. Since the Japanese Americans on the islands were not evacuated, they assumed they were safe. In May, however, the university administration advised us to get ready to leave the campus and to report early in the morning with our belongings at the local railroad station.

On May 23, 1942, seven of us boarded a train not knowing where we were going. Two of us who had parents living in inland states were assured that we would be reunited with our families soon. However, we were told that we would have to go to the relocation center first while arrangements were made. So our expectation was that our stay in camp would be very brief. When we arrived in Poston Camp I in Arizona, there was no Camp II or III. There was barely a Camp I, because we were the early internees, and the men were used to build the barracks. The two of us who expected a brief stay decided we didn't want to be housed in the women's dormitory next to the unruly bachelors' quarters. We negotiated to be housed with a family of four from Redlands. Their daughter was a graduate of the University of Redlands, so we had much in common. It enabled them to choose the two additional people that otherwise might have been assigned to them randomly. At this early stage, six people were placed in a unit.

The brief sojourn in camp took four months, and during that time I was busy helping my former pastors, also internees, organize church activities. My job assignment was to publish the church newsletter. Being young, naive, and perhaps a bit dramatic, I thought of this period in my life as a testing period akin to the Jewish people wandering in the wilderness with Moses as described in the Bible. The Arizona desert felt like a good fit with the Sinai desert. Despite the heat, dust storms, lack of privacy, unfamiliar diet and people, and separation from my family, this time in camp was not that traumatic for me. Each day I had the hope that my leave clearance would come through, and that my incarceration would not last too long.

In the meantime, my two mentors were busy making contacts with the American Baptist Home Missions Society trying to get me transferred to one of the Baptist colleges in the East. Since the student worker was a graduate of Denison University in Ohio, he succeeded in arranging for me to transfer there. In September 1942, my leave clearance papers finally arrived and I was released. Since, however, it was too late for me to make the fall semester, I went to Salt Lake City to be with my parents until the spring semester. As my mother was able to transport a portion of her inventory and her sewing machine, she could carry on a small business there. My step-father, in the meantime, took up gardening and they were able to maintain themselves in a small apartment. Our family was fortunate in that our home in Gardena was rented out and the Caucasian pastor of the Baptist church was the overseer. My parents always knew they were going back and expected to pick up their lives as before the war.

En route to Granville, Ohio, I decided to visit my brother and sister, who by this time had been transferred to the camp in Rohwer, Arkansas. I took a Greyhound bus from Utah to Arkansas by way of Kansas and Missouri. The problem I had on that trip was more a nuisance than anything very serious. There were a lot of military personnel on the bus, and these men were inclined to have wandering hands or would try to borrow my shoulder as a head rest. However, one night the bus suddenly stopped in the middle of nowhere, lights flashed on, awakening all of the passengers. Two or three military police marched down the aisle and we all wondered what was going on. They came and stood over me and demanded to see my identification. It wasn't until after the incident that fear crept into my whole being. What would I have done if they had removed me in these Kansas wheatfields, in the dark hours of the night. Whatever they wanted, I must have satisfied them with all the documents I had been carrying. On any of the international trips I have taken, even to communist countries, this type of experience was never repeated.

My life at Denison University was a dreamlike, storybook life. Granville is a small college town in rural Ohio. I had the great fortune of spending my first semester in the home of the dean and his wife, Cyril and Alice Richards. Margie, their daughter who was also a student at DU, thought of me as her college roommate, sharing all our secrets, hopes, and aspirations. Being so close to campus, there was no need for her to live in a dorm, which she regretted and having a roommate meant a lot to both of us. The Richards were some of the most influential people in my life. Their home was like a novel about America's heartland in a college setting. They took me in as a daughter, including me in all their activities and their affection. My attitudes toward social justice and political concerns were developed and nurtured during this time. My narrow theological beliefs were broadened to integrate new learnings that I was acquiring in college. I began to develop my own philosophy of life. It was a period of awakening to the world and the responsibility that each of us has to make it a better place for humanity. I was now able to articulate these ideas that had been forming for the past years. Efforts I had made trying to share some of these thoughts with my mother always ended in frustration because of the language barrier.

Denison University Dean Cyril Richards and his wife, Alice, in Granville, Ohio, 1943. The Richards had tremendous influence on Tai Shigaki's attitudes toward social justice and political concerns.

271

Again I was content to be a typical college co-ed, active in a variety of campus organizations with newly found friends. It was not until years later that I learned that my presence in the college community had created a turmoil in connection with my eligibility for sorority membership. Denison was a strong Greek campus, and a number of my friends had evidently tried to no avail to get me into their sorority. Being goal-oriented and realistic about my socio-economic situation, it had never entered my mind to consider pledging. I knew I couldn't afford the time or money. It was not until after I graduated and another Nisei came to campus and wanted to pledge but was not rushed that I learned the sororities were not ready to take us in.

In the summer of 1943, my sister was expecting her second child. As her husband had left camp for employment in Michigan, she was to be alone to have the child. The plan was for her to join him as soon as she was able to travel. I went to Rohwer, Arkansas, to be with her, awaiting the delivery. In the meantime, I worked as a welfare worker assisting families with their problems. There was no reservation on my part about reentering camp, because I knew I was free to go whenever I desired. But I realized how trapped the people were who were still interned there with no expectation of release or knowledge of what the future had in store for them when that time came. Shortly after her second child, Margaret, was born, I accompanied my sister, her first daughter JoAnn, and her newborn baby to Michigan. By this time my brother had joined my parents in Salt Lake City, so there was no one in my immediate family still detained in camp.

The second wartime horror story happened the following summer. Upon graduation from Denison University, I went to the Crow Indian Reservation in Montana to participate in the Baptist Student Work Project. One hot Saturday afternoon, 15 of us decided to go to the local municipal swimming pool. As I entered, I noticed a conclave of the life guards. At the dispersion, one guard came to inform me that I could not remain in the pool. The debate had evidently been to determine whether the rules stipulated that this was a white-only pool, or that only Indians were excluded. Where did I fit in this scheme? This incident emitted indignation and vocal objections by my fellow workers. My memory is that I was rather accepting of the affront and didn't feel the outrage that the others were expressing. Again, I was in the eye of a storm but felt removed from the hot debate that ensued for some time thereafter. I seemed to have been cushioned from the indignity and coped very calmly. Or it may be that I didn't permit myself the luxury of feelings.

Tai Shigaki attired as a Crow on the Crow Indian Reservation in Montana, where she participated in the Baptist Student Work Project, 1944.

My Baptist mentors continued to pave the way for my educational and vocational pursuits. John W. Thomas of the American Baptist Home Missions Society arranged for me to go to Andover Newton Theological School in Newton Centre, Massachusetts, to earn a professional degree. Living in New England and in an erudite community of the seminary, my eyes were opened even more to a wider world community. I managed to meet my degree objective, but the

273

blow came when I could find no employment upon graduation. Ironically, the only job interview I had was in the same city where I was not welcomed in its local swimming pool. I was rejected by the church. I assumed it was because I was the wrong sex, color, and theological hue. So I had to go home with no job prospects.

I am sure my parents hadn't understood why a daughter insisted on a college degree and then persisted on going on for a graduate degree in religious education. What good was six years of higher education that resulted in no job or husband? Some of my friends and relatives made subtle efforts to resolve the latter problem by introducing me to a number of eligible Japanese men, but it never "took." Finally, I did get a call to a church, the first Japanese Congregational church in Honolulu. That job was an eye-opening experience where I faced blatant prejudice, taking the brunt of the island vs. mainland Japanese antipathies.

*Tai Shigaki at the Nuuanu Congregational Church
in Honolulu, Hawaii, 1950.*

*Tai Shigaki departing from Honolulu, Hawaii,
to return to the mainland, 1950.*

Labeled a "kotonk," a derogatory name the Hawaiian Japanese GI's gave the mainland Japanese GI's, I settled in Hawaii for three years, enjoying the leisurely pace of the islands. I realized that unless I intended to spend the rest of my life in Hawaii, I needed to return to the mainland. By this time, my sister had moved to Minnesota following her husband who was stationed at Fort Snelling. With that attraction and a job offer at a church in Minneapolis, I came to Minnesota in 1950. My claim to fame in that year was the establishment of a community center in the Whittier neighborhood where I helped organize the first senior citizens club in the state. From that assignment, I went on to work as a program director at the Unity Settlement House in North Minneapolis. One year was spent as a group worker at the International Institute in St. Paul, where I counseled Japanese warbrides. Considering my education, it was my desire to use all of my knowledge and skill. When the opportunity arose to become the director of the University of Minnesota YWCA, I took advantage of it. As my career thus far had combined my religious training with group work, I decided to return to school and get a Master's degree in Social Work from the University of Minnesota.

Tai Shigaki with Brownies in front of the Unity Settlement House in Minneapolis, Minnesota, circa 1953.

Tai Shigaki (back row, far right) serving as a group worker for Japanese women married to U.S. servicemen at the International Institute in St. Paul, Minnesota, 1955.

Upon completion of that degree, the only door that opened to me was with the Minnesota Department of Corrections as assistant superintendent of the Women's Reformatory in Shakopee. In the 1960's, the Reformatory had 60 to 70 women and about 20 severely retarded children housed on the campus. The women cared for the children, learning how to be nurturing care givers, which many of these women were not to their own children. Having experienced incarceration myself, I was very aware of the fact that the worst thing about imprisonment is not poor living conditions but the removal of freedom. Having a sense of that deprivation, I was able to empathize with the inmates and help them not only to get beyond focusing on their plight, but also to learn how to control the behavior that resulted in their imprisonment.

Assistant Superintendent Tai Shigaki with Superintendent Ruby Benson of the Women's Reformatory in Shakopee, Minnesota, circa 1964.

For 25 years I worked in the Department of Corrections in a variety of administrative positions. From Shakopee, I moved up to the central office as director of staff training for all state correctional facilities and probation/parole officers. I was the only woman in a managerial position at this time in the department, which was completely male except in the girls' and women's institution. During my tenure as staff training director, we were able to get a stipend program that sent more than 30 professional employees to get Master's degrees in Social Work. We were also able to professionalize the guards through a newly created training academy which continues to be operational today. Upon reflection, I feel these were the most successful years in the field of corrections, and the Minnesota Department of Corrections gained a national reputation.

Tai Shigaki, Assistant Personnel Director at the Minnesota Department of Corrections in St. Paul, Minnesota, circa 1980.

Following the directorship of staff training, I became the program director in a juvenile facility. I supervised the Minneapolis juvenile probation/parole office and then returned to the central office to develop the Corrections Group Home standards that regulated the operation of these facilities. My professional career was concluded with nine years as assistant director of personnel and the department's affirmative action officer.

When it became possible for Japanese Americans to return to California, my parents and my brother's family returned to Gardena into our old home. My brother opened a dry cleaning shop, and my mother continued her sewing business. My sister stayed in Minne-

Tai Shigaki with her colleagues at the Minnesota Department of Corrections in St. Paul, Minnesota, 1987.

sota where she worked as a librarian in St. Paul, while her husband worked as a mechanic and later for the Minnesota Department of Transportation. Her two daughters both have successful careers: one as a social worker and the other as a librarian. My brother has a son, Richard, who resides in Colorado and is a consultant for a computer firm. My brother's daughter, Betty, is the director of the Rochester Art Center where she has worked for the past 20 years. Both of them received their higher education at the University of Minnesota. Two grandnieces returned to Minnesota to attend and graduate from Carleton College.

Reflections

As my biographical history reflects, my World War II experience did not leave a strong negative impact upon me. Because I really had very few worldly possessions, I lost very little unlike many people. Perhaps it took a year of my life when my education was disrupted. And perhaps I lost a husband and family that I might have had, had life proceeded in the course it was going before Pearl Harbor. But I gained an education beyond my expectations back then. And more importantly, I gained a world view that continued existence in Southern California may not have made possible.

When I read the stories of other Issei and Nisei, I am keenly aware of the great hardship suffered by many people. I realize the toll that the evacuation experience took on the members of my family, and I feel badly about the scars that still remain. But I have to be honest and admit this was not my plight. What transpired probably trained me to respond to slights, rejections, and animosity with minimal distraction to the inner sense of direction and goals that I had set for myself. It may be that I have cushioned myself from the affronts and not permitted myself to recognize, admit, or give in to feelings of hurt. These survival skills have enabled me to not become bitter and angry, for which I am grateful.

Minnesota was a breath of fresh air because I felt accepted and not put down. I was in many situations where I was a novelty, and as such, doors were opened to me. Once permitted in, I made the most of the opportunities to be my own person and to help others discover that our differences need not be a barrier. In the process, I hope I was able to bridge the gap of understanding with individuals and groups that may not have exposed themselves to outsiders.

After 41 years of residence in Minnesota and having travelled in 49 of the 50 states, I am always happy to return home. I appreciate the openness of the people here who continue to take in refugees in large numbers from all over the world. The way the Minnesotans respond to human needs and remain in the vanguard of reaching out to suffering peoples is phenomenal. Our human services, criminal justice, and educational systems are superior. I am not so naive as to not recognize that we are not without shortcomings. Compared to other parts of the United States, however, Minnesota is tops in my book. The quality of life and the moral, ethical values that I hold dear still matter.

I have not been active in the Japanese American community, so I cannot assess how things have changed. But this very fact is significant in that some of us have felt sufficiently at home here not to need to cling to each other for support. We are comfortable and adjusted, so we can do our own thing with freedom and no sense of restraint. The isolation from the new wave of immigration from the Pacific Rim countries does delay us in learning and appreciating the impact of the shift in world power and the cultural changes that are occurring in our country. Our successful adjustment in American society could be useful in helping these newcomers, many of whom come out of oppression, find a home here as we have found.

MARTHA INOUYE OYE

My father and mother did not cross the Pacific together to our western shores. Father, Yasuzo Inouye, was born in Fukuoka, Japan, in 1882 and came to the U.S. via Canada after the death of his parents. He was 18 years old at that time. He then moved to Portland, Oregon, where he worked at the home of Mr. and Mrs. Lippman and completed grammar school. It was 13 years later that Mother, Mitsuye Inouye, a native of Kumamoto, Japan, crossed the Pacific. She was the youngest of six children and came over as a picture bride at the age of 18.

During their residency in Portland, my parents had four children: Mabel, George, Mary and me, Martha. Dad initially ran a grocery store and later owned an Oriental gift shop. About the time World War I ended, Mother and Dad moved to Seattle with their offsprings. On board the train were war veterans returning from Europe. Mother reminisced as to how these soldiers enjoyed playing with the four of us. My father went into the lumber exporting business after settling in Seattle. He went into partnership with an Irishman, Patrick Lyon, and named their company U.S. Trading Company. It was located in the Central Building in downtown Seattle. In 1990, my husband and I made it a point for our daughter, Audrey, and our granddaughter, Emiko, to see this building which still looks good on the outside, when we traveled to the Pacific Northwest es-

A wedding picture of Martha Oye's parents, Mitsuye and Yasuzo Inouye, in Portland, Oregon, May 2, 1913.

*Martha Oye's father, Yasuzo Inouye, ran this Oriental gift shop
in Portland, Oregon, in the early 1900's.*

pecially to show them our old stomping grounds as well as to introduce them to our friends.

Henry, the youngest child of our family, was born in Seattle.
Our growing-up years were mostly ones of positive experiences. We
lived in an integrated middle-class neighborhood. Across the street
from our home were the St. Mary's Catholic Church and school, plus
a large residence for nuns. We had fairly easy access to our public
schools as well as to our Japanese language school.

In 1926, we had the opportunity to travel on a Japanese steamship to Japan to meet my maternal grandmother and other relatives
in Nagasaki. We had memorable experiences on that trans-Pacific
voyage, especially on our return trip two years later when we traveled first-class. One night the ship's captain invited our family to
have dinner at his table. We also had the opportunity to socialize
with the chief engineer in his cabin. The chief steward who had

responsibilities for our rooms was artistically talented and creative. Every morning we could hardly wait to return to our room to see what he had created for us using the extra blankets we each had on our bed. Using *origami* (folding paper) technique with the blankets, he created flowers, animals, and all sorts of interesting items to be placed on top of our beds. We loved his creations and thought they were works of art! We also had the opportunity to see from the deck spouting whales following our ship. There was a time on that voyage when some passengers complained about not sleeping well after having eaten green tea ice cream for dinner. The caffeine in the tea made it difficult for them to sleep. This was the first time I was made aware of the effects of tea in one's system.

In the early 1920's, Martha Oye's father, Yasuzo Inouye (second from right), was engaged in the lumber export business in Seattle, Washington.

My father's business thrived until the early 1930's. Due to the Depression, it tapered off. Dad kept himself actively involved in a number of community organizations, such as the Japan America Society, Japanese Chamber of Commerce, Seattle Buddhist Church, Fukuoka Prefectural Association, and golf and fencing clubs.

Martha Oye (far left) with her siblings, (from left to right) Mary, George, Mabel and Henry, in Seattle, Washington, circa early 1920's.

I took a secretarial course at a business college after graduating from Garfield High School. I secured employment as a school clerk at both Ravenna School and Roosevelt High School.

In September, 1940, the United States imposed an embargo on exports to Japan, including lumber. By the following summer, the U.S. Government froze Japanese assets, adding oil and high octane aviation fuel to the list of embargoed goods. When this happened, my father did not have any means of making a living for his family. He had to close his office. Being the eternal optimist, Dad never gave up hope of continuing his lumber exporting business again some day in the future. Rather than sell his office furniture and equipment, he stored them and opened a dry cleaning establishment in Seattle in the fall of 1941. This venture lasted but a few months because World War II broke out.

About 11 p.m. on December 7, 1941, my father was awakened by an FBI agent and three uniformed men who came to our home. They searched my parents' bedroom and took my father's wallet, several personal checks, and other papers. He was then taken to the U.S. Immigration Office. We did not see him until several days later when we were given permission to visit him. My father was not the only person to be treated this way. All Japanese men considered to be leaders in the community were rounded up that night. Years later, after my father had passed away, I was to learn, from information provided by the Justice Department under the Freedom of Information Act, that the FBI had been gathering information on Dad because he was considered to be a community leader. It is not surprising that he was apprehended so quickly. It should be noted that my father's dossier showed nothing to justify his incarceration.

I was not home on December 7. I had received an invitation from my friend, Tom Oye, who was attending Law School at Willamette University, to visit him in Salem, Oregon, that very weekend. I took a train to Salem. Early Sunday afternoon while we were eating lunch, we heard on the radio of the Japanese surprise attack on Pearl Harbor. This news was repeated over and over again. I didn't have the slightest idea of how drastically this incident was going to affect my life. When I got to the Portland railroad station for my return trip to Seattle, my world literally caved in. A couple of FBI agents stopped me to inquire if I was Japanese. When I answered in the affirmative, they proceeded to tell me that I could not board the train. How terribly angered and frustrated I was! Not only did I feel that this situation was unwarranted, but I felt I was a fool to have been so honest. How could these men tell whether I was Japanese, Chinese, Korean, Vietnamese or some other Asian when I myself couldn't identify the specific ethnic background of an Asian simply by looking at him or her? As an American citizen, my civil rights were being violated.

Luckily I had an aunt and uncle living near Salem, in the town of Independence. I surprised them by unexpectedly appearing at their door with Tom. They kindly took me in and I stayed with them for about three days until my brother, George, drove from Seattle in the family car to pick me up. It was only then through George that I first learned that my father had been detained in the Immigration building. We were permitted to see my father once before he was sent with other Seattle leaders to an Army base in Missoula, Montana. Dad was then transferred to a detention center in Louisiana and subsequently to New Mexico before being released two years later.

I regret now in hindsight that I never really got my father to recount stories of his confinement years. The messages I received from him were few and far between. He generally wrote to me on postal cards. I am sure the reason for his sending me the postal cards instead of letters was to avoid censorship. Dad said very little on those cards. I don't think he was mistreated; I hope he wasn't. Dad spoke and read English fluently, so I am sure he had no difficulty communicating with the military police.

With the outbreak of the war, Japanese Americans could no longer travel about freely. We were restricted to travel only five miles from our homes. No longer was I able to go to work at Ravenna School or to Roosevelt High School. The distance there far exceeded the limit we were allowed to travel.

In 1984, I was surprised to learn through the Seattle chapter of the Japanese American Citizens League that they were earnestly lobbying for a bill which would make possible the release of funds presently held in escrow for secretaries of Japanese ancestry who had unjustly been fired or voluntarily resigned in lieu of dismissal following the Japanese attack on Pearl Harbor. They had been involved in this redress effort for the preceding ten years, hoping to assist 35 state, three city and 25 school district employees. H.R. 1415 was finally passed on April 25, 1984. In September 1984, I received my reparation in the amount of $2,500 from the Seattle Public Schools.

When military notice was posted that all persons of Japanese ancestry on the West Coast were to be evacuated due to military necessity, we had great difficulty accepting this order. America was also at war with Italy and Germany, but neither Italian Americans nor German Americans were evacuated en masse. Neither were Japanese Americans in Hawaii with the exception of some 1,000 people. It was surprising too that the public at large voiced so little opposition to our government's plan to put us away. I have often wondered if there would have been greater objection had all the present-day modern communication systems been in place. Years later we learned that had it not been for our government's campaign to suppress, alter, and destroy crucial evidence, the U.S. Supreme Court might have been persuaded to rule unconstitutional this massive evacuation of 120,000 Japanese Americans. Apparently it was not so much a matter of security, but an attempt by some groups to gain economically.

On April 28, 1942, the mass evacuation of Japanese Americans from Seattle began. Families were evacuated according to the district in which they resided. My family was in the first contingent to be moved. We had but a few weeks to move out of our four-bedroom house, where we had lived for some 15 years; to dispose of much of our belongings; and to move what we didn't sell or give away to the basement of our dry cleaning establishment. Much of our property was practically given away, since buyers who appeared at our door knew we had no alternative because of the impending exclusion. The owner of the dry cleaning building promised to take good care of our possessions. This didn't turn out to be the case. Four years later when evacuees were finally permitted to return to the West Coast, my mother went back to the building to check on our belongings. She found many of our valuables had disappeared.

The Wartime Civil Control Administration instructed each evacuee to bring only two suitcases. We who were in the first group to be evacuated met at an empty lot near the Beacon Hill Bridge. A few friends from the nearby area came to see us off. At the appointed time, we were loaded into buses with military escorts. This evacuation scene was repeated many times. Only those people who were patients in tuberculosis sanitariums or mental institutions were allowed to remain in Seattle. It took a month to complete the exclusion of some 7,000 Japanese American residents. Our destination was not disclosed beforehand.

Our family's destination turned out to be the Puyallup County Fairground's parking lot. This place was designated Area B. We saw for the first time the many hastily constructed barracks with knot holes, one of which was to be our dwelling place.

People walking outside the barracks could easily see in, especially at night, when the one hanging lightbulb in the center of the room was lit. Inside the barracks, the partitioning walls that separated us from our neighbors' rooms were only six feet high. If we stood on our cot, we could see what was going on next-door. Six families were quartered in each of these barracks. Dreadful as our room was, we felt lucky in comparison with some Seattle residents who were assigned to Area D where they were placed in animal stalls, fraught with the stench of earlier occupants.

One of the first things I did upon arriving at the Puyallup Assembly Center was to write to my Seattle friends who had not yet been evacuated. I wanted them to know what to expect when they arrived here and also what they should bring. An Army sentry was good enough to mail my postal cards. I had no idea whether my messages would be censored, let alone mailed. Later, when my friends arrived at the center and thanked me, I realized my messages had gone through.

My brother, Henry, who was a senior in high school at that time, was allowed by the Seattle School Board to graduate, as were others in the same situation even though they were missing the last six weeks of school.

Our regimented existence was much like a soldier's, except, of course, that we were held captive. We quickly learned that it was going to be a continual line-up for everything: line-ups for meals, washroom and laundry room, as well as for mail and medical services.

Our first meal was served to us in a very disorganized fashion. It consisted of Vienna sausages, potatoes, and bread. Meals on the whole were pretty starchy fares. It wasn't unusual for us to get on our plate macaroni and rice, or spaghetti and rice. What we missed most were fresh fruits and vegetables. Family life deteriorated at meal time, too. Everyone ate pretty much when he or she pleased and with whomever they cared to sit. Parents lost control of their children and table manners were forgotten.

Sleep was difficult at night in the barracks. One could hear loud snores, family quarrels, grinding of teeth, babies crying, laughter, and giggling. On cold nights, the one blanket issued to each of us was not enough and we got up to put on extra clothes. Washroom facilities were few and inadequate. Toilet stalls lacked doors.

During our five-month incarceration at the Puyallup Assembly Center, we experienced many surprises. We learned for the first time that Japanese residents from Alaska had been evacuated and placed in our camp. Under Executive Order 9066, 151 Alaskan Japanese met the same fate as we. Fifty of these Alaskans were seal and whale hunters and were of either Japanese-Indian origin or Japanese-Eskimo background. The criterion used by our government for evacuating Alaskans was that anyone with one-half Japanese blood was to be evacuated.

Another surprising revelation for me was to find that internees with social diseases were segregated in Puyallup. They were placed in a separate area within our center and could not associate with others not segregated. We were also taken aback when we learned that agencies, such as the Red Cross, had been permitted to come to our Assembly Center, asking for blood donations for the war effort. We wondered out loud how recipients of our blood would feel if they found out they were injected with Japanese blood.

When the war started we were angry and upset. We thought our alien parents, who were deprived of U.S. citizenship rights, might possibly be treated differently. However, we never dreamed that we, who were American citizens by birth, would be placed in the same position as our parents. Didn't our citizenship assure us of our rights and liberties as guaranteed under the Constitution?

I have also wondered what black employees working on the railroad as cooks, waiters, and porters thought as we came on board and had to be transported to our permanent concentration camp in September 1942. Again, we were not informed of our destination. We were sent to the camp called Minidoka, a place near Twin Falls, Idaho, which is located about 90 miles from the famous ski resort, Sun Valley. Our train passed Portland, Oregon, my birthplace, and then followed the Columbia River. To this day I can't describe exactly the route our train traveled, because most of the time, especially when we were going through any town, our window shades had to be drawn. We traveled with military police escorts, the majority of whom were courteous, but some seemed embarrassed about the whole thing. Our trip lasted two days, and it wasn't until we reached our destination that we finally knew where our permanent camp was.

The camp's official name was the Minidoka Relocation Center. Minidoka, I believe, is an Indian word. I don't know what it means. However, to the Japanese it sounds similar to their phrase, "*Mina do ka?*" which translates, "How is everyone?" Evacuees all thought that was a big joke..."How Is Everyone Relocation Center?"

This permanent camp of ours was laid out in a long, winding fashion some seven miles long. The U.S. Government had built barracks to intern some 7,000 evacuees from the various assembly centers. Unlike our assembly center barracks, these buildings were constructed more durably. Each room had a black potbellied stove and Army cots set up for members of the family who were to be assigned there. The camp was situated on dusty, barren lands. Like the Puyallup Assembly Center, the Minidoka Relocation Center was surrounded by barbed wire fences and guard towers. However, military security at Minidoka wasn't tight. The administrators of our camp were right in assuming that the highly visible internees would not go A.W.O.L. No one in Minidoka, during the five months I was there, made any attempt to escape.

For a city girl, it was the first time that I heard the lonely howling of coyotes at night. I was scared to go out to the washroom unless I had someone accompany me. During the day, some adults and children passed their time catching rattle snakes and jack rabbits. Once, a friend of my mother caught one of these jack rabbits and gave it to her. She cooked it and tried to pass it off as chicken to us, but from the odor we knew better.

Comfort was uppermost in the minds of the people when they first arrived here. As at the assembly center, talented and creative evacuees built partitions and furniture from discarded lumber and materials picked up around the barracks to make their rooms more habitable.

The camp administrators made work available to those who wished to keep busy. There were great needs for cooks, waitresses, dishwashers, office workers, and teachers, as well as for medical professionals like doctors, dentists, and nurses. Those who worked were paid $12, $16 and $19 a month, depending on their job classifications. Doctors and dentists were among those in the top pay bracket, receiving $19 a month. I worked as a secretary for one of the procurement officers at the monthly salary of $16. Most people, with the exception of the aged, the infirm, and children, worked to keep busy.

Farmers from nearby communities came to recruit workers, too. Idaho farmers who grew mainly sugar beets and potatoes were suffering a wartime labor shortage. Topping sugar beets was no easy task, but to be free and on the outside was the deciding factor for many of the Nisei men who signed up for work.

My brother, Henry, worked at the camp medical clinic with doctors, medical students, and nurses, who in the main were internees. I remember how excited Henry was the first time he got to see an evacuee's cadaver. He pursued a medical career after being released. He retired recently from the position of medical director at Illinois Bell Telephone Company in Chicago.

Classes for elementary and secondary school students were made available in some of the barracks. Caucasian teachers from nearby towns and college-educated internees staffed the classes. George, my older brother, who had graduated from the University of Washington in Business Administration, helped teach some of the high school classes. One cold, sub-zero day, George got his ears frostbitten when he walked back to his barrack after teaching. My sister, Mary, assisted at the general store or canteen which was opened in one of the barracks. There one could purchase a few snack foods, such as Ritz crackers, peanut butter, and jelly. Sears and Montgomery Ward set up a mail order catalog business. They really did a landslide business since they had captive customers. Evacuees had to dig into their own savings for these purchases. Economically it was rough on families with limited resources.

The one and only time our family was given permission to leave Minidoka for a few hours, escorted by the military personnel to the nearest town, Twin Falls, was when George and Ritsuko, his bride, were married. The Rev. Terakawa, a former minister of Portland's Buddhist Temple, performed the marriage ceremony before a dozen friends and relatives at the Rogerson Hotel.

Similar to most communities on the outside, various church denominations were formed in the camp, and evacuees had opportunities to worship in the church of their choice.

Other group activities that were organized at Minidoka included Americanization classes for our alien parents, flower arrangement and dance classes, brush painting and other arts and craft classes. Baseball was the favorite outdoor sport. Internees provided for their own baseball equipment. For entertainment, talent shows were produced on some Saturday nights. Young folks also managed to have dance parties, providing their own music by using phonograph records or having a group of musicians play their instruments. Some of the music groups developed into very fine dance bands.

Periodically, old movies would be secured for us by the camp administrators. The one and only movie I remember was "Citizen

Kane" starring Orson Wells. The movie, which is considered a classic, is supposedly about newspaper publisher William Randolph Hearst. It was rather ironic that we should be watching the life story of a man who did so much to inflame prejudice and bias against the Japanese with his yellow journalism. His granddaughter, Patricia Hearst, later participated in a bank robbery as a member of the Symbionese Liberation Army. She was convicted and served a prison term. Another irony of fate was that the woman, with whom Patricia Hearst was arrested while a fugitive, was Wendy Yoshimura who was born in an American concentration camp during World War II.

Five months after we were brought to Idaho's concentration camp, President Roosevelt announced that volunteers from internment camps would be accepted into a Japanese American combat unit, and that other internees, who could secure educational and employment opportunities in receptive communities outside, would be released after proving their loyalty to the United States. This occurred about the time that camp and government officials were being pressured by taxpayers on the outside. The taxpayers were beginning to feel the pinch of the costs associated with the operation of ten permanent internment camps scattered in the western half of our country. The first year's operating costs amounted to about $150 million. There was also a critical need for Japanese linguists and translators to serve and help the American military intelligence in the Pacific Theatre of Operation. The last and perhaps the most important reason for the anxieties of the Roosevelt Administration was that the Supreme Court might rule the imprisonment of the Japanese Americans to be unconstitutional.

So about a year into the internment program, internees began to apply for permission to relocate. With clearance from the FBI, those released were permitted to go only in one direction—eastward. The West Coast was still considered off-limits.

In order to qualify for leave clearance, internees had to write to their friends on the outside for references. Years later, upon writing to the U.S. Justice Department for personal information under the Freedom of Information Act, I was deeply moved by a letter which my dear friend and public school teacher, Eleanor Writt, had written for me on February 14, 1943. The letter read as follows:

> War Relocation Authority
> Washington, D.C.
>
> Gentlemen:
>
> Your recent form letter relative to Martha Teruyo Inouye, #10752, Minidoka 41-8-C, has been received. I am happy to recommend the above mentioned as a genuinely sincere American citizen. I have known her and the other members of her family over a period of years which began when the children attended Grammar School. Raised as she was in a fine home where American customs were taught, her Americanization carried on the way of life taught in our public schools.
>
> She is a young woman of much individual worth. She is not afraid of hard work. At one time she served as a domestic in order to earn her living. She served as a clerk in the school where I am now employed. Given an opportunity, she will prove her loyalty to her country and contribute her utmost in productive activity.
>
> Sincerely yours,
>
> Eleanor Writt

Shortly after Eleanor Writt had mailed her reference letter, I was released from the Minidoka Relocation Center in February 1943 to marry Tom Oye who was stationed at Camp Crowder, a U.S. Signal Corps base near Joplin, Missouri. I was escorted to the Twin Falls train station by one of the civilian personnel. I paid for my own transportation out of Minidoka and also for expenses incurred en route to my destination.

A week prior to my departure for Missouri, my sister Mary had left to seek employment in Chicago. Mother joined Mary several months later. George, his wife Ritsuko, and Henry headed for Detroit, Michigan. Henry did not remain long in Detroit as he was accepted by Bates College in Lewiston, Maine. George opened a haberdashery near the Wayne State University campus.

Regarding students who left the internment camp to continue their education, the so-called Big Ten universities did not accept students of Japanese ancestry during the war. This includes our own University of Minnesota. Many students, therefore, applied to small private colleges, many of which were church-affiliated.

Here in Savage, Minnesota, the Military Intelligence Service Language School was established to train Nisei soldiers about the same time that the 442nd Regimental Combat Team, a segregated Japanese American fighting unit, was formed in Mississippi. One of my nonethnic Minnesota friends remembers seeing the MIS Language School in Savage as a young girl. For many years, she had been under the impression that it was a Japanese prisoner of war camp. The fact of the matter was that thousands of U.S. Army recruits were brought here from the ten American concentration camps. The cadre and staff came from various service units throughout the United States.

Tom Oye and I were married at the First Methodist Church in Joplin. The Rev. Ridpath performed the service, and his wife and another church member stood up for us. The Martins who were members of the First Methodist Church befriended quite a few of us Japanese Americans. They invited us to their home and made us feel welcome in the community.

Tom was transferred for combat training by the fall of 1943, so I joined my sister and parents in Chicago. I was pregnant with our first child when I left Missouri. My sister assisted in every way possible when my labor and delivery time began. During the war, telephones were not readily available. Mary, therefore, had to make many trips to the public telephone at the nearby elevated train station to call my doctor, hospital, and taxi. Unable to secure a cab, Mary called the police. They arrived at our home in the middle of the night with their big van and flashed bright spotlights on our front door steps. As we boarded the van, Mary and I felt like criminals being hauled away. When I finally got to the hospital and my labor and delivery were completed, I remember Mary crying. What she went through for me was quite a traumatic and emotional ordeal.

Martha and Tom Oye shortly after their marriage in Joplin, Missouri, 1943.

Three months after our son, Thomas Asa, was born, I took him by train to introduce him to his father. Traveling to the Southern city of Anniston, Alabama, by train was another eye-opening experience. I had heard and read about the Mason-Dixon line, but on this trip I learned that blacks still had to move to the rear when the train crossed the boundary between Pennsylvania and Maryland. Upon reaching Anniston, I noticed separate drinking fountains and rest rooms for blacks. Riding the city bus, I was also made aware that blacks sat in the rear of the bus and whites up front. Having been subjected to internment, I decided to sit in the rear. Some of the white passengers gave me strange looks, but no one said anything. The American Civil War which lasted from 1861 to 1865 had not yet abolished disparate treatments. These experiences occurred in 1944.

Shortly after relocating to Chicago, Mother suffered a stroke while traveling by herself on the elevated train line which operated a block away from our home. We don't know how she managed in her condition to make it home. As her clothes were all dirty, we surmised that she must have had to crawl. Mother was paralyzed on the right side and could not talk. We had a physical therapist come to our home to help her recover. Mother, being in her early 50's when she suffered the stroke, was lucky. Her recovery was fairly quick.

Mary, while in Chicago, married a Japanese national, Paul Katsuro, who had been evacuated by the Peruvian Government and sent to the United States for detention in the Crystal City, Texas, interment camp operated by the U.S. Justice Department. He was one of over 2,000 Peruvian Japanese whom the U.S. Government contemplated using as pawns to be exchanged for American prisoners of war in Asia. Fortunately for Paul, he was not used for this purpose. When Grant Woods' art exhibit was held at the Minneapolis Institute of Arts, we met Jerre Mangione, the uncle of the famous musician, Chuck Mangione, who had served during World War II with the Immigration and Naturalization Service. Jerre Mangione had come in contact with Japanese who were evacuated from Central and South America for the purpose of POW exchanges, which never materialized.

Mabel, my oldest sister, spent the war years in Japan. Graduating from Seattle's Garfield High School, she was enrolled in a college in Kyoto, Japan. She married a Japanese national, Francis Suzuki, whom she had met in Seattle. He was studying Civil Engineering at the University of Washington. The Japanese Exclusion Act of 1924 excluded Francis from becoming a permanent resident in the United

States, thereby making it impossible for him to get a job after graduation. For this reason, he returned to Japan upon completion of his degree objective. Mabel was spared internment, but suffered tremendous hardships in Japan due to food shortages. Moreover, she had to raise her four young children without her husband who had been drafted by the Japanese Army. In 1956, Mabel and Francis were finally able to return to the United States with their family and joined us in Chicago.

The first Japanese to settle in the United States arrived in California in 1869. It took Congress 83 years to pass the Walter-McCarran Act which made naturalization possible for the Japanese. The right to citizenship was finally granted in June 1952, seven years after World War II ended. Dad was 72 years old when he finally became eligible for naturalization. He cherished his new status of being an American citizen and discharged his civic duty by voting at every election. Mother felt she was too old to apply for citizenship. She lived to the age of 95.

As a member of the 100th Battalion/442nd Regimental Combat Team, Tom served in the European Theatre of Operation, mainly in Italy and France. Nisei soldiers in this famed unit fought gallantly and died for the United States while their families were imprisoned in the American concentration camps without due process of law. The members of the 442nd Regiment received numerous medals and citations for their outstanding services.

During their deployment near Riviera, France, Tom's unit was headquartered in the home of a wealthy American family. The owners were not there, but their housekeeper was, and she was most hospitable to this group.

Tom was appointed Battalion Sgt. Major after peace was declared in Europe. He received his discharge from the Army on November 28, 1945, and went back to school to get his law degree at De Paul University in Chicago. On March 27, 1950, he was commissioned a Second Lieutenant in the Army Reserve. With a total of

Martha Oye's husband, Tom, was a member of the highly decorated
442nd Regimental Combat Team, in Milan, Italy, July 5, 1945.

some 27 years of service, Tom was transferred to the Retired Re-
serves with the rank of Lt. Colonel on November 19, 1971.

While attending De Paul University, Tom worked part-time
at the American Bar Association's headquarters. Upon receiving his
J.D. degree, he secured employment with General Mills as Credit
Manager. In 1959, Tom was transferred to the General Mills headquarters in Minneapolis for one year in their management development program. We bought a home in the suburb of St. Louis Park
and lived there with our son, Thomas Asa, who was 15 years old, and
our daughter, Audrey, two years old.

On the day we moved in, our neighbor next-door, an elderly
lady, was in our yard removing dandelions. In a subtle way, she was
giving us the message that weeds were unwelcome neighbors.

When Tom was promoted to National Credit Manager in the Grocery Products Division at Park Ridge, we moved back to Illinois and rented an apartment in Skokie. We lived there for six years until the Credit Department was moved to the company's headquarters in Minneapolis. We were delighted to be back again in Minnesota and purchased a split-level house in Edina.

Martha Oye's husband, Tom, with other members of the Board of Directors of the National Food Manufacturers Credit Association in Fort Lauderdale, Florida, circa 1981.

Tom retired from General Mills in 1985 after 30 years with the company. He is involved in many community organizations such as the Edina Human Relations Commission, Edina Chemical Health, Good Samaritan United Methodist Church of Edina, and several committees at the University of Minnesota. My mother used to comment that Dad had been my role model and that I married a man much like Dad who thrived on community service. Tom served on the National Food Manufacturers Credit Association Board of Directors for some 15 years. He still attends the board meetings as an ex-officio member.

During the six years we spent in Illinois, prior to our transfer back to Minnesota, our family joined the Central Methodist Church of Skokie. Tom taught Sunday school to 7th graders. To him it was a learning experience to hear from his Gentile students remarks of being a minority in a predominantly Jewish community.

Shortly after our second move back to Minnesota in 1966, I joined the Edina League of Women Voters. The League conducts national, state and local studies and research, and promotes responsibility through informed and active participation of citizens in government at the national, state, and local levels. I find my involvement with the League to be a great learning experience. I am also a member of the World Affairs Council, United Nations Association, Interfaith Peacemakers of Edina, and Good Samaritan United Methodist Church of Edina.

Periodically, I do work as proctor for the Minnesota Board of Nursing at their state licensure examinations for Registered Nurses and for Practical Nurses. My friend, Kimi Taguchi Hara, whom I knew in Seattle, recruited me. She was an Assistant Director for the Minnesota Board of Nursing at that time. For me it is interesting to observe that since the Vietnam War there has been an increase in the number of men going into the field of nursing. State licensure exams are open to persons with dyslexia and other physical disabilities.

Eight years ago, my dear friend, Zelma Gray, introduced me to Elderhostel, a fairly new movement in American adult education. Elderhostel, a non-profit adult education program, offers inexpensive short-term academic programs hosted by educational institutions here in the United States and around the world. Individuals 60 years of age and older are eligible. The accompanying spouse or companion of an eligible participant must be at least 50 years of age. I enjoy Elderhostel because it encourages diversity and welcomes people of all races, colors, and religions. I have taken courses every summer with my Minnesota friends at different colleges and universities mainly in Minnesota, but have ventured outstate to the University of Wisconsin-Milwaukee and the University of Chicago.

We have lived in Edina, in the same home for over 26 years, and have enjoyed getting together with our neighbors to play bridge.

On Labor Day, neighbors on our Countryside Road would participate in a street social party where we had potluck dinners and games
for the children. With the passing of years, there have been changes
in the makeup of our neighborhood. When we first moved here,
there were as many as 90 children living on our two blocks. Now
many of us are "empty nesters" and some families have moved away.
So we do not socialize as much as we did in the past. However, on
Christmas Eve, we all love the opportunity to put up Luminaria—
decorating our yards with white candles and lighting them at night-
fall. Returning home from our church's Christmas Eve service, it
uplifts us to see the many candles along our streets glowing, and it
reminds us of the One who is a source of light to us who believe.

*Martha Oye attending an Elderhostel class at the
St. Paul campus of the University of Minnesota, 1989.*

Reflections

Our family is happy that we were transferred to Minnesota.
We find residents here extremely friendly, kind, and willing to accept people of diverse backgrounds. In the last couple of decades,
the number of Korean children adopted by Minnesotans has increased.
Furthermore, tens of thousands of Vietnamese and Hmong have been
able to come here as refugees. There is now talk that some 200 Ti-
betans will be coming soon.

I believe job opportunities are available in Minnesota for qualified persons. Nisei are socially accepted; they have been able to participate in state and city governments. Many have successfully engaged in entrepreneurial ventures. From our experience of living in other states, we think Minnesota Japanese Americans are fortunate, socially and culturally, to be living here. This area provides a climate for individual pursuits and for closer contact with the majority community.

In August 1992, my brother George and his wife, Ritsuko, celebrated their golden wedding anniversary in Chicago, and some 40 relatives and 30 close friends attended the celebration. The weekend weather was beautiful, and we were kept busy with many interesting activities which were planned for us by their daughters, Anne and Joyce. Saturday night we were invited to a wonderful banquet at the University of Chicago's Quadrangle Club, where my brother Henry is a member, and Henry and Tomi's daughter, Mariye, emceed for this memorable occasion. In another era, it would not have been possible for us to be entertained at a setting like the Quadrangle Club. Henry would not have been asked to be a member.

Martha Oye's daughter, Audrey, at the house of her aunt, Maye Uemura, in Roseville, Minnesota, 1991.

Audrey, our daughter, was especially happy to have had the opportunity to meet so many of her cousins which this 50th anniversary presented, but regretted that her relatives are now so scattered due to the wartime evacuation. Her cousins came for this celebration from the states of Massachusetts, Connecticut, New York, Washington, Oregon, California, Alabama, Ohio, Illinois, and Michigan.

Our son, Asa, his wife, Karen, and their daughter, Emiko, who live in Parma, Ohio, regretfully were unable to join us in Chicago since they were taking Emiko to New York to enroll her at Syracuse University. Our granddaughter, who has received several scholarships, is going to major in Fine Arts for which Syracuse is well known.

Martha Oye's son, Asa, with his wife, Karen, and daughter, Emiko, at her Valley Forge High School commencement in Parma, Ohio, June 9, 1992.

Asa met his wife, Karen Brenner, while attending Morningside College in Sioux City, Iowa, and is not alone amongst his third generation cousins to intermarry. Seven of his cousins have also intermarried. This is not an unusual occurrence for Japanese Americans today; a majority of his generation has married outside the Japanese American community.

Reflecting upon these many happenings in the postwar period, I view, with mixed feelings, the Executive Order that moved us to new scenes and experiences. Will the price we paid earn for our posterity and the generations to come a rightful place in this Democracy? We can only live our lives to the fullest and leave the rest to history.

GLADYS ISHIDA STONE

Both of my parents were from Oita-ken (prefecture), Kyushu, the southern-most island. My father was born in 1891 in Kitsuki-machi (town), and my mother was born in 1891 in Saiki-machi. They were both educated in the primary and secondary schools in their hometowns. However, for their college education, they both left Kyushu; my father went to the Imperial University at Sapporo, Hokkaido, and my mother attended Ochanomizu University in Tokyo.

Mother was the youngest of three children; her brother and sister were considerably older than she by some 17 and 11 years. For a young woman of that period, she was allowed considerable freedom and independence. For example, she traveled to Korea when she was a teen-ager because her brother, a journalist, was stationed in Seoul.

When my mother was ready to go to college, she was allowed to attend Ochanomizu University, a prestigious private women's college in Tokyo. She majored in American literature. After the first year, she transferred to another college which was intellectually more rigorous and the students were more serious. She apparently was headstrong and probably ahead of the times, an early women's libber! In Meiji Japan, this was a period when there was a great interest in westernization and the flowering of women's literary groups.

My relatives tell me that my mother was quite a liberal and talented person who not only associated with her male cousins, but also their friends who were studying at the Imperial University in Tokyo. No wonder she chose to come to America!

I remember that Mother helped us kids with our homework, especially Math and Art. She taught Japanese on Saturdays whenever the small Japanese community could not raise enough money for a full-time teacher of the Japanese language.

After the Relocation Centers closed in 1945, Mother came to join me in Chicago. She found a job rather quickly. It was one in commercial art; she painted faces on figurines, an imitation of the Hummel. Her art training in Japan helped. She continued to work for this company for 17 years until retirement. But after she retired, she then proceeded to take courses in oil painting at the Chicago Art Institute. She continued to paint in her studio until her health no longer permitted. Her last paintings reflect her love for Van Gogh and the Impressionists.

My father was the second of five children. Apparently, Father's dream as an eight-year-old was to go to America. To fulfill his dream, he raised squash on his father's land. In the ensuing years, he continued to save his squash money toward the eventual trip to America. Father really planned ahead!

The core of my father's reason to immigrate to America was the opportunity for expansion and growth. He kept repeating that Japan was such a small country that there was a limited chance of growth. His prophecy has been played out; the land where he grew his squash is still there, but little was growing when I visited Japan in 1989. No wonder Father decided early on to prepare for his trip to America where he envisioned a future of expansion.

At the turn of the twentieth century, the Imperial University at Sapporo in Hokkaido was the place for American agricultural training. Several American professors taught courses in extensive farming methods and techniques. Father matriculated at the University in 1909, and graduated four years later. He left Japan soon after graduation and immigrated to California in 1913.

Gladys Stone's father, Henry Raiji Ishida,
in Modesto, California, circa 1915.

Between his arrival at San Francisco and his marriage in 1922, Father experimented with a variety of jobs: school boy (a Japanese American term denoting a household servant), tenant farming with partners, and farming small acreages. After their marriage, my parents worked together as tenant farmers, always looking for farm land to buy. For an Issei person wishing to purchase land, the obstacle was the Alien Land Law of 1913, which prohibited aliens ineligible for citizenship from owning real property. The only way for an Issei to own any land in California was to register the land in the name of his offspring, his Nisei child. When my father died in 1940, the land he thought was registered to me, the oldest of the three citizen children, was registered in the names of my father's Caucasian attorney and his mother!

Gladys Stone's father, Henry Raiji Ishida, on his farm, Winafred Orchards, in Modesto, California, circa 1920.

Japanese farm hands making mochi (rice cake) on Winafred Orchards in Modesto, California, circa 1920.

I was born in 1923 in Modesto, California. Before the wartime evacuation, I lived with my widowed mother and two younger brothers on a 180-acre orchard, called Winafred Orchards, growing apricots, peaches, and grapes. But, in February 1942, our family was forced to leave the orchard by my father's trusted attorney, because he had presumably paid us off for my father's share of the ownership of the orchard. This was my first real encounter with an unscrupulous, greedy character.

Soon after Pearl Harbor, my father's Caucasian attorney came to the orchard on Sunday, December 7, 1941, to harass my mother into destroying certain legal papers which would tie the ownership of the orchard to my father's estate. At that time, he clearly stated that my Issei mother was now an enemy alien who had no rights, and that the children were minors and, therefore, had no legal rights without a guardian.

Between February 1941 and April 1942 when our family evacuated, there were numerous meetings with different attorneys, business associates, appraisers, and friends of the family, who tried to help us bring about a fair settlement of the property. However, all the cards were stacked against the widow and her three minor children. We took what my father's lawyer was willing to pay us; it was a paltry sum indeed!

After the war, we went to District Court of Appeals in California, but without sufficient documentary evidence, it was of no avail. The fruition of my father's dream was not realized.

Modesto was a small town where people were friendly and helpful. The neighbors who lived adjacent to our orchard were European ethnics. We had some good times and good relationships with them. Since we lived five miles north of town, we were bussed to the high school in town. This was a relatively untroubled, carefree, and happy period of my life. I was invited to Caucasian friends' homes to study as well as for parties. My mother also took three of us children to Japan for six months. We stayed with my father's relatives in Kyushu.

Since I was still young, my mother worried about my dating. When I drove, she would send my brother to chaperon. Usually I dropped him off at the movies and picked him up later. He was a good sport. During this period, I was not very sensitive to prejudice or discrimination; therefore, I do not remember any specific incidents.

Although I stated earlier that I was carefree and happy, during my last three years in high school, my father was in and out of the hospital; he had six major surgeries during that period. This was a constant worry for the family.

The Ishida family in Modesto, California, circa 1937.
From left to right, Calvin, Julius, Henry Raiji, Suye, and Gladys.

When the war broke out between the United States and Japan, I was completely traumatized with uncertainties and frustrations. My family consisted of my recently widowed mother, two younger brothers, and myself. As the eldest child, I had to provide emotional and physical support to my mother, even though I was as naive and ignorant about financial and legal matters as she. Moreover, the war had suddenly changed my mother's status from resident alien to enemy alien. Similarly, all Isseis were affected since they were aliens ineligible for citizenship. Therefore, the oldest citizen son or daughter was likely to become the legal representative of the family; many Issei parents felt they lost their authority within the family.

In 1942, I was living in my hometown, Modesto, California. It had a small Japanese community consisting of a grocery store, two cleaners, a barbershop, and several rooming houses/hotels. The Japanese American farmers lived in the outlying areas of Stanislaus County. By March 1942, our family moved into town, since the final settlement of selling the orchard was completed. Though the payment was far from satisfactory, our advisors concluded that there was no way a fair settlement could be achieved, given the chaotic times and the uncertainties of the war. Many Japanese Americans were victims of wartime hysteria.

For most of my Nisei classmates at the Modesto Junior College, this period between the bombing of Pearl Harbor and evacuation was a very confusing period, especially because of rumors. It was difficult to distinguish between facts and rumors. However, I continued to attend classes and carry on as normally as possible. I continued to participate in social activities until the Army imposed a curfew on all persons of Japanese ancestry, which inhibited our social life. I had to be home by 8:00 p.m. Some evenings I barely reached home before the FBI check.

In the early spring of 1942, I still had high hopes for the future. Given the development of the war, perhaps, my thinking was naive. Nevertheless, I took an entrance examination for admission to Stanford University. This took place before the evacuation orders were out. Surprisingly, I passed the exam, but discovered I could not be matriculated there since the university was located in Military Area No. 1. This was a great disappointment to me.

I evacuated with my family from Modesto to the Merced Assembly Center, a former county fairground. Our baggage was limited to what each of us could carry. Therefore, this meant that all of the household goods—furniture, appliances, dishes, cars, etc.— had to be packed and stored at the Buddhist Temple. For some reason, we decided to store our household goods, I guess, hoping for a short war. What an illusion! Other families sold their belongings at a fire sale.

In the initial evacuation process, each member of the family was given a family number and labeled just like baggage. Finally, at a designated place, we reported and boarded a Greyhound bus to be transported to the Merced Assembly Center.

In Merced, we lived communal-style; we were put in a hastily built living unit made out of existing structures like horse stalls. To accommodate the overflow, they built rows upon rows of tar-paper-covered barracks. The residential section was divided into blocks comprised of a dozen or so identical barracks measuring 120' x 20' each. A unit the size of a small bedroom accommodated a family of three, while the larger one, 20' x 25', housed seven people. The floor consisted of either cement or bare boards. A bare bulb hung in the center of the unit. Each of us was supplied with an Army cot. We had to supply our own bedding. For heat, a pot-bellied stove was installed in one corner of the unit. Each block had a mess hall, latrine, laundry facility, shower room, and a recreational hall.

Despite the uncertainties of the times, I finished my sophomore year at the college and graduated in early June 1942. A special graduation ceremony was held for the Japanese American graduates at the Merced Assembly Center where we were awarded the Associate of Arts degrees. Thanks to the formation of the National Japanese American Student Relocation Council in May 1942, it became possible for Nisei college students to continue their education in the Midwest or East. Thus, the Council assisted me in gaining admission to Washington University, St. Louis, Missouri.

I spent four months at the Merced Assembly Center. After a month of feeling bitter and very depressed, I decided to take a job as a recreational worker at the fabulous salary of $16 a month! This decision was good therapy for me, and it filled in time and kept me busy. The main purpose of the recreational program was to keep young people busy and out of trouble. The department provided a wide range of diversions available to them. Among the programs were community singing, movies, get-together rallies, G. I. Hops, etc. In addition, weekly Saturday night dances were sponsored. Part of our job was to chaperon and make sure the participants returned home safely.

In early September 1942, my brother and I went with the advance crew to the Amache War Relocation Center in Colorado, a permanent camp for the duration of the war. Mother was determined to see her three children off to college. She was willing to subsidize our education. Shortly after we arrived at Amache, we received our leave clearances which enabled us to matriculate at Washington University in St. Louis, Missouri, for the fall semester 1942. My youngest brother subsequently left Amache to attend Wooster College in Wooster, Ohio.

Gladys Stone at Washington University in St. Louis, Missouri, 1942.

Leaving the Amache Relocation Center for St. Louis was worrisome and full of anxiety, since I had no idea what to expect or who might cause trouble. This Greyhound bus trip was the first trip without parents or friends. Nevertheless, we arrived in St. Louis without exciting problems, although it was arduous and wearisome. On arrival, two students met us and drove us to the dormitory at Washington University.

I resettled in St. Louis, a border city with cultural characteristics of the North and the South and a large black population. It took me a while to get accustomed and comfortable with this environment. My first year at the University was a terribly busy one, combining academic and extracurricular activities. There were only seven Japanese American families and they were invisible to the St. Louis community. Hence, many of the Nisei students at Washington University were expected to be ambassadors of good will and were invited to speak about the incarceration of Japanese Americans before a variety of church, civic, and community organizations. It was a very frenzied and busy time for many Nisei attending college. Concurrently, we had to adjust to the University, dormitory life, the city and its environment, but what an exhilarating experience it was!

Gladys Stone studying in her dorm room at McMillan Hall, Washington University in St. Louis, Missouri, 1942.

I finished my undergraduate work and was awarded a Bachelor of Science degree in Business Administration from Washington University in February 1944. Then, I moved to Chicago where I was accepted for graduate work at the University of Chicago. I had problems with military clearance, since the University was conducting atomic bomb research, which was unbeknown to me at that time. For a while, I could not matriculate immediately at the University, because certain buildings were not accessible to me. In addition, I was interviewed by an FBI agent whose central question in the two-hour interview was: "Why do you want to pursue International Relations for your M.A. degree?" I concluded that, for some reason, a Japanese American who wanted to take a degree in International Relations could be subversive. I did pass the scrutiny. It took me six months for the clearance, but I did register for the fall quarter in 1944.

HERE AND THERE IN ST. LOUIS

JAPANESE-AMERICAN GRADUATES / Eight of the nine students of Japanese ancestry who were graduated today from Washington University, to which they were admitted through efforts of the National Student Relocation Council. They are, from left, front row: Setuko Matsunaga, Gladys Ishida and Lillian Tsukie Kubota; back row: Hiroshi Kisamoto, Shotaro Tsuruoka, Tsuyoshi Itano, George Matsumoto and Yoshio Matsumoto.
—By a Post-Dispatch Staff Photographer.

Gladys Stone (center) with other Japanese American graduates from Washington University in St. Louis, Missouri, 1944. The National Student Relocation Council was instrumental in having these students admitted to the university. Yoshio Matsumoto (far right) later married Alice Matsumoto, nee Abe, one of the contributors to this anthology.

319

By mid-August 1945, after the bombing of Hiroshima and Nagasaki, the war was over. As I look back on those years, Mother must have endured some lonely times, but she never complained. She must have had some very supportive friends in camp. Mother utilized her time in crocheting beautiful tablecloths and doing watercolor paintings and other crafts. In her own mind, she was determined to do battle with the policy of evacuation and internment. She was determined to stay at the Amache Relocation Center in Colorado until its closure. She said that the government put her in camp, and thus she was going to stay and live off of the government until the bitter end and she did! My mother joined me in Chicago in September, 1945. She continued to live and work in Chicago until her retirement, and lived to the ripe old age of 90.

When World War II ended on August 14, 1945, I was a graduate student at the University of Chicago, and living at International House. Within a month after the end of the war, I began to look for an apartment so that my mother could relocate and join me in Chicago. Fortunately, a Nisei friend of mine, Frank Miyamoto, received a Ph.D. in Sociology from the University of Chicago and accepted an appointment at the University of Washington about the same time I was looking for an apartment. His place was ideally located, close to public transportation—the Illinois Central and the elevated—and two blocks from the University of Chicago. What perfect timing for both of us!

After receiving a Master of Arts degree from the University of Chicago, I began to look for a job. I remember sending resumes; I wrote letters to the international division of the Chamber of Commerce. The executive at the Chamber of Commerce took me under his wing and tried to help me. One of the first interviews was with the Alsdorf Import and Export Company which exported Cory coffee brewers as well as other kitchen appliances. I was hired as a trainee to become an export manager. At the time, I thought I could combine my backgrounds in International Relations and Business Administration. But, after working six months, I decided that I did not belong in the business world. The ethics and morality of a corporation selling faulty equipment or making an "extra buck" at the expense of people's health or the environment were despicable to me.

From 1946 to 1949, I took a job as a research assistant for the Committee to Frame a World Constitution at the University of Chicago. This Committee's Executive Director was Professor G.A. Borgese, an Italian scholar of Dante who had fled Italy in the 1930's during the dictatorship of Benito Mussolini. The Committee consisted of Robert Hutchins, President of the University of Chicago; Robert Redfield, an anthropologist at the University of Chicago; William Benton, publisher of Encyclopedia Britannica; and scholars from Stanford University, Columbia University, and Yale University. Elizabeth Mann Borgese, Harris Wofford, and several others were research associates. Research papers and monographs addressing constitutional issues were published and distributed to the Committee members and the public. Periodically, the Committee met in Chicago to discuss, clarify, and reflect on cultural, political, social and economic issues, in the context of what would be desirable in a world constitution. The idealism, the life style, and the cosmopolitan nature of the staff were invigorating and indeed most challenging.

In 1949, I resigned from the Committee and returned to graduate school in Far Eastern Studies at the University of Michigan. After two years of course work, I was awarded a Traveling Fellowship from the Center for Japanese Studies to conduct field work for my dissertation. Hence, I left for Japan in 1952 for one year. I interviewed 45 Japanese American renunciants in Okayama Prefecture at the Center for Japanese Studies' field station, located in Okayama City. Originally, I intended to do a comparative study of renunciants in five different prefectures, but my advisor felt that it was too ambitious. As the weeks and months went by, I agreed with him.

The year's sojourn to Japan was very fruitful. In addition to research, the Center family was frequently invited to a variety of seasonal celebrations and cultural events, such as *kabuki*, *noh*, *bunraku*, and many festivals. Some contacts developed into real

Gladys Stone basking in the sun on the shore of a lake near the University of Michigan campus, 1951.

Gladys Stone with her fellow graduate students in front of Angell Hall at the University of Michigan in Ann Arbor, Michigan, circa 1950.

friendships, and, therefore, we were invited to attend weddings, funerals, and traditional tea ceremony (*chanoyu*), as well as to experience Zen cuisine (*shojin ryori*) at a Zen temple. Indeed, a year's stay in a foreign country enables an exposure to four seasons and various ethnic holidays. As a Nisei, I had opportunities to visit with relatives, which resulted in a close bond with them. My parents were the only ones who immigrated to the United States. As a consequence, all my cousins, aunts, and uncles live in Japan, though some have visited me in the United States in recent years.

Gladys Stone at a traditional Japanese dinner in Okayama City,
Okayama Prefecture, Japan, 1952.

Gladys Stone attired in traditional kimono
in Kitsuki Town, Oita Prefecture, Japan, 1951.

On my return home I took the long way via Europe. I traveled on a Dutch freighter, leaving from Kobe, Japan for Rotterdam, the Netherlands. There are advantages and disadvantages of freighter travel. It stops to pick up freight wherever it is scheduled. Thus, the passengers do not know precisely where it will be stopping to pick up freight at the time of booking their trip. For example, I anticipated visiting Calcutta or Bombay, India, but, instead, from Hong Kong, we went to the Philippines—first to Manila and then to the Island of Cebú. Fortunately, I could look up a friend in Manila; she was a chum from graduate school at the University of Chicago. Helena and her husband entertained us royally. We visited the Presidential Palace and museums, and saw water buffaloes, their beasts of burden. Ruins of World War II still existed. I was struck with the poverty—so many young beggars; it was difficult to go shopping with so many beggars following us.

From Cebú, we went directly to Aden, Yemen, since the ship was full with cargo. We took on fuel, then proceeded to go through the Suez Canal. My friends and I decided to disembark at the Town of Suez and took a Thomas Cook tour which enabled us to travel by

Gladys Stone aboard the Ryndam on her way back from her dissertation research in Japan, 1954.

324

land to see the pyramids, Cairo, and Alexandria. Since we had three or four days for sightseeing, we could spend considerable time at the British Museum, where I ran into another friend who worked at the Oriental Institute in Chicago. What a small world!

Embarking from Alexandria, we headed for Genoa, Italy, the birthplace of Christopher Columbus. After the four of us toured Genoa, two friends decided to travel together and left for Venice. Louise Antonou and I left for Rome, Naples, and Florence. We decided that it was easier for two people than for four to travel together. There was much to see in Rome and Vatican City: the churches, museums, the ruins of the Holy Roman Empire, etc. For an American, it is remarkable to see how these structures have withstood the ravages of weather and time.

In Italy, the serendipity of running into fellow students and former colleagues was extraordinary. I could not have planned these

Gladys Stone with the captain of the Ryndam at the dinner table on her way back from Japan via Europe, 1954.

encounters any better. In Rome, I ran into a Japanese law student who was a colleague at the University of Michigan; he was returning home via Europe. We had an opportunity to get together for supper to exchange our experiences and to get caught up. In Florence, I had the pleasure of having lunch with a former colleague, the youngest daughter of Thomas Mann, a German writer. Her home was located close to the Medici summer home, which overlooked the Arno Valley where the famous 442nd Regimental Combat Team had fought so courageously during World War II.

As student travelers, we stayed at inexpensive pensions or student housing, such as the American House in Paris. I remember distinctly my roommate remarking how wonderful the hot showers felt during our stay at the American House. In the 1950's, the pensions in France usually had old-fashioned tubs; often hot water did not come from the tap. Water was boiled in a large pot in the kitchen and poured into the tub, so it took a while to have enough hot water to bathe. Before we went out for the day, we made reservations for a bath.

So many people rave about Paris, but I enjoyed Rome far more than Paris to this day. Louise and I took the various tours, and then proceeded to travel south to Nancy and Grasse, where we visited unique castles and palaces.

Soon, I would embark for home, so we spent a few days in London, where we called friends and were able to visit with them. Of course, we went on some of the tours, including the historical buildings, theaters, museums, and Cambridge and Oxford Universities.

By late December of 1953, I was ready to embark on the Holland America Line from Rotterdam to return to the United States. I have vivid memories of the New Year's Eve celebration on board the rolling ship. It was a venturesome affair.

Taking the long way home for two and a half months enabled me to appreciate the diversity of peoples and cultures in Asia, the Middle East, and Western Europe. If it had not been for the evacuation and subsequent Midwestern and Eastern exposure, I do not know whether I would have taken risks or been curious about other cultures, or whether I would have had the courage to get involved with human beings different from my background.

Soon after my return to the United States in mid-January 1954, I had to find a part-time job and finish my dissertation. My mother gave me tremendous support, emotionally and financially; how many mothers would have supported such a venture of traveling overseas alone? I guess Mother trusted me. There was no way out but to complete the thesis. Thus, in 1956, I completed my degree.

Shortly before finishing my Ph.D., I applied for a job with the American Friends Service Committee (AFSC) in Chicago. This service organization did so much to help and comfort the evacuees during the Japanese American evacuation and internment. I wanted the satisfaction of returning their generosity and kindness extended to the evacuees. I did get the job in their college program. It required travel to the States of Illinois, Wisconsin, and Minnesota. My job involved setting up programs, symposiums, panel discussions, and conferences on non-violence, pacifism, humanness, Quaker values, and questions of ethics and morality, and recruitment for the AFSC's summer projects.

A year of serving the AFSC was an enriching experience, but after a year, I had to decide whether or not I should continue for another year. In consultation with close friends, I decided to give academia a try. Since 1957, I have had appointments at a number of colleges and universities: University of Wisconsin—Stevens Point, University of California at Los Angeles, Augsburg College, University of Minnesota, and University of Wisconsin—River Falls. I have taught or carried on research for 30 years. I retired in 1987 and am a Professor Emeritus of Sociology at the University of Wisconsin—River Falls.

Professor Emeritus Gladys Stone chatting with her colleague during her retirement party at the Uniersity of Wisconsin-River Falls, 1987.

My first academic appointment was at the University of Wisconsin—Stevens Point as Assistant Professor in Sociology and Political Science from 1957 to 1960 and Associate Professor from 1960 to 1962. From 1961 to 1962, I was the chairperson of the Department of History and the Social Sciences, simply because the men in the department were so factionalized that it was difficult to conduct business at hand.

The five years at the University of Wisconsin—Stevens Point was an extraordinary learning experience for me. There were congenial colleagues with whom I had stimulating conversations on many facets of life. Specifically, these friends helped me understand the politics of the department, the various factions, and how they were likely to vote on certain issues. I thus learned how to plan strategies for certain issues.

In 1962, I left the University of Wisconsin—Stevens Point for Minneapolis, Minnesota, where my *fiancé* was teaching at the University of Minnesota. Gregory P. Stone and I were married in

1962 in Chicago. My family—mother and two brothers—lived there. Since Greg and I had attended the University of Chicago, though not at the same time, we had friends in the Chicago area. Greg studied there in the postwar period on the G.I. Bill. He earned a Ph.D. in Sociology during the heyday of the department. I received my Master's degree in International Relations in 1946. When we were married, Greg was an Associate Professor of Sociology at the University of Minnesota. Within a few years, he was promoted to Professor with tenure.

We settled in Minnesota, partly because we both had tenure at our respective universities. We both liked the populist quality of political life. The people were friendly and easy to meet and were accessible. Our family enjoyed the outdoors and sports. Minnesota was a perfect take-off place for the wilderness for camping, fishing, and hunting.

Both of my children live in the Twin Cities. My son, Mead, works for Cub Foods as Director of Targeting. My daughter, Susan, is employed as a client accountant at Ruhr/Paragon, Inc., an advertising agency. Altogether I have four grandchildren.

Between 1962 and 1965, I had an appointment as Associate Research Sociologist with the Japanese American Research Project (JARP), located at the University of California at Los Angeles. However, I worked out of the basement of our home in Minneapolis. The object of the JARP was to obtain national data involving a stratified sample of Issei before they died off. Every Japanese American Citizens League chapter in the United States was asked to compile a list of Issei names and addresses in their community. In my mind, it was necessary to interview Issei from the upper, middle, and lower strata living on the West Coast, in the Midwest, and on the East Coast.

Next, a questionnaire was constructed which would examine a variety of regional experiences, gender differences, professional/job history, etc. Because the Issei were a dying generation, the questionnaire was an instrument which would explore and acquire as ex-

tensive facets of their lives as possible. It was a very long questionnaire which required many hours to administer.

Ordinarily, a research project hires trained interviewers, but
the Japanese American Research Project required bilingual skills.
Wherever JACL chapters were located, the JARP recruited bilingual
volunteers who were willing to be trained. Among one of my responsibilities was to train these bilingual volunteers. In my career,
this period of my life was an exhilarating one, in spite of the tremendous travel schedule.

In late 1964, my husband was invited to present a paper at the
International Sports Conference at Warsaw, Poland. Our family decided that it was the last chance for our son to travel with his parents.
Hence, on our way to the conference, we took this trip as an opportunity to visit seven cities in Western Europe: London, Brussels, Paris,
Copenhagen, Cologne, Amsterdam, and Warsaw. In three weeks, we
visited the highlights of the cities—churches, museums, government
buildings, universities, retail shops, etc. Warsaw intrigued us; the
churches were being restored so meticulously. Yet, it was a communist country at that time. Another phenomenon was the memorial for
600,000 Jews who were killed during World War II.

In my academic life, one of the most memorable research
trips was to spend six weeks with the Sanema Indians in Venezuela,
45 miles from the Brazilian border. My husband received a grant
from the University of Minnesota's Institute of International Studies
to study the play of Sanema children in the summer of 1969. Mean-
while, I became interested in the role of women in the Sanema culture. I accompanied and participated with them. I went to their farms,
gathered firewood, went fishnetting, watched their cooking, and observed how they took care of their children.

In the early period of our residence in the Indian village, the
four of us on the research team had to find a way of learning some
basic Sanema language. Henri, a French artist residing in Venezuela, drew a picture of a man and a woman with children, then asked

Dr. Gladys Stone and her late husband, Dr. Gregory Stone,
showing off the marlin they caught off the Venezuelan coast, 1969.

for the Sanema words. In this way, we learned nouns but encountered difficulties with verbs and tenses. Non-verbal communication helped, but not totally. Counting numbers in their system was another challenge, because it was one, two and more than two. We managed to accumulate several hundred words with which to communicate with them.

Toward the end of our stay in the Sanema village, we began to appreciate these people, not as primitive people, but as human beings. Of course, they were as curious about us as we were about them. We participated in their activities and in their daily lives, interpreting their behavior as we observed them.

In this Sanema village, it was very difficult for us to achieve privacy. We slept in hammocks like they did. By daylight, however, they came to "hang out" around our hut to check us out. They were fascinated with books with photos and pictures.

One midday, my husband and I thought that the villagers were all working and doing their chores. This would be our chance to bathe and shampoo our hair. We thought we went quite a distance from the village along the river. As we proceeded to bathe and shampoo, heads and bodies popped out of the bushes. The young folks noticed that we were using shampoo for our hair, and they wanted a sample to wash their hair, too. Our supply of shampoo dwindled! For the duration of our stay in the village, we never succeeded in achieving complete privacy from curious onlookers.

Reflections

As I reflect in 1992, it's been 50 years since the Japanese Americans and resident alien Japanese were forced to evacuate from the West Coast and interned in concentration camps. This event has been considered one of the most shameful episodes of our history, not only for Japanese Americans but for all Americans, which blatantly violated our Constitution, especially the democratic ideals for which our country was founded. More recently, historians, sociologists, and Asian/Pacific scholars, now having access to heretofore classified materials, have made revelations about pernicious policies and forces which had led to the passage of racially discriminatory laws in the early 1940's.

Even before the forced evacuation and internment in 1942, one of the most striking denials of Civil Rights was directed against the Japanese resident aliens (Issei) who were ineligible for citizenship under U.S. naturalization law. Likewise, the California Legislature enacted the Alien Land Law in 1913, which resulted in widespread deprivation of civil rights. This legislation prohibited "a Japanese alien ineligible for citizenship from acquiring, possessing, enjoying, using, cultivating, occupying, transferring, transmitting, inheriting real property or having in whole or part directly or indirectly any beneficial interest therein." (Japanese American Citizens League, *Brief of Amicus Curiae, Japanese American Citizens League, in Support of Contention of Appellant Sue Ishida* (Filed with the District Court of Appeal, State of California, Third Appellate District, 3

Civil No. 8946, September 5, 1957, pp. 14-15). Both of these laws had egregious consequences on Issei like my father who was an entrepreneur and dreamed of owning land in America since he was eight years old.

For the 23 years of my father's life in the United States, he was a successful agriculturist and was considered a leader in his community. But because of these two pieces of legislation, my father could never fulfill his dream of acquiring title to a piece of California land. Finally, in 1952, and thanks to the Japanese American Citizens League (JACL) and other Japanese American leaders, Congress passed the Walter-McCarran Act abolishing racial barriers to naturalization. By 1952, furthermore, both the U.S. Supreme Court and California Supreme Court ruled that the Alien Land Law was unconstitutional. For my father, these changes were much too late, but, at least, Japanese can now purchase land and become naturalized citizens of the United States. In the past 50 years, our country has made some changes at the behest of organizations such as the Japanese American Citizens League, the American Civil Liberties Union (ACLU), and other civil rights groups.

Urged by the Japanese American leadership, our country has tried to rectify the wrongs of wartime evacuation and internment. President Gerald R. Ford signed a proclamation rescinding Executive Order 9066. His proclamation stated in part: "Not only was evacuation wrong, but Japanese Americans were and are loyal Americans ... We have learned from the tragedy of that long-ago experience forever to treasure liberty and justice for each individual American and resolve that this kind of action shall never again be repeated." In the future, I hope that no other ethnic or minority group shall ever go through such experiences as the Japanese did during World War II.

In addressing the issue of redress, the JACL successfully organized a campaign to have President Jimmy Carter and Congress establish in 1980 a Commission on Wartime Relocation and Internment of Civilians. In 1981 the Commission conducted a series of regional meetings to record the testimony of Japanese Americans

333

who were interned during World War II. It took another seven years before President Ronald Reagan signed the Civil Liberties Act (redress bill) into law on August 10, 1988. My mother was eligible to receive $20,000 in personal compensation as provided by the Act, but she passed away six weeks before the redress check arrived.

Curiously, my mother remained in Amache for the duration of the war (1942-45), but she encouraged all three of her children to leave camp and go to college. Apparently, she did not want us to waste precious time; she perceived some manifestations of negative family values in camp over which she had no control. I believe she thought that college was likely to exert a more powerful influence on us than stagnating in camp.

Throughout her internment, my mother maintained the moral and ethical values that sustained her all her life. She was quite a feminist; she had a mind of her own. She was well-read for her times. In camp, she took up interest in arts and crafts. She attended classes in crocheting, sculpturing lamp bases, and water color painting. Even after relocating to Chicago and in retirement, she attended classes in oil painting at the Chicago Art Institute; she liked Van Gogh.

Gladys Stone's mother, Suye Ishida, with her son, Julius, and his cousin, Noriko Watanabe, in Chicago, Illinois, circa 1985. She passed away a few months before receiving reparation for her unconstitutional wartime evacuation and internment.

Even though my mother was extremely disappointed with the financial settlement of the fruit orchard, she never lost the purpose of her life. She lived long enough to become an American citizen in 1954.

I was one of those Nisei students who left Amache for college in time for the fall semester 1942. I was glad to be released from camp, but felt a tremendous burden to do well, not only for myself, but to be a good representative of Japanese Americans.

In St. Louis, we were received and accepted with warmth and caring by representatives of the Campus YMCA. At the Washington University campus, I lived at MacMillan Hall, a women's dormitory. Its residents were friendly and accepted us with kindness. As we made friends, they invited us to their parents' home during the holidays and on special occasions. Other kind folks became our surrogate families during our residence in St. Louis. It was a very hectic period of my life; I did not have the luxury of getting homesick!

As I reflect now, I think what made the difference in our St. Louis relocation experience was two people, Dean of Women Adele Starbird and Arno Haack, the Campus Director of the YMCA. They were both extraordinary human beings who cared so much and provided Nisei students with time and all kinds of assistance. They offered friendship and understanding—a triumph of the human spirit.

The forced evacuation and internment broadened my view of the world. Before this, the trips I took were with my family. Thus, traveling from the Merced Assembly Center to the Amache Relocation Center in Colorado, under protective custody, was an immense undertaking for a rural-based, small town girl. It was scary. I was apprehensive, but, at the same time, I felt a sense of adventure and independence. I believe this initial experience of having to travel to college in the Midwest gave me exposure to a wide range of ethnic, racial, and minority peoples. Meeting these individuals was a source of enlightenment. After being deprived of my civil rights, I became more aware of racial and peace issues. For over 50 years, I have continued to be concerned with injustices; therefore, I support volunteer efforts in these areas.

However, racism has not abated, homicides have increased, and prisons have become overpopulated. It seems as though understanding of the human condition has not improved much in the last 50 years. Instead, we continue to stereotype people without knowing one another as human beings. The United States is made up of fascinating native-born citizens, immigrants, refugees, settlers, and undocumented immigrants, who make up the land of the free. And as we must negotiate on a global level, we must be able to communicate and be understood.

In spite of the wartime incarceration of the Japanese Americans, understanding Americans who were opposed to the evacuation policy provided support and relief to the evacuees. Among these peace-loving and fair-minded people were the Quakers who were generous and helped relieve the monotony of camp life; they provided news from the outside world. They visited some of the camps regularly and provided homey things such as cookies, sugared nuts, glazed fruits, and other items not found in the camp stores. For the evacuee friends, these good-hearted Caucasian visitors provided hope and caring at a time when disillusionment and despair prevailed.

Another group of Americans who had the foresight and courage to act upon their beliefs was the educators, namely, the presidents of colleges and universities on the West Coast. These leaders recognized the necessity of rescuing a generation of bright Japanese American students numbering some 3,800. Soon after the Executive Order 9066 was announced, the educators, together with the leaders of religious and civil rights groups, called a series of meetings from early March through May 1942. They worked very rapidly and decided to establish the National Student Relocation Council (NSRC). Under the able leadership of Clarence Pickett, this organization raised funds for scholarships and administrative expenses. The NSRC did all the paperwork to enable the Japanese American students to matriculate at colleges in the Midwest and East. Some Nisei students were placed in Ivy League universities. A dream became reality for some, thanks to the efforts of the NSRC. What would our lives have been like if it had not been for these foresighted EDUCATORS?

Marriage brought me to Minnesota. My late husband, Gregory, was an Associate Professor in the Department of Sociology at the University of Minnesota when we married. I taught at the University of Wisconsin—Stevens Point in the Department of Sociology and served as chairperson of the Department of History and the Social Sciences. I resigned the position as Associate Professor to live in the Twin Cities. Concurrently, I began a new position as a Research Associate for the Japanese American Research Project located at the University of California, Los Angeles. I worked out of my residence with frequent trips to UCLA. I was with the project for three years until I returned to teaching again.

For us, settling down in Minnesota was a good choice, because it is a state with a populist tradition. We have participated on the local level, meeting and working with the likes of Walter Mondale, Hubert H. Humphrey, George Latimer, Don Fraser, city council members, etc. We found people to be friendly and helpful. The school system was a good one, where innovation and creativity were encouraged. I also like the Twin Cities because philanthropy provides the community with support for the arts, theater, and music, proportionately more than New York. Furthermore, my husband and family enjoyed the outdoor sports, and Minnesota accorded many camping areas, and deer hunting, fishing, and boating opportunities. It is not difficult to take off for the wilderness in Canada.

In the past, I have stated elsewhere that Minnesota's Japanese American community is different from its counterparts in other parts of the United States. Since it is a small group, the Japanese American community participates in a variety of civic and community activities. It is not quite as parochial as other communities with a larger Japanese American population. Hence, these activities provide us with opportunities to reach out for contacts in the wider community, and to work on projects alongside majority members of American society.

MAYE
MITSUYE OYE
UEMURA

For 21 years, my father, Inokichi Oye, lived in a small mountain village named Takasu, Maebaru-machi in Fukuoka Prefecture, Japan. I had always been told of its beauty, and I discovered in July 1992 that indeed it is a beautiful spot. His father was a rice farmer, and my father worked on his farm in the rice paddies. His education was limited because he was needed on the farm, but he educated himself by reading newspapers and writing letters.

At the age of 21, in the year 1900, he set out for America by steamboat and arrived in Seattle, Washington, on May 8, 1900. Upon his arrival, he began working for the railroad, building tracks, along with other Japanese men like himself. From there, he went into logging with some friends.

After working seven years, he had saved enough money and it was time for him to think about sending for a wife. Through a "go-between," a marriage was arranged for him with a young woman from a neighboring village. My mother, Tao Nakamura, who was selected for him, was almost the same age as my father. She was a daughter of a rice farmer, and also grew up working in the rice paddies.

My mother had a very difficult trip on the steamboat, and arrived in Seattle on April 27, 1907. The wedding took place on

May 4, 1907. My mother and father started their life together in the logging camp. People who worked together, especially immigrants, lived communally, much like the migrant workers of today.

For immigrants like my father, it was a matter of saving enough money to move on to the next step. Thus, when my father had adequate funds, he started a sawmill business with two brothers, also from Fukuoka. Funds were embezzled by one of the brothers, however, and the business failed. After that, he went to work for the Hillsdale Fuel Yard, which was a business that cut wood and sold it by the cord for fuel.

By this time, some of the Japanese had settled on truck farms in Troutdale, Oregon. Many of these people were from the same village as my parents, and they had become friends. Consequently, my father went to work for them for a few years. Farming was what he knew and he seemed drawn to it.

One of these close friends had helped him financially in his business venture. This friend decided to move to Independence, Oregon, to start a berry farm of his own. My father wanted to repay him and help him in his new venture, so he moved to Independence with him. He got a job on an adjacent hop farm and worked there for two or three years until the debt was repaid.

By this time, it was time for him to think of ways to establish himself. He decided to be a truck farmer. So, in 1925, he moved to a small community outside Salem, Oregon, to work for Mr. Fukuda, who ran a truck farm. He worked for this man in order to learn about truck farming. In a couple of years, he was able to lease his own land, adjacent to Mr. Fukuda's, and started farming on his own. The major crop was celery, along with various other vegetables. This is where the family settled and lived until World War II.

In the preceding years, my mother had seven pregnancies but only two surviving children. Due to poor medical facilities, the children who were born before my brother and myself did not live beyond their first year. My brother and I were the last two to be born and the only two to survive.

When my parents lived in Independence, Oregon, I came into the family. It was on the 23rd day of February in the year 1923. When I was two years old, my family moved to the farm near Salem,

Maye Uemura with her brother, Tom Oye, in Salem, Oregon, circa 1930.

Oregon, mentioned earlier. I grew up in this small farm community, mostly among other Japanese people, until we were forced to leave in 1942.

As a small child, I spoke only Japanese, because neither my mother nor father spoke English. I don't remember how I learned English, but I suspect I learned it from my brother who was older than I. Also, two Nisei neighbor girls who were older than I took me under their wings, and I learned a great deal from them, including English.

Ours was a simple life and I had what I consider a happy childhood. I grew up wandering the woods and countryside by our home. I loved spring, when we could go into the woods and find all kinds of wild flowers. In the summer, we had fun picking wild berries and nuts. We played simple games that required little or no equipment.

I attended elementary school in a small, four-room rural school called Keizer. I loved school. It opened up a whole new world for me. I had new friends who were non-Japanese, and I had the opportunity to learn so many new things about the world.

I was conscious of being Japanese, but the other children did not make me feel that way. It came out in little ways. For example, we had to fill out charts in my grade school days, indicating our nutritional and health habits. We were required to write down our breakfast menu for the week. I was embarrassed that my breakfast was different than those of my friends. Our breakfast of rice and *misoshiru* (Japanese soup) certainly was different from the oatmeal and cornflakes my Caucasian friends may have had. I reasoned, however, that rice was cereal, and the egg in the *misoshiru* was no different than their fried egg, so I made my chart fit the American menu.

The Caucasian children and I all played together harmoniously. This may be partly due to the fact that teachers in that period had a great deal to do with not only academic training but our moral training as well. They were always with us, and I'm sure they knew each of us very well. They went out at recess with us, and played with us, and taught us how to deal with social relationships.

I went to this elementary school for eight years. The same children, except for an occasional newcomer, were my companions for all these years. Yet, I was not close to any of these children because we had no contact outside of school. Being in a rural area, we were all fairly isolated and there was no going back and forth to play.

From the time I was in second grade, my summers were spent working on the farm, along with my parents and brother. We were poor, and everyone had to do his or her own share. It made for closeness in the family, but at times, as a small child, I wished for more time to play.

Summer was also the time Japanese teachers came to town to run the language school. I was able to attend this school for a half day for a few weeks. I always looked forward to this. It was a time for me to get better acquainted with the other Japanese Americans who lived farther away. I loved learning Japanese and some of the Japanese arts.

In my teen-age years, I attended junior high and high school in the town of Salem. It was an exciting time for me to go from a four-room school to a large school where we attended each of our classes in different rooms with different teachers. I participated in many activities in these schools and studied hard. I felt I was treated well and given an equal opportunity to do almost anything I wanted. I was elected to a few positions which proved to me that the students did not hold race against me.

Although I never experienced direct prejudice during these years, I was well aware of being a Japanese American. We interacted freely with everyone in school, but socially there was no mixing. Perhaps we were at fault. The Nisei grouped themselves together during the lunch hour and study period. This was probably due to the fact that the people we knew well were Nisei because we had contact with each other outside of school. After school, there was no social interaction with Caucasian students.

All of my social activities were centered around the Japanese American Christian Church. The church was a place to gather, not only for worship and study, but for many social activities. Through the church, I met Nisei not only from our town, but from other cities in Oregon and Washington. I found my church experiences very memorable and happy.

After graduating from high school in 1941, I enrolled in Willamette University, a college in town. My father did not think a girl needed a college education, but I was determined and found ways through scholarship and work to enroll.

In college, I found myself mixing much more with Caucasians. We traveled together through speech activities, and through organizations such as the YWCA. We had many activities where we interacted freely without reservation. The one area where I knew I would never be accepted for membership was the sororities. At any rate, I could not afford the membership fee, and did not believe in the exclusiveness of the sororities, so I never tried. Perhaps I avoided any blatant rejection this way. Nonetheless, I had an exciting few months at this college until the war broke out on December 7, 1941.

When the news came that Pearl Harbor had been attacked and war had broken out between Japan and the United States, I was shocked and frightened. It was truly the darkest day of my life. I remember it still, for it was literally a dark and gloomy day, and the fear and depression heightened the gloom. It was one of those days when I felt completely helpless. I was on the Willamette campus at the time. The college football team had just gone to Hawaii to play the University of Hawaii, so concern and fear for the players was tremendous. I felt immediately ostracized. Students with whom I had been friends began gathering in little groups whispering among themselves. I couldn't understand how people could do such an about-face. I was deeply hurt and frightened.

The only ray of light came when the Dean of Freshmen called the school together in an assembly. He talked to the students about the seriousness of the war and the fact that there were several Japanese Americans on campus. He said these students had nothing to do with the war and, indeed, were Americans like the rest of the students. He asked for tolerance and understanding toward the Japanese Americans. I was grateful and relieved that the air had been cleared. Whether the students reasoned the same way or let their emotions take over, someone from the administration had taken a clear stand and I never forgot what Dr. R. Franklin Thompson did. The atmosphere around the campus was definitely more restrained afterwards.

My parents were definitely frightened like they had never been before. It was bad enough when my brother was drafted into the Army a few months before. They were dependent on him for handling their business affairs and marketing some of the vegetables. They were left without this help or transportation. Now, with the war, they had fear for him as well as for themselves and me. They felt helpless and were at the mercy of the U.S. government.

Even before the evacuation orders were issued, our neighbor was taken away as a prisoner of war. No one knew where or why he was taken away. He was a sweet man who could harm no one. There was the lurking question of who would be next or what would happen next.

When the FBI came to search our house, my parents were shaken. They couldn't understand why the agents had come and what they were trying to find. Not understanding anything, my parents didn't even ask for their identification. It was especially difficult for my parents, because they did not understand English too well and these strange men were coming into our home and invading our privacy.

There were only the three of us, since my brother was away in the Army. I was staying in town at the YWCA in order to continue my college education, due to the curfew against Japanese Americans. I was left without transportation, too, with my brother gone. In the YWCA, I lived with three other girls who were not college students. These people were very supportive and sympathetic.

Although things were very uncertain, and all types of wartime restrictions and practices were all around us, I continued with school. We had the curfew, blackouts, sandbags around the buildings, and it was unsettling for everyone. I worked along hoping and praying I would at least complete my first year. Then the evacuation order came. We were to report to the train depot on May 18, 1942. This was three weeks before the term was up. I talked to my professors and each one allowed me to take tests early and complete the term. They were very considerate about it. When my grades came, there was only one teacher who had docked me for leaving early. It was the gym teacher who had reduced my grade for not being in attendance. I was furious at her insensitivity. She knew it was impossible for me to be there, and yet did not excuse me for it.

When one of my friends learned that I would have to leave the state, she gathered a few people together and gave me a send-off. I was very much touched at her generosity and kindness. We are still in touch with each other.

With only a few weeks to get ready for the move, we had to sell all of our household goods and farm equipment. I was now the translator for the family, so I had to go home from college to help make these sales. I remember putting everything in the yard and people coming by to pick up their "bargains." Recently, I ran across a bill of sale for the farm equipment and was appalled to note how little we had gotten for it. Yet, I do know that at the time, there was nothing we could do.

On May 18, 1942, we went to the train station with our few possessions which had been marked with the ID number we had been assigned. We registered again and were given tags to wear before boarding the train. We had absolutely no clue of our destination. It was a strange feeling to board a train and not know where we were going. There was no way to get a clue, for the shades were drawn all the way. We arrived the next morning and saw this camp with tar-papered barracks, surrounded with a barbed wire fence with guard towers. We learned we were in Northern California.

My parents and I found out we were in an internment camp called Tule Lake. It was located in a desert in Northern California.

When we arrived there, the camp had not yet been completely built, so there was much confusion all around. They assigned us to a room in a completed block. The room we were given was 16' x 20' with four army cots and a pot-bellied stove. This was our beginning.

We went to the common mess hall to have our meals. We sat at what looked like picnic tables and were served family style. Our toilet and bath facilities were in a common bath house.

Eventually, we made our barren room look a bit more homey by building our own furniture with the help of a neighbor boy. My father made some benches, a table, screens, and a closet.

The day of our arrival, we were told we could have jobs, so, as tired as I was after the night-long train ride, I went to the administration building to apply. I was given a job as a clerk, which paid $12 a month. My job was to keep a record of the time cards which were turned in. It was a tedious and somewhat pointless job, but I liked the idea of keeping busy. After a few months at this job, I went to work in the warehouse where I kept track of invoices. There, for the first time, I encountered what we now call "harassment" by my Caucasian boss. It was verbal harassment, but I could not stand it and went to the head boss. Surprisingly, my boss was immediately removed from his position. To me this was an indication that there were Caucasian employees in the camp who held the internees in contempt, and of course others who were sensitive to the issue. From there, through one of my ministers, Daisuke Kitagawa, I got a job working for a sociologist, Marvin K. Opler. He had come to the camp to make a sociological study. This was a job I found very satisfying.

Outside of work, I was very involved in the church and the YWCA. I taught Sunday School, sang in the choir, was active in the youth group, and put out the church paper. I was 19 and had never worked with young children before, so it was new to me to be teaching Sunday School. They taught me a great deal. The Youth Group met every Sunday, and we had many interesting programs.

Somehow, the YWCA leader in camp learned of my past connections with the "Y" and recruited me to head a group of young girls. Again, I was totally inexperienced and learned as I went along.

The YWCA and the YMCA had a Spring Conference for the Western Area at Estes Park, Colorado. In their effort to learn about Japanese Americans and to build better relationships, they invited a few of us from camp to attend this conference. Through the efforts of Daisuke Kitagawa, there were five of us who were given permits to leave the camp and go to Colorado. It was a bit scary to leave the camp and head for an area unknown to me. We arrived at Estes without incident, and it was a wonderful experience. We were received warmly, and I felt the students were genuinely open and accepting. I felt very privileged to have been given the opportunity that others did not have.

Aside from these activities, I took classes in sewing and learned a very valuable skill that helped me in later years. Because of all my activities, I was too busy to brood over being in camp.

*Maye Uemura (center) with the Rev. Daisuke Kitagawa (far left)
and other delegates to the YMCA-YWCA Conference
for the Western Area held in Estes Park, Colorado, 1943.*

My father worked with the farm crew, and he enjoyed the companionship of the other workers. He also liked the idea of keeping busy.

In the summer of 1943, due to the controversy arising from the bungled administration of loyalty questionnaires, we were again moved to another camp. We were allowed to choose where we wished to go. We selected Amache, Colorado, because it was a bit closer to Joplin, Missouri, where my brother was stationed in the Army.

Amache was also in the desert, but when we arrived there, we were pleasantly surprised at how home-like the residents had made it. There were flowers in front of some of the barracks. The rooms seemed a bit more cozy.

I was transferred to the same sort of job with a sociologist, John Rademacher. I was not there long, because I had applied for a student leave and had been accepted at McPherson College in McPherson, Kansas.

I left for college in October of 1943. I was late for the fall term, but the professors were very kind and helped me catch up with the rest of the class. I was very well-accepted at the college and made many fine friends, but we were cautioned about going into town where we might not be so well-accepted. Most of the Nisei students stayed close to campus. However, I do recall going to a downtown movie theater one day with another Nisei, and we were required to sit in the balcony. This was where the black people were also required to sit. I never went to a movie again during my stay in McPherson.

I had two jobs while in college. One job was with a woman in town. She was a nurse who needed me to clean her house once a week. She was very kind and appreciative of my work. Her husband, who was home on occasion, was a gruff truck driver with a

Maye Uemura (center) with her fellow Nisei students at McPherson College in McPherson, Kansas, 1944.

booming voice and quite intimidating. He drove the route to Colorado and passed the Amache Relocation Camp regularly. He was very interested in the camp and asked me many questions. I soon learned that once you got beyond the gruff exterior, he was genuinely interested in learning about the internment and the camp.

I also did secretarial work for the Director of the Board of Education of the Church of the Brethren. His office was in his home, across the street from McPherson College. When I reported to work on the first day, his two little sons were playing in the yard. When they saw me approaching the house, they ran into the house shouting, "The Japs are coming." They were genuinely frightened. For some reason, this supposedly educated man had not educated his children about the Japanese American students at the college.

While in college, I was asked to speak in many communities, to educate people about Japanese Americans. I went with other students and faculty, and usually spoke to church groups. They were receptive and interested on the whole.

After a year at McPherson College, I learned that people in the camps would be "relocated" in preparation for camp closing. I was told by the Reverend Daisuke Kitagawa about Yellow Springs, Ohio, and what opportunities were there. I talked this over with my parents and they consented to going there, even though my father wanted to stay in Colorado and work on the sugar beet farms. I thought that at 65, he was too old for this kind of hard labor.

I left the college in Kansas and returned to Amache to help my folks with the move. In the summer of 1944, we arrived in Yellow Springs, Ohio, a small college town of 2,000. As small as the town was, there were already three other Japanese families there. We had never been in the Midwest and were, once again, frightened of the unknown. However, when we arrived in Yellow Springs, we found a group of warm, concerned people, who helped us in every way they could.

Even though he was 65, my father worked as a gardener for the Fels Institute. My mother worked for the Dean of Women at Antioch College as a housekeeper. I worked at the Fels Institute, a Child Development Research Center, as a research assistant.

Maye Uemura's mother, Tao Oye (far right), with her Issei friends in Yellow Springs, Ohio, circa 1946.

I worked at Fels for six months in order to save enough money to return to school. I had applied and was accepted at Ohio Wesleyan University in Delaware, Ohio, where I resumed my education in the second semester in 1945. The classes were very stimulating and the students, on the whole, were friendly and accepting. I became active in the YWCA and as a result had the opportunity to meet people who were interested in discussing current affairs and worldly problems. I went to many conferences, representing the University. I met my husband at one of these conferences.

I studied Sociology and Psychology and was very idealistic about "saving the world" and helping others. By the time I had almost completed my B.A., I decided I didn't know nearly enough, so I made plans to continue my schooling. Selected as University Scholar, I pursued and completed a Master's degree in Clinical Psychology at Ohio State University.

*Maye Uemura with her roommates, Garry, Jeanne
and Esther (left to right), at Ohio Wesleyan
University in Delaware, Ohio, 1946.*

The postwar period brought many changes in my life and took me to many places where I had never expected to be. After receiving my Master's degree at Ohio State University, I went to work for the Children's Home Society in Cincinnati, Ohio, as a psychologist. My job was to evaluate children for adoption and counsel prospective parents. There were no problems of acceptance in my job with the professional people or the clients.

However, Cincinnati was basically a Southern city with segregated housing, buses, and restaurants. It was not a comfortable atmosphere for me. It was the real world that the idealist had to face.

Maye Uemura and her roommate, Phyllis Edwards, at Ohio State University in Columbus, Ohio, 1948.

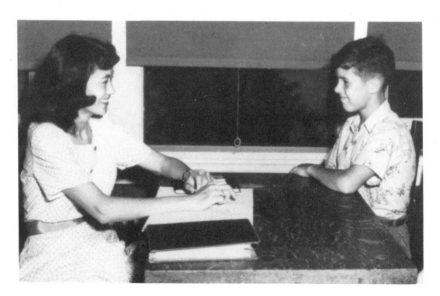

Maye Uemura counseling a boy in her office at the Children's Home Society in Cincinnati, Ohio, 1948.

A group of Japanese Americans had settled in Cincinnati, and as far as I know they were treated well. After the war, the American Friends Service Committee had established a hostel to help the Japanese Americans resettle there. This Quaker group was still active at the time of my move, and I was offered help in looking for housing. As it turned out, I took a room with a kind, elderly lady named Mrs. Diehl, whose only concern was whether I smoked or drank. There was no concern of race or color. She treated me like her daughter.

I had a close college friend, Marie Newby, in Cincinnati, so I participated in activities with her and other friends from college as well. Some activities were serious and political, and others purely social. The Japanese community also provided activities in which I participated. Lorraine Takayama Tokimoto, one of my closest Nisei friends from Oregon, had also relocated to Cincinnati. She took me in, and we did many things together.

I left Cincinnati and my job after one year, because I was married on September 10, 1949, to Joseph Uemura in Yellow Springs, Ohio. We had met as students at the National YMCA-YWCA Conference at Urbana, Illinois, during the Christmas vacation in 1946. He was a student at Denver University in Denver, Colorado, and I was a student at Ohio Wesleyan University in Delaware, Ohio. We corresponded for three years and visited each other three times before our wedding. Because of the great distance, his family could not be with us, but my parents and my brother's family, who lived in Chicago, attended the wedding. Marion Garrison, my roommate and closest friend at Ohio Wesleyan, was my maid of honor. Joe's best man was my brother, Tom Takeshi Oye.

After my marriage, I moved to Denver, Colorado, where my husband was completing a graduate program in Theology while working for the Colorado Conference of the Methodist Church. I worked as a psychologist for the Children's Home Society and as a research assistant for the Child Development Research Center at the University of Colorado Medical School.

Denver was Joe's home. He had grown up there since he was three years old. Most of his family was there, although his parents had moved to Fresno, California, to serve the Japanese Methodist Church. There was a fairly large, close-knit Japanese community there. The Reverend Seijiro Uemura, Joe's father, was the minister of the Japanese Methodist Church from 1929 to 1947, and helped many Japanese Americans from the West Coast and the Relocation Centers resettle in Denver. He worked closely with the Caucasian community and state officials, notably Attorney General Charles Morrissey and Governor Ralph M. Carr, to prepare them for the influx of new Japanese Americans into the State of Colorado. Colorado was the first state, and Governor Carr was the first governor, to announce the acceptance of "evacuees" from the West Coast (Military Area No. One). The Rev. Uemura's relationship with Governor Carr was crucial. Consequently, there was a good relationship between the Japanese American relocatees and the citizens of Colorado. The result for me was an easy adjustment to my new home. Joe's sisters, Maggie, Lillian, and Ethel, all welcomed me into the family.

In the fall of 1950, we moved to New York City because my husband received a fellowship to do graduate work in Philosophy at Columbia University. Neither of us had lived in the East, and especially in a city as large as New York. It was a culture shock at first. Once we got settled, however, we found it very liberating. We got to know people of various cultural backgrounds and all walks of life, with whom we shared a great deal. For instance, for a couple of years, we shared an apartment complex with two other couples, a Czechoslovakian Jewish couple, the Krayks, and another American Jewish couple, the Bakers. We learned a great deal from them in many ways.

While studying at Columbia, Joe worked at the Japanese Methodist Church as an assistant pastor for Dr. Alfred Saburo Akamatsu. We had a good time working with the young people and the Sunday School in the Church. I worked as a research assistant at the New York University Medical School for Dr. Donald Mainland. I met some very fine people there and enjoyed my work very much.

In spite of the reputation New Yorkers have of being rude and impersonal, we met some very kind people. We were impecunious students and many people were very helpful and considerate.

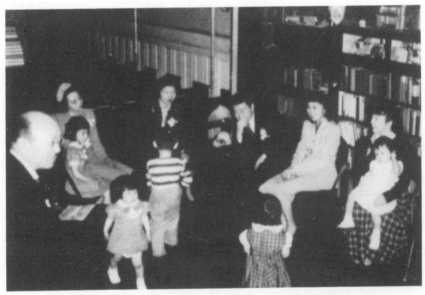

Joseph and Maye Uemura (center) with Dr. Alfred Akamatsu and members of his congregation at the Japanese Methodist Church in New York City, 1951.

Maye Uemura with her Sunday School children at the Japanese Methodist Church in New York City, 1952.

For instance, when I became quite ill with rheumatoid arthritis shortly after our arrival in that city, I received excellent medical treatment free of charge. I had the name of a well-known arthritis specialist, Dr. Joseph Bunim, because my former boss, Dr. Marsh in Denver, had suggested that I contact him. When I went to his office on Park Avenue, I knew it was someone we could not afford. However, he told me about his experimental program at Bellevue Hospital which would cost nothing. A group of doctors were trying to find a treatment for the disease, and were testing many things on patients, such as gold salts, blue dye, steroids, and the new drugs, ACTH and cortisone. Thus I chose to become a "guinea pig." Only after these experiments was cortisone given approval for general medical use in America. I remained in the hospital for three months, and, in the long run, it was an excellent treatment for me.

Our son, Wesley Makoto, was born in New York City. The experimental group was delighted, not knowing if the treatment would affect pregnancy. But again, we would be helped substantially, being charged only a minimal fee by a very prominent Fifth Avenue doctor, Dr. Ronald Gepfert. Our hospital fees at New York Hospital were also a minimum. Furthermore, Dr. John Franklin, our pediatrician, gave us an excellent treatment at minimal cost because we were connected with the research group and were graduate students. We never expected such treatment in this "heartless metropolis!"

When Wesley was nine months old, and we had been in New York for three years, Joe was offered a teaching position at Westminster College, an inter-denominational Protestant college in Salt Lake City, Utah. Dr. Richard Palmer, his friend from Colorado days, had become the president of the college and thought of Joe. The West was familiar to us and the prospect of rearing a child in New York City was a bit daunting, so we made the move. Going to a small college community made the adjustment easy for us. Dr. Palmer personally saw to it that we felt at home and part of the college family.

Maye Uemura with her son, Wesley, in front of their new house in Salt Lake City, Utah, 1953.

Joe was very busy at the college and in the community. I did some teaching at the college, and along with an old Cincinnati friend, Jean Van Dilla, organized a cooperative nursery school and taught there. Wesley went to nursery school with me.

While we were in Salt Lake City, my parents came to live with us from Yellow Springs, Ohio, by reason of their poor health. They liked it there because there was a Japanese community in Salt Lake City. They made friends and were able to visit other Issei for the first time in a long time.

Salt Lake City had a beautiful physical setting, and in many ways it was a pleasant place to live. However, it is a predominantly Mormon city, and we were not Mormons. There were constant pressures from the Mormon Church permeating all aspects of life in the city. We were in a college community of like-minded people, but in the community as a whole, we felt ostracized and discriminated against, both racially and religiously. We could see that it would be very difficult for our son in a predominantly Mormon community. Mormon students reported Joe many times to their Ward Bishops for his teachings which were not all in compliance with the Mormon doctrines. We did not find much neighborliness from our Mormon neighbors.

When we decided to leave Salt Lake City in 1959, after being there six years, we had a very difficult time, for instance, selling our house. We concluded finally that it was because we had a Protestant realtor.

Maye Uemura with her parents, Inokichi and Tao Oye,
in Yellow Springs, Ohio, 1953.

We moved to Sioux City, Iowa, where Joe was offered another teaching position at Morningside College, again by President Palmer who had moved there. We were virtually the only Japanese American family in Sioux City, except for a couple of warbrides from Japan. We were a novelty at first, and people went out of their way to be nice to us. However, it was difficult for my parents to make the move, because they knew there would be no Japanese community in Sioux City. The only consolation for them was that they were a bit closer to Chicago where my brother Tom and his family were living. They managed to adjust to a somewhat isolated life. They did get around the neighborhood, and people got to know them and were very thoughtful and kind.

For my own family, it was much easier to get acquainted, for the college community was there to welcome us and help us get resettled. Our son enrolled in the second grade without any problems. Joe became very involved in college life, as well as in the church and community.

I worked as a public school psychologist and a counselor at Morningside College. I was also involved in college life, and the church, and various community activities. We had a very good time in Sioux City, and made many close and lifelong friends there. Our daughter, Charissa Keiko, was born there on August 30, 1963.

Seven years later, Hamline University in St. Paul, Minnesota, offered my husband a faculty position. We thought it was an exciting prospect to move back to a metropolitan area, where there would be more cultural and educational opportunities for our children. The position itself was a new challenge for Joe. We also looked forward to the fact that there was a Japanese community in the Twin Cities area. Consequently, we made the move in August of 1966.

For my parents, also, it was a good move. Coincidentally, my brother, Tom Oye, and his family were moving to Minnesota at exactly the same time. This meant that for the first time since the War, my parents would be in the same community as their son. They were also happy that they would be able to be with other Japanese once again.

After we decided on the move, we came to Minnesota one weekend to look for housing. At that time, we felt one of the realtors we contacted showed us only certain kinds of houses in certain areas. Finally, we found a house ourselves, through a newspaper ad, that we wanted to see. Unlike the other real estate agent, the realtor connected with this house was nice and accommodating. He knew we were from out of town, and even offered us supper in his home before we returned to Sioux City.

So, we settled in a fairly new neighborhood in Roseville. We were welcomed warmly by our neighbors and made to feel at home. We joined the Centennial United Methodist Church nearby and even found three Japanese families to be members there, the Itos, the Sembas and the Tanis. Wesley now was in the ninth grade, and it was a great change for him. But he made new friends through his sports activities, as well as through the church and school. Regrettably, the Japanese community being scattered throughout the Twin Cities, he did not meet many Sansei. Nevertheless, there seemed to be a new challenge in the schools. Charissa was three and eager for playmates, too. There were several in the neighborhood, one of whom was Shannon Schroeder. She is still among my daughter's closest pals. Charissa also enrolled in one of the first Twin Cities Montessori schools, and she liked it immensely.

I got a job teaching at the Red Robin Nursery School. I taught there for 12 years and liked having this long-term relationship. I got to know the children and their parents and still see them from time to time in the community. The director, Ethel Graham, and the teachers with whom I taught over the years, keep in close touch. We have a get-together twice a year.

After my retirement from the nursery school, I went to work for the Deluxe Corporation and stayed there for ten years. I found there a warm friendly atmosphere and a genuine concern for each individual employee, something I did not expect in a big corporation. I attribute this to a very caring plant manager, Frank Matchina. His care contributed to inculcating the same sort of attitude in the employees.

Our move to Minnesota and settling here has been, I think, the right thing for me and my family. We have lived for 25 years in the same house in Roseville. Many of our current neighbors are the same people that were here when we moved in. Our children went through high school here and got a good education. We have all been enriched with good theater, music, and art. We have enjoyed the cultural events and the opportunity to learn a bit of the Japanese arts. My daughter, Charissa, and I have taken some lessons in Japanese brush painting from Reiko Shellum.

We changed our membership to the Hennepin Avenue United Methodist Church in Minneapolis, because of their fine educational program. We have been members and have attended church there for 22 years. My parents lived and died in Minnesota and are buried at the Lakewood Mausoleum. My husband has been teaching for 25 years at Hamline University. It is his longest term of teaching at one college, and it is the longest we have lived anywhere, so we feel this is our home.

Minnesota is home for our children also. Charissa, our daughter, is a photographer and has settled in St. Paul. Wesley, our son, returned to Minnesota for a few years after college, and is at present a graduate student at Cornell University in Ithaca, New York. He considers Roseville, Minnesota, his home base.

Maye Uemura flanked by her son, Wesley, and his wife, Makiko, while visiting her paternal relatives' rice farm in Takasu, Maebaru-machi, Fukuoka, Japan, 1992.

Maye Uemura (center) with her paternal relatives in front of their family home in Takasu, Maebaru-machi, Fukuoka, Japan, 1992.

Reflections

Many times, I have pondered the question of how I was affected by World War II. As I reflect back on my childhood and youth, I see myself as an extremely naive person.

I grew up believing in the flag, the Preamble, and the Constitution of the United States. In the four-room elementary school that I attended for eight years, we stood by our desks each morning, saluted and crossed our chests, and pledged our allegiance to the flag. I memorized the Preamble and studied the Constitution, and particularly the Bill of Rights. I took great pride in it. It was impressed upon our young minds that we lived in a democracy and the Constitution was what we lived by.

My parents lived in this country respecting the presidents of this country. In our living room, we had a big poster with pictures of all the presidents with their names and dates of service. I loved that poster. I studied it and memorized the names of all the presidents from George Washington on.

I had grown up feeling secure. I believed in freedom and justice, love and friendship. When the United States declared war on Japan on December 7, 1941, everything was immediately changed. It was as though the world had come tumbling down on me. I found my so-called "friends" gathering in groups and whispering behind my back. I realized that the war had made me an instant "enemy." There was no rational explanation for it. It was only that I was a Japanese American. However, the American part had been forgotten and ignored.

I realized then that things would be difficult for me, my family, and everyone of Japanese ancestry. However, I never dreamed that in a democracy, the government created on the principle of checks and balances could issue an order to remove an entire group of Japanese Americans from the West Coast without due process of law. I never dreamed that all of our property and possessions could be confiscated, and that we could be sent to a camp in a barren desert. I was devastated.

It made me grow up fast and think seriously about life, and what was in store for me and my family. It made me wonder about the meaning of democracy, and what I could have done to prepare myself for such an eventuality. It made me wonder about relationships and what I might have done to understand people's reactions and motives. It seemed to me that the life of another human being meant very little to some people. It was most frightening to think that we had become one big lump of people with no individual faces or names. From the day the war began, I didn't know what I could depend on.

I was more determined than ever to complete my college education, because I felt there was so much about the world that I didn't understand. It also became clear to me that one's personal possessions could easily be taken away and would then mean nothing, but that one's thoughts and ideas could never be taken away. I needed to develop these thoughts and ideas more freely in order to begin to understand human relationships. Human relationships seemed to me basic to the understanding of society and the ills created in it.

It wasn't at all clear whether I would ever have the option to continue my education when I went to camp. However, in about nine months the option came through the National Student Relocation Council. Several colleges opened their doors, and at the time, I chose McPherson College in McPherson, Kansas, because it was within a day's bus ride of Amache. This was where we lived at the time and where my parents would be.

While studying at McPherson College, I decided to major in Sociology. I think I was influenced by Dr. Bittinger, my Sociology professor, a caring man with compassion for all human kind. I had begun my college career at Willamette University, considering Journalism as a major. As a sophomore, writing about events no longer held my interest because, on the whole, I was not delving into human problems deeply enough. Sociology dealt with problems of human relationships and dynamics of society. It dealt with problems of prejudice, poverty, crime, and war. I wanted to learn how to deal with problems of this type. It was a subject matter in which compassion and concern for others seemed to be at the base. I liked that notion.

When I transferred to Ohio Wesleyan University in Delaware, Ohio, I continued with my study of Sociology. Under the tutelage of Dr. Milton Yinger, I learned a great deal about the workings of society and the problems in it. He also had great compassion for humanity. I tried to learn as much as I could about how to deal with prejudice, poverty, crime, war, etc. In and out of class, we researched peace issues and tried to educate others on these issues.

In the process of my education, I also became interested in Psychology. I was interested in learning about the mind and how it works in forming certain attitudes. I majored in Psychology in graduate school. I felt that by working with individuals, I could help people handle human relationships on a personal level. If people could learn to deal with themselves and with each other, I thought it would be a step in finding answers to society's problems.

As I moved about the country and worked at various jobs, my focus turned to children. I loved working with small children in a school setting, because their minds were so open and uncluttered with preconceived notions. We could talk about, and set examples of, such concepts as love, kindness, generosity, honesty, and peace at an early age. And these small children were very often wiser than their years. They had very wise things to say about very big issues.

I lived in many communities after the war and had an opportunity to work with children in these communities. However, my move to St. Paul has enabled me to have a long-term relationship in a nursery school setting. It has been fun to observe their growth and see what fine human beings many of them have become.

I have also tried to think how the war affected my parents. My parents never discussed the evacuation and how they felt about it, so I never knew what pain they endured. When they talked about the camps, it was only to relate incidents that took place there. They accepted what was meted out to them and did the best they could with it. They were Buddhist and their philosophy was to accept whatever life brings and live with it without complaining.

When I had to move my parents to a nursing home because of several falls and a near fire, I explained as carefully as I could where they were going. Of course, they could not understand. My mother kept talking about once again going to "camp." I was hurt and offended to think she would think I would do such a thing to her. However, as I thought more carefully about what she was saying, I realized how deeply hurt she had been with the internment. This was the first time I had an inkling of how she really felt. It was subtle but clear to me. It was heartbreaking, and I spent many a sleepless night thinking about it. To place them in the nursing home was one of the hardest things I ever had to do. This was 33 years after the evacuation.

The war years were difficult and I kept busy in camp to avoid brooding or thinking too much about our situation. However, it was not just keeping busy that prevented me from becoming completely cynical and skeptical. There were the few friends who were faithful and kept in touch. There were people who did not know me but reached out in friendship. I have a friend, now in her late 80's, who became my "pen pal" during the war because she wanted to write to someone in camp and extend her understanding. Her name is Ruth Rietveld, and she had gotten my name through some pen pal club or her church. She wrote regularly, and though she never mentioned how she felt about the war or the camps, I felt there was love and understanding being extended to me. It went a long way to sustain me in those uncertain times.

We continued our correspondence after the war. After nearly 45 years of writing to each other, I finally went to visit her in De Ruyter, New York, on August 8, 1987, along with my husband, daughter, son and his wife. When we arrived at her home, she greeted me with a warm hug as though we had been much more than pen pals. She welcomed my family just as warmly.

Maye Uemura, accompanied by her son, Wesley, and his wife, Makiko, visited her pen pal, Ruth Rietveld, after 45 years of writing to each other, at her home in De Ruyter, New York, 1987.

When we went into the house, we learned that she had no telephone, no electricity or running water; she lived a truly simple life. As we talked, however, it became evident that she had done many things in her life to help others and to promote world peace. It was somewhat of a puzzle to know how she could be so much in tune with the world when she had no television or radio. She did have books and magazines neatly stacked in a bookcase.

During our visit, she kept saying she could not believe we had come on this very day, August 8. It was the day the atomic bomb had been dropped on Hiroshima. It was quite by accident that we had chosen this day, but it was significant to her. Then she told us that she had planted a thousand Japanese larch trees on the hill on her farm beginning on August 8, 1945. She called it her Peace Garden. It has been her wish that nothing like that would ever happen again.

She took us for a walk through her beautiful flower garden and the forest of larch trees. She had written me about the larch trees, but I had no idea of what a larch tree was and how extensive her forest would be. It was very touching, as we stood in this beautiful forest with the sun filtering through the larch branches, to think that here on this quiet farm in the hills of New York was a symbol of peace.

My entire family came home deeply touched and with a sense of hope.

ALICE ABE MATSUMOTO

My father, Toyoji Abe, was born in Yamagata, Japan. He was a graduate of Keio University in Tokyo where he majored in Philosophy and Asian History. In 1910, he came to the United States to attend the University of Washington to work towards a Master's degree. As he was the second son of the Abe family, he was able to leave his home in Japan to study abroad.

After a year of study at the University of Washington, Father was asked by the Japanese community in Portland, Oregon, to take over the publication of the Japanese language newspaper in that city. He accepted the invitation and became the editor and publisher of that paper. With the newspaper business running successfully, he then returned to Japan to marry my mother.

My mother, Yuka Shima, was born in Yokohama. She had two sisters and two brothers. Her father, a physician, died when the children were quite young. It was therefore necessary for my grandmother to find work to support the family. As my grandmother was among the first to graduate from Ochanomizu University, she was able to obtain a position as tutor in the royal family of Count Yanagisawa. Grandmother took my mother along with her whenever she went to the Yanagisawa residence. Therefore, according to my aunt, Mrs. Toku Tanaka of San Diego, Mother herself became

*Alice Matsumoto's parents, Yuka and Toyoji Abe,
in Portland, Oregon, circa 1914.*

well educated and cultured as a result of these visits. She later graduated from Aoyama Gakuin University and became a teacher herself.

Soon after they were married, Father brought Mother to the United States. They made their first home in Portland, Oregon. Their first four children were born there: Sophy Teruko, Roy, Victor and myself. Our family enjoyed a happy life in Portland among good friends and neighbors. My mother especially loved the roses for which Portland is famous.

When I was still a young child, my father decided to leave the newspaper business and return to Japan to become a member of

*Alice Matsumoto with her mother, Yuka Abe,
in front of their house in Portland, Oregon, 1920.*

*Alice Matsumoto with her neighborhood friends
in Portland, Oregon, 1922.*

373

the House of Representatives of the Japanese Diet (Parliament) from Yamagata Prefecture. All of our things that we wanted to take with us to Japan were packed and shipped off to San Francisco where we were to board a steamship for Japan. When we arrived there, however, we were told that a terrible earthquake had struck Japan, and that the ship's departure therefore had to be canceled. Unfortunately, half of our belongings had already been shipped off to Japan on an earlier ship. My mother remembers her precious sewing machine being among them.

Shortly thereafter, my father again was asked by some friends to take over a San Francisco Japanese language newspaper, the *Shinsekai Asahi Mainichi* (*New World Sun*). He arranged the purchase and became the president, publisher and editor of this Japanese language daily newspaper. Our family was settled in San Francisco and two more children, Martha and Hana, were added to our family. We lived in San Francisco until the evacuation in the spring of 1942.

We lived in the Japanese area of San Francisco. I attended a Japanese language school and was a member of the Japanese YWCA. Our family belonged to the Japanese Reformed Church. My contact with Caucasian people was limited to school and the YWCA camps and conferences I attended. I realized much later that Japanese could not own real estate in San Francisco, which explained why we al-

Alice Matsumoto (far left) in a play at the Japanese Reformed Church in San Francisco, California, 1935.

ways lived in a rented house. Our social life almost exclusively revolved around fellow Japanese.

I attended public schools in San Francisco. We were asked to go to a school not in our district in order to achieve some racial balance. I was asked to attend Pacific Heights Elementary School. After completing elementary school, I chose to attend Lowell High School, a college preparatory school. Surprisingly, even in those early days we were able to choose the schools we wished to attend.

After graduating from Lowell High School, I attended the University of California at Berkeley. Even at UCB, our social activities were mainly with other Nisei students, which we did not think particularly strange at the time.

On Sunday, December 7, 1941, I was studying at the UCB campus when I heard the news on the radio about the Japanese attack on Pearl Harbor. I rushed home to San Francisco to find my father had already been arrested by the FBI. I couldn't believe they would take my father, but as the FBI file showed (which we were able to obtain recently under the Freedom of Information Act), my father had been under surveillance for some years prior to Pearl Harbor.

Father was a member of the Japanese Committee on Trade and Information and represented the Japanese Association, the *Heimusha Kai* and the *New World Sun* at the 2600th year anniversary celebration of the Japanese Empire in Japan. Father headed the party from the United States to attend the celebration and was welcomed by former consuls and leaders who had served in America. While in Japan, he received a second rank medal with selected appointment treatment from the Emperor in the Empire Jubilee Ceremony. He was permitted to view the Loyalty Hall within the Imperial Palace in Tokyo and entered the Higashi Kurumayose Hall to sign the great registry, generally regarded as a high honor.

While in Japan, he was approached in secrecy by a coalition whose aim was to maintain the peace between Japan and the United

Alice Matsumoto (first row, second from right) with members of the planning committee for a Japanese American student conference at the University of California, Berkeley, circa 1941.

States. They sought Father's advice and proposed to attempt to have him appointed as Japanese Ambassador to the United States. The coalition failed in this attempt due to the predominance of military fervor in Japan at that time.

Back in the United States, he entertained Ambassador Kichisaburo Nomura and held several discussions with him regarding the relationship between Japan and America.

As a result of the above activities, Father was apprehended by the FBI as a dangerous enemy alien and was ordered by the Attorney General to be interned for the duration of the war.

At our home, the family was in deep shock over the unexpected attack on Pearl Harbor and the apprehension of Father. We had no knowledge as to where the FBI had taken him. The family urged me to go back to the university to continue with my studies in Dietetics. Some Nisei had already left the campus for home. I continued with my classes until the evacuation orders were posted. I went to see my instructors who were very kind and sympathetic. Some let me take early examinations, while others waived the examinations. One instructor gave me a letter of recommendation for employment in the camp. I do not recall any negative treatment toward me while on campus.

My brother, Roy, was serving in the U.S. Army when the attack on Pearl Harbor occurred. He was among the first draftees in 1940 as his name was drawn during the first drawing. Father and Roy were the only family members not with us during the evacuation.

In March 1942, our family was taken by bus to the Tanforan Race Track in San Bruno, California, just a few miles south of the San Francisco city limits. This area was renamed Tanforan Assembly Center by the War Relocation Authority, and all Japanese families from the San Francisco Bay area were housed here as the first stage in their evacuation from the West Coast. What a shock to discover that we were to be housed in horse stalls! With typical Japanese determination and fortitude, we scrubbed and cleaned the floors and walls of the stall to which we were assigned, and filled mattress ticks with the straw that was provided.

Our brother, Victor, who had graduated from the Hastings Law School at UCB, was selected as one of the block captains in the Assembly Center, so we were eventually moved to a room in one of the tar-paper barracks. With blankets and sheets draped over the exposed joists, we tried to establish some sort of privacy within our small room.

When I took the letter from my instructor to the job procurement office, they placed me in the Diet Kitchen. This primitive Special Kitchen, situated under the grandstand of the racetrack, provided diets for all diabetics, hypertensive and ulcer patients in the center.

In the Assembly Center, there was a spirit of comradeship and togetherness. There was entertainment put on by the residents every week in the grandstand area. One of our most popular entertainers was Goro Suzuki who was a professional night club singer in the prewar days. His professional name was Jack Soo and he later became nationally known for his character part in the television series Barney Miller. Some of the Issei men created a Japanese garden and pond in the infield of the racetrack even complete with a Japanese bridge over the pond. Softball, tennis, badminton, volleyball and even fencing were popular sports among the young people.

Yoshio Matsumoto, who was to become my husband, was allowed to leave the Assembly Center to go to St. Louis, Missouri, where he was able to continue his studies in Mechanical Engineering at Washington University.

We remained at the Tanforan Assembly Center from March to September of 1942. In September, we were transported by train to the Topaz Relocation Center in central Utah. What a shocking first impression it was to see that desolate barren camp with rows upon rows of black tar-papered barracks enclosed within barbwire fences and guard towers! The wind and accompanying dust storms were unrelenting. The sand sifted through the doors and windows and through cracks in the walls. Our belongings were constantly covered with fine dust. We could feel our spirits match the desolation of our surroundings.

Our one hope was to get clearance from the War Relocation Authority to attend a college which would accept us. Our Reformed Church offered us scholarships, and the American Friends Service Committee, through their National Student Relocation Council, assisted us in the selection of a suitable school. In March 1943, my sister, Martha, got her clearance first and was accepted at Elmhurst College in Illinois. There she majored in Technical Laboratory Science. Shortly thereafter, Dr. Park Johnson, a Presbyterian minister, sponsored me for the Kansas City College in Kansas City, Missouri. But this college did not offer a degree program in Dietetics, so I worked at the lovely Johnson home during that summer.

Alice Matsumoto with her classmates at Temple University in Philadelphia, Pennsylvania, 1943.

Through the National Student Relocation Council, I was able to gain acceptance to study Dietetics at Temple University in Philadelphia. In the fall of 1943, I left Kansas City for Pennsylvania, and there I went to live at the manse of Dr. Rex Clements, another Presbyterian minister and his family in Bryn Mawr, a suburb of Philadelphia. In exchange for my room and board, I cooked and cleaned house for the family of Dr. and Mrs. Clements and their two young sons.

After having been a student at the University of California, a very large university, I enjoyed this smaller school where I knew everyone in the class and had closer contact with the instructors. It was easier to make friends among the Caucasian students when you were the only Asian. The two Presbyterian minister families who were so kind to me are still my dear friends.

After graduation from Temple University, I applied for an internship and was accepted to Montifiore Hospital in the Bronx. Miss Lenna Cooper, the Director of Food Service, took me under her wing, and I, with the other 11 interns, spent a rewarding year in New York City. I remember even going to Times Square with them on V-J Day.

In the meantime, we had received letters from my father in New Mexico, and we were glad to hear he was in good health. Then my mother and two sisters, Sophy who was later to marry a Congregational minister, and Hana who was still in high school, were able to join my father in Family Camp at the Crystal City, Texas Interment Camp.

My brother, Victor, had gone to Chicago seeking employment in a law firm. He was later joined by sister Sophy. Brother Roy completed training at the Military Intelligence Service Language School at Fort Snelling and was sent to Japan with the Occupation Army.

While in Texas, my father had surgery for a brain tumor and did not survive the operation. Sadly, I and some of the other members of our family were not able to see him again after he was taken away by the FBI on December 7, 1941. After his death, my mother, brother Victor, and sisters Sophy and Hana returned to San Francisco. My mother found work as a seamstress at I. Magnin Company. Victor started private law practice, Sophy married the Reverend Norio Ozaki, and Hana entered the University of California at Berkeley.

While I was a dietetic intern at Montefiore Hospital in 1945, Yoshio, who was by then in the U.S. Army, received orders to transfer to Europe. We decided to get married right away although my superior, Miss Cooper, advised me to consider my career and to postpone our marriage. During the weekend that I didn't have to work, I took a train to Philadelphia and met Yoshio who had arrived from Fort Belvoir near Washington, D.C. On September 14, 1945, the two Reformed Church ministers, who were so helpful to me during my school days in Philadelphia, performed our marriage ceremony

After completing her dietetic internship, Alice Matsumoto went to visit her sisters, Sophy (center) and Martha (right), in Chicago, Illinois, 1945.

at the Old First Church. After the wedding, I returned to Montefiore to continue my studies, and Yoshio went to Europe and was attached to the 252nd Combat Engineering Battalion in Berlin, Germany.

After finishing my internship, I decided to accept the position as a therapeutic dietitian at New Grace Hospital in Detroit. Yoshio's parents were living there at the time, and he was planning

Alice Matsumoto's three sons, David, Steven and Joseph (left to right), in Royal Oak, Michigan, circa 1960.

Alice Matsumoto with her husband, Yoshio, and three sons, David (back), Joseph (front) and Steven (right), in Woodbury, Minnesota, 1962.

to return there when he was discharged from the Army. When he came back to the United States in the fall of 1946, he returned to his job as a mechanical engineer in the Advance Planning Division in the City of Detroit Engineer's Office. After two years, he joined Smith Hinchman and Grylls, an architectural and engineering consulting firm in Detroit.

We purchased a home in Royal Oak, a suburb of Detroit, and raised our three sons, Steven, David and Joseph. They enjoyed activities and school with Caucasian friends and neighbors. I gave up my job at Grace Hospital so that I would be with the boys while they were growing up. I was active at our church, the Evangelical and Reformed Church of Royal Oak, the local PTA, and Cub Scouts.

In 1962, after 18 years with Smith Hinchman and Grylls in Detroit, Yoshio accepted a position with Minnesota Mining and Manufacturing Company in St. Paul, Minnesota. At first, the boys and I were very sad leaving our friends and relatives. For several years, the boys continued to root for the Detroit Tigers baseball team and

Alice Matsumoto with her husband, Yoshio, son, Joseph, and Jean-François Dreyfus, an AFS (American Friends Service) student from France her family hosted, at their home in Woodbury, Minnesota, 1962.

the Detroit Lions football team, and I ran up big telephone bills calling back to Michigan.

Our sons were enrolled in the St. Paul Park Schools. At that time, I remember one of the teachers commenting that our sons were the first Asian students, but expected no problems. Their experiences at the school were satisfactory and they were well-accepted, as shown by the fact that Steven won a Science Scholarship; David was the valedictorian and first-chair clarinet in the band; and Joseph had an AFS (American Friends Service) brother from France. They were active in the St. Paul YMCA, where they took *judo* and swimming.

We have now lived in the Twin Cities for 30 years, longer than we have lived in any other city. We have found the Twin Cities to be the best place in which to live and raise our sons. They have received a very good education, grown up in a friendly and healthy environment, and made many friends. They all graduated from the University of Minnesota.

Our eldest son, Steven, received a B.S. in Chemistry from the University of Minnesota, and an M.S. and a Ph.D. in Biochemistry from Cornell University in Ithaca, New York. Presently he is a researcher for the Allergan Co. in Irvine, California.

Our second son, David, majored in Psychology at the University of Minnesota and received a Bachelor of Arts degree. He then entered the University of Minnesota Law School and received a Juris Doctor degree. He was admitted to the bar in Minnesota and California and was employed by the Southern Minnesota Legal Assistance Office.

Our youngest son, Joseph, majored in Asian Studies at the University of Minnesota and received a Bachelor of Arts degree. He then entered the Mayo Medical School in Rochester, Minnesota, and received a Doctor of Medicine degree in 1979. He interned at Hennepin County General Hospital and did his residency in Neurology at the Mayo Clinic.

While attending the University of Minnesota, our sons worked in the University Hospital as kitchen helper, nurse's aide, and laboratory aide, as well as in the central supply service to cover a part of their school expenses. They enjoyed attending the University which they felt offered superior instruction, excellent courses, and a variety of cultural experiences. We shall be forever grateful to Minnesota for the excellent education our sons have received.

In the fall of 1978, David married Susan Tsuchiya, the daughter of Frank and Helen Tsuchiya of St. Louis Park, Minnesota. As Susan and her parents were of the Buddhist faith, David converted to Buddhism, and the marriage ceremony was performed by a Buddhist minister. Susan had also attended the University of Minnesota, and, after graduation, was teaching at an elementary school in the Burnsville Eagan Savage School District in Minnesota. In the spring of 1980, Susan tragically died of cancer. After her death, David decided to become a Buddhist minister. He received a scholarship from the Buddhist Church of America to study at Ryukoku University in Kyoto, Japan, where he graduated and was ordained in 1988.

While studying in Kyoto, David met and became engaged to Diane Hane from Milbrae, California. Diane was a graduate of San Jose State University where she majored in Art, and she had gone to Kyoto to study Japanese textile making under a master in that field. Diane and David were married in Kyoto in the spring of 1987. They presently live in Stockton, California, where he is the assistant minister at the Buddhist Church of Stockton. They have one son, Davey, born to them in February 1989.

In the fall of 1978, Joe married Jane Marie Sexton, his classmate at the Mayo Medical School. Jane is the daughter of Jack and Peggy Sexton of Janesville, Minnesota. Jane graduated from Brandeis University in Boston and spent one summer working on Senator Walter Mondale's staff in Washington, D.C. Jane and Joe were married during their last year at the Mayo Medical School. She did her residency in Pediatric Radiology at the University of Cincinnati and completed her training in 1990. She is presently on the staff of the

Radiology Department at the Mayo Clinic. Jane and Joe have four children: Peter, Molly, Martha, and Andrew.

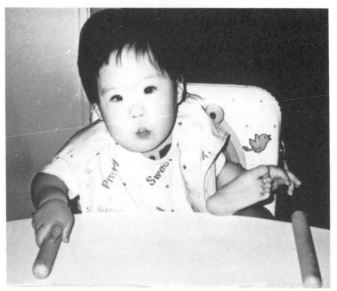

Davey Matsumoto, David and Diane Matsumoto's son in Stockton, California, 1991.

Drs. Joseph and Jane Matsumoto's children, Martha, Peter, Andrew and Molly (left to right), at their home in Rochester, Minnesota, 1991.

During our early days in Minnesota, I enjoyed attending the St. Paul YWCA and participating in their programs which Ruth Tanbara had organized as Program Director. I was also volunteering at Gillette Hospital during that period. I then decided to take some refresher courses in Nutrition at the University of Minnesota since I thought I would like to return to work as a dietitian. After completing the courses, I applied for employment at St. Joseph Hospital in St. Paul and was accepted for the position of clinical dietitian.

I worked at St. Joseph Hospital for 20 years until my retirement in 1986. My work involved patients on the Cardiac Floor. In addition to managing patient diets, I was a team member for the education of cardiac patients. I gave lectures and demonstrations covering low-fat, vegetarian, low-cost, and low-calorie cooking at cardiac support group meetings and also at senior citizens centers, the YMCA, and the Town Square building in downtown St. Paul. I also gave classes on prenatal, postnatal and breast feeding nutrition for the maternity patients. I was a member of the American and Minnesota Dietetic Associations and served on their Career Guidance and Minority Recruitment Committees.

Alice Matsumoto demonstrating how to cook healthy food at Town Square in St. Paul, Minnesota, circa 1982.

When we moved to St. Paul in 1962, we joined the United Church of Christ on Summit Avenue. Our three sons were confirmed in this church. My husband and I are still members of this church. Yoshio has served on the Church Council and I have served on the Women's Guild. This church is an integral part of our lives.

Reflections

On the 50th anniversary of the Japanese attack on Pearl Harbor, I had feelings of sadness in recalling the events of that fateful December day, the fear and confusion we experienced, and hardship that our family and other evacuee families had to endure. I am still uncomfortable with the fact that the country of my parents, Japan, committed that act of aggression against my country, the United States.

Although the evacuation was a humiliating experience, for many of us it also had a positive side. Many Nisei and Issei eventually resettled in other parts of the United States and became better integrated into American society. At Temple University in Philadelphia and at Montifiore Hospital in Bronx, I enjoyed the interaction with people of other social, ethnic and economic backgrounds. In Michigan we lived in a neighborhood of middle-class Caucasian families and developed a close friendship with them. Our sons seemed to thrive in that environment too.

My husband and I have now lived in Minnesota for almost 30 years. Minnesota, with its liberal political background, provided the right climate for us. We were then, and still are, members of the Democratic Party. What a thrill it was to meet Vice President and Mrs. Hubert Humphrey at their home in Waverly, Minnesota, during a Democratic beanfeed, and Vice President Walter Mondale in Afton, Minnesota, during his presidential campaign!

We are members of several social and cultural organizations in the Twin Cities including the Japanese American Citizens League, Japan America Society, St. Paul-Nagasaki Sister City Committee, and the Como Park Japanese Garden Club, and enjoy participating in the activities of these organizations. We are supporters of the Minnesota Science Museum, Walker Art Museum, Minneapolis Institute of Arts, and the Minnesota Zoo, and we enjoy regularly attending the performances of the Minnesota Orchestra, the St. Paul Chamber Orchestra, and the Guthrie Theater.

Now that we both are retired, we enjoy visiting our two sons, Steven and David, my sisters and brothers, and our many friends in California. The Japanese community in the Bay Area is reminiscent of those days before World War II, although the Nisei, who resettled there after evacuation, and their offsprings, now have better jobs, homes, and socio-political status. Although we enjoy visiting California, we have decided to continue living in the Twin Cities, at least for the foreseeable future, as we have many very dear friends living here, as well as our youngest son, Joe, his wife, Jane, and their four children, who live in Rochester, Minnesota. We love living in Minnesota with its friendly people, its lakes and forests, and the beautiful change of seasons.

CHISAKO JOYCE HIRABAYASHI

I t was in the early 1930's when Japan invaded Manchuria and Mainland China, that I realized that I was quite different from my classmates, and that my parents' background and the country they left would play a major role in my thoughts and feelings, as well as in my line of education.

Dad, Yuzaburo Higuchi, was born on November 7, 1883, in a small village of Yukiha-gun, Fukuoka, Japan. In his family there were around ten or twelve children, and Dad was in the middle. The eldest son was the only child who was given the privilege of going on to university and eventually inheriting the family estate.

Dad, at the age of 17, left Japan for America by ship, along with his brother and their two cousins. Dad and his brother disembarked from the ship in Washington State, while their cousins continued on to California. This information was related to me by the father of Francis Higuchi during my visit to Heart Mountain in Wyoming, an internment camp euphemistically called "relocation center," where many of the American people and their parents of Japanese descent were incarcerated during World War II. I met Francis Higuchi, third cousin to me, at the University of Colorado where my husband and Francis taught in a special program for U.S. Naval Intelligence officers during 1942-43.

There was a time when all immigrants, including those from Japan, were able to apply for American citizenship. The group of people with whom Dad associated said that they should apply for citizenship because it was rumored that they might not get it if they waited too long. Dad made his application and got his first paper.

Declaration of Intention to Become a Citizen

UNITED STATES OF AMERICA.

STATE OF NORTH DAKOTA,
County of Williams. } ss.

Yuzaburo Higuchi personally appeared before the subscriber, the Clerk of the District Court of Williams County, State of North Dakota, being a Court of Record, and made oath that he was born in *Japan* on or about the year eighteen hundred and *eighty-two* ; that he emigrated to the United States, and landed at the port of *Seattle* on or about the month of *August* in the year *ninety-nine* ; that it is bona fide his intention to become a citizen of the United States, and to renounce forever all allegiance and fidelity to any foreign Prince, Potentate, State or Sovereignty whatever, and particularly to the *Emperor of Japan* whereof he is a subject, and that he will support the Constitution and Government of the United States.

Yuzaburo Higuchi

Subscribed and sworn to this *27th* day of *July* A. D., 190*3*

Geo Bruegger
Clerk of District Court, Williams County.

By _____ Deputy.

United States of America, }
STATE OF NORTH DAKOTA, } ss.
COUNTY OF WILLIAMS, }

I, *Geo Bruegger* Clerk of the District Court of Williams County, North Dakota, certify that the foregoing is a true copy of a record now in my office.

IN TESTIMONY WHEREOF, I have hereunto set my hand and affixed the seal of said District Court, this *27th* day of *July* 190*3*

Geo Bruegger Clerk,

By _____ Deputy.

Joyce Hirabayashi's father, Yuzaburo Higuchi, applied for U.S. citizenship in 1903 at the Williams County District Court in North Dakota. However he returned to the State of Washington before his application was acted on.

392

But before he could get his citizenship, the U.S. Supreme Court ruled that all people of Asian background were excluded from citizenship.

After spending some time in America, Dad's parents called him back to Japan to get married to Katsumi Takanami, also of Fukuoka, Japan. Mother's recollection of meeting Dad was not in Dad's favor. Dad must have grown sloppy leading a bachelor's life in the wilds of America.

After their marriage, they came to the United States and took up residence in Tacoma, Washington. My sister, Suzy, was born

Joyce Hirabayashi's mother, Katsumi Higuchi (nee Takanami), as a small child with her father and grandmother in Fukuoka, Japan, circa 1903.

Joyce Hirabayashi's mother, Katsumi Higuchi (far left), as a young lady with her friends in Fukuoka, Japan, circa 1916.

at the Massasoit Hotel in that city. The family then moved to Napavine, Washington, where Dad worked as a lumber man. During their stay there, I was born.

There must have been a downturn in the lumber business, for the family again was on the move. This time it was to Steilacoom, a village about 13 miles south of Tacoma. My brother, Sam, was born, and all of us children grew up there and enjoyed the community life.

Dad found work with the Steilacoom Sand and Gravel Company, a firm owned by William Thompson, Sr., an immigrant from Wales. The friendship between Dad and Thompson grew to be a close one. Thompson visited our home frequently, and Dad was invited to pick apples from his boss's orchard. Mother and Dad would wrap these apples individually and put them in a large barrel to be eaten throughout the winter.

Joyce Hirabayashi (center) with her sister, Suzy, and her mother, Katsumi Higuchi, in Napavine, Washington, circa 1923.

Mother, from the time that I can remember, was always helping others. During the flu epidemic, she helped others who were left motherless. She made shirts for two such boys and clothes for other children. She would invite children, especially those from the cities, for the summer so they could enjoy the salt water and the outdoors. There were so many who contracted tuberculosis in those years.

Not only did Mother do all that, but Dad would lend money to friends who needed it for spring planting on the farms, or to help buy equipment, or for someone's schooling.

Joyce Hirabayashi's father, Yuzaburo Higuchi, with his employer,
William Thompson, Sr., who owned the Steilacoom Sand and Gravel Company
in Steilacoom, Washington, circa 1926.

A half block away from our home, lived the Reverend West, our minister, with his wife, adopted daughter and grandmother (his mother-in-law). I enjoyed the grandmother so much that I was there at her home quite often. I learned to love flowers by helping with her gardening. Dad, too, enjoyed flowers and started my sister and me on our own terraced flower garden since our lot was on a steep hill.

On top of this hill was the home of William Thompson, Jr. and his family. They had one daughter named Catherine, who was much younger than my sister or I. William Thompson, Jr. was expected to take over the Sand and Gravel Company after his father retired.

Next to the Reverend West family home lived the Jack family, immigrants from Scotland. They had three children, James, Kenneth and Isabella. The daughter was in the same class as my sister, but I was included in the same play group. The boys, out of mischief, would put boxing gloves on us and they enjoyed seeing us box. However, I can't remember enjoying this.

Also Mother would take us down to the beach for swimming lessons. I can still see us in our maroon cotton bathing suits and Mother trying to help us swim.

That was a time when our lives were happy and peaceful. Mother would take walks and bring home scotch broom for part of her flower arrangement display. She made silk macramé purses for us and articles for the home. Not only did she take English lessons, but also tried to teach us Japanese.

The aura of contentment did not last long. By the time I was nine, Dad was in the hospital due to injuries from an accident at his work. While shoveling sand through the hole to fill the truck

Joyce Hirabayashi (left) with her sister, Suzy,
in Steilacoom, Washington, on Easter Sunday, circa 1925.

below, the hole closed after the truck was full. But Dad fell in the hole while the hole was closing and he was crushed. Hannah Thompson, the daughter, rushed Dad to St. Joseph's Hospital in Tacoma. He was there for about six months. Shortly after he returned home, the stock market crashed. That was in October 1929.

The Thompson family, too, had come into some misfortune. Their son, William, Jr., who was to take over the management of the company, died unexpectedly from a tooth infection. Since the elder Thompson was hoping to have his son carry on, there was no other successor, so the Gravel Company came to an end.

Now Dad and Mother had to think of what to do. The Great Depression was on us. The Jack family moved to California because the paper mill where the father worked closed and, of course, William Thompson, Jr. was dead.

Since Dad had his spinal column crushed and his ribs broken from the accident, the type of work he could do was limited. In the early 1930's, he was able to lease the beach which the Gravel Company had made in the process of producing sand for sale. After his son's death, William Thompson had sold his property to the Pioneer Sand and Gravel Company. Dad leased the beach and called it Sunny Beach.

From then on there would be no more freshly baked bread and wonderful dinners Mother used to make. We all had to pitch in and help. It was up to us to carry on in the home. Going to the farm for health and social reasons was put aside. But Suzy and I did go out to a friend's farm for the last time to help out—Mother did not come with us. It seemed as if we came home with some Japanese words which Mother was not fond of. However, we did get to see and make Japanese American friends of our parents' prefectural friends.

Clearing the artificial beach was the biggest task but Dad never complained. He built four one-room camp houses with a stove for warmth and cooking. He ordered 12 custom-made round bottom row boats to add to the one which the family had before the accident. He put up a building to house the boats. He built family picnic tables along the shore of the beach and two huge organizational or club picnic tables, one on each end of the beach. All of the picnic tables had a roof for shade from the sun or protection from rain.

Since renting the beach facilities to visitors did not bring in enough money to keep a family of five together, Mother found work as a clerk in a friend's grocery store in Tacoma. Now Dad was home taking care of the beach and us kids.

My sister, at the age of around 13, also went to work as a clerk on Saturdays along with Mother. My brother and I stayed at home. We helped Dad with his work on the beach, cleaning the debris washed ashore from the tide of Puget Sound and doing any other tasks that needed to be tended to.

Janet C. Tait, my grade school principal in Steilacoom, was of English descent. She taught the 7th and 8th grade classes. She was very strong in History, English and Mathematics. She wanted all of her pupils to do well not only in History but all other subjects that she taught. At that time, we had state exams. I've always said that I learned the most in the 7th and 8th grades under her tutelage. She was a taskmaster, but an excellent teacher.

The students in our local school were made up of mostly immigrants. The families all started out on equal terms, more or less. The only difference was that the Higuchi family looked different. We were all in the same boat, just being kids trying to live and play together.

After graduation from the eighth grade, there were three of us who went to Jason Lee Junior High School in Tacoma. I had to get up at 6:00 a.m. to catch the 7:00 a.m. bus, because there was a 15-minute walk to the bus line. After getting off the bus, I caught a street car from downtown Tacoma to the school. On the way home,

I could stop at the Tacoma Public Library to take out books for the weekend.

Joyce Hirabayashi with her 8th grade classmates
at Steilacoom Grade School in Steilacoom, Washington, circa 1934.

At Jason Lee, I found out I was the only Japanese American student in the class. One Japanese American girl had graduated one-half year before I graduated, so she was never in any of my classes. When I graduated, I was still the only Japanese American student.

After one year of junior high school, I was off to Stadium High School. Since the girls whom I became acquainted with at Jason Lee also went to Stadium, we kept up our friendships. At one time when I first entered Stadium, I thought and wanted to get acquainted with my Japanese American classmates. To my surprise they all spoke Japanese and I just felt excluded. So I rejoined my friends from Jason Lee and a few others from Mason Junior High School. We kept our friendships until we graduated.

There was more and more news at that time on the war between China and Japan, as well as the war in Europe. It was in high
school that I changed my mind on what I wanted to take up for my
future vocation. I had started to take courses at Jason Lee in preparation for the medical field and I continued it in high school. But it
seemed that nobody was interested in trying to help keep the friendship and peace between the United States and Japan, or within Europe. And, the ties between the United States and Japan were getting
strained. My thoughts were that I wanted to try to keep Japan and
the U.S. on friendly terms, i.e., between my parents' country and the
country where I was born. I thought that the Japanese Americans
could try a little harder to understand the whys and wherefores of the
situation. I therefore changed my vocational goal from the medical
field to Political Science.

Given my little knowledge of what could be done, the only
solution appeared to be through the diplomatic channel. Mother
thought it would be impossible for me to get into a diplomatic career,
and probably she was right. She discouraged me from changing my
professional goals, and she was disappointed that I did not continue
my preparation for the medical field.

Nevertheless, high school life with friends was still carefree and some of us were thinking of continuing our education at a
university or college. I thought of going to the College of Puget
Sound. I was, however, told in no uncertain terms that since my
sister, Suzy, had already started at the University of Washington, I
had to attend the same school. Obligingly, I did so. Initially, I was
so homesick I think I went home every other weekend, or I wanted
to.

Since I had not attended any Japanese school, the only Japanese I knew was what I had learned on the farm and from my parents. Thus, I decided to study the language at the University under
Professor Henry Tatsumi.

It did not take long to adjust to university life. There were eight girls from outside of Seattle who "batched" together. Two in each room except for my sister and me. We roomed with another student. We took the largest room with a window facing the campus.

During my first year, Sat (Satoshi) Hoshi, a friend of Martin Hirabayashi's who was also a YMCA member, asked him if he had anyone in mind to take to the "Y" social. Sat said if not, he knew of a person Martin might ask. Since Sat knew my sister and had asked about me, a blind date was set up. That was my introduction to Martin. We dated for the rest of the year while Martin was an undergraduate.

After Martin graduated, he left for Japan to do some studying. He was able to get a scholarship to Kyoto University, where he studied under Professor Abe in the Electrical Engineering Department. While there, he also studied the Japanese language. He, too, did not have much knowledge of the language before going to Japan.

In the meantime, the war situation between Japan and China continued to deteriorate. There was news of alleged atrocities committed by Japanese soldiers in China. Also, the war in Europe widened into open conflict with the United States taking an active part.

Martin returned home in April 1941 on the next to the last ship that left Japan for the United States, prior to the outbreak of the war between the two countries. The American consulates in Japan had advised all American citizens to return to the United States.

Martin again enrolled at the University of Washington for graduate work since there were no jobs available. While in graduate school, he served as an assistant to Professor Macy Skinner in an international trade course and to Professor Dean Preston in a banking course.

Martin had gone to his University office to grade "blue books" on Sunday morning, December 7, 1941. So a classmate of his had asked me to go with him to the University Museum. After enjoying the Museum, we walked over to University Avenue, when I heard the paperboy on the corner of 40th Street and University Avenue calling out "Pearl Harbor bombed! War declared with Japan." What a jolt!

Now what was I to do. I was about 50 miles from home. Although my parents were frantic and anxious to get me home, I could not move. No traveling of any kind beyond a five mile radius was permitted and a curfew was imposed. However, I did get home somehow. I don't remember the details of how I made the trip back home, but my parents were relieved.

As soon as I returned home, we had to get ready to sell what we could and move all of our belongings. Thank goodness, we knew the minister and his wife from the time we had moved to Steilacoom. We were able to store our furnishings in a barn on their property. The store which Mother ran and owned in Tacoma also had to be sold. Dad had to sell the rowboats and put things in order at the beach. Somehow, everything was accomplished. But in the meantime, my sister had married, so she was not with us when we went to the train station to await the train, which took us to our first destination, the Pinedale Assembly Center in the San Joaquin "Desert" in California.

Before leaving for the Pinedale Assembly Center, Mrs. West, the wife of the minister, who had attended Earlham College before her marriage, suggested that I attend that college. She wrote to her classmate who was now an English professor there. I thus established contact with her. Furthermore, Professor Floyd Schmoe at the University of Washington had a relative in Richmond, Indiana, where Earlham College is located.

After settling down at the Pinedale Assembly Center, the American Friends Service Committee was right there to help in any way they could. For many of the college-age students, it was a blessing to have this organization to help them get started on finding colleges to attend. Since I had made my contact back in Washington State, I did not have to wait long to get out. My stay in the Assembly Center was during late spring and early summer. The desert, the sand, the hot winds blowing were an experience I'll always remember, especially coming from a cool temperate climate of western Washington. I remember the straw mattress which we had to sleep on; each family was given only one room with no dividers. One could not keep the door closed during the day because it was so hot. But then, you get all the sand and dirt from the hot wind that blew into the room. Depressing, and this word is not strong enough to describe the living conditions.

I can't remember when the rumor began that the people in the Assembly Center would be moved to a more permanent internment camp at another location. In any event, we did move to a camp called the Tule Lake Relocation Center in northern California where the climate was better and the camp area was larger. Among the residents at the new Center were many from California, some of whom were rumored to be violently protesting their internment. We were not involved with them, because we were put into an area called "Alaska" which was separated from the area of the above group by a huge drainage ditch.

Just before I left the Tule Lake Relocation Center, there were people trying to organize classes and projects to keep the people busy and usefully occupied. English language teachers were recruited, and I was among those called upon to teach. Before I had a chance to do that, I received word that I could leave the Center to attend Earlham College.

The family sent me off with tears in their eyes. Mother thought she would never see me again. I can still see her tearful eyes saying to herself that something terrible could happen to me. She knew she had to let me go, because Martin was out in Montana at a dude ranch owned by Professor Dean Line, Dean of Business School at the University of Montana in Missoula. Martin was able to avoid life in the Relocation Center by leaving the West Coast before the

404

deadline for the internment of all persons of Japanese ancestry living on the West Coast. Martin was to come to Richmond, Indiana, and marry me "to rescue and protect me from harm." Letters flowed from Mother more than once a week. She was so anxious that I not be alone in this frightening world.

The bus ride from Tule Lake to Reno was "bumpy and dusty." I don't think civilization (especially in roads) had come to this part of the United States at that time. We called the Japanese road from Tokyo to Nagoya a "*Suribachi* Road." This was the same. While on the bus, I talked to a Caucasian girl who was familiar with this part of the country. When we arrived in Reno, she told me to hang on tightly to my purse and guided me through the gambling house, since I had never been to a gambling casino. The shock of a huge cage of silver dollars in one of the houses probably awaiting for some winner took me by surprise.

The train trip from Reno to Chicago was another eye opener. The train was packed full of wounded and shocked military men coming home to be treated. I talked with one of them. His legs were bruised by leeches.

There was also fascinating and impressive scenery from the train window. The vast Rocky Mountains, the upheavals in the terrain exposing red granite rocks, the barren areas with no plants or trees, and then the miles and miles of corn in Nebraska. The first thing I wanted to find out was all about geology when I enrolled for classes at Earlham College. My eyes were opened to the wonders of God's creation.

At Earlham, in addition to preparing for my studies, I had letters flying in from Tule Lake which needed to be answered. But I had to prepare for my wedding. The Davises—Mr. Davis was a cousin of Ruby Davis and Professor Floyd Schmoe of University of Washington—assisted me in preparing for the wedding. They served as foster parents in place of my parents, and at the shower and wedding, Mr. Davis had movies made to be sent to my parents in camp.

After the wedding, honeymoon and more cramming to prepare for the exams, I was invited to go to Philadelphia for Christmas with a classmate, Meg Bowman, who was adopted by the Watsons. Her parents died while serving with the Quakers in Europe when Herbert Hoover, a Quaker and later President of the United States, distributed food and clothing after World War I. So there we were in Germantown, a suburb of Philadelphia, after an overnight train ride from Richmond, Indiana. The Watsons, the hosts, took us up to Buck Hill Falls near Philadelphia for Christmas. This was a resort which was used by the Quakers. It was a wonderful Christmas!

Joyce Hirabayashi with her Earlham College classmate, Meg Bowman,
and Mrs. Harold Watson at Mrs. Rigpath's house
in Philadelphia, Pennsylvania, Christmas, 1942.

Vacations had to end, and Meg and I headed back to school again. More letters were flying this time from Mother and Martin.

Martin was asked to teach the Japanese language at the Navy Intelligence School, University of Colorado at Boulder. So off he went after the brief honeymoon. I was to follow after the school term ended.

Seeing the vast dry arid land and huge rock formations from the train and now living in it in Boulder were two different things. I loved the greenery of Washington, the beautiful fall scenery in Indiana, but I was not prepared for the high altitude and cooking problems generated by the altitude. But it was not long before I felt and saw the beauty of the flat iron range, the clear blue sky, the wonderful soft water to drink, and the small town atmosphere of Boulder. There was so much to see and explore.

To my amazement and Martin's, we met former students from the University of Washington at the Navy Intelligence School. My quiz instructor in Economics and two other classmates who had been neighbors of mine off-campus were enrolled in Martin's Japanese language class. We had many of his students, including enrolled WAVES (Women's Appointed Volunteer Emergency Service), over for dinner during the time we were in Boulder.

At the so-called Relocation Centers, there was much change taking place. The interned residents were getting out to seek new housing and work. My brother came to Boulder for a short while and then went to eastern Washington where my sister and her husband had relocated. Sam entered Gonzaga College. Martin's sister Ruth was able to get out and stayed with us. Martin's other sister and her husband also visited us for a while. In the meantime, Tim was born to us. Martin and I took Tim to the Topaz Relocation Center, to which our parents had been transferred from the Tule Lake Relocation Center, so that they could see their first grandchild.

After two years of course work in Japanese, the Navy Intelligence School laid off many of the teachers for lack of sufficient funding or of suitable high-caliber language students. Martin was one of the laid-off teachers. However, he was asked to go to Columbia University in New York City to do some research and translation work for a Navy Research unit stationed there. So off he went once again, and Ruth, our son Tim, and I stayed behind to get things packed.

Joyce and Martin Hirabayashi visited her parents,
Yuzaburo and Katsumi Higuchi, at the Topaz Relocation Center in Utah, 1944.
Katsumi is holding her first grandson, Tim.

New York City was hot and humid in August and a disappointment. Housing was horrible; there was no elevator to our fourth floor apartment on 100th Street, just off the Riverside Drive. It meant climbing up and down four floors of stairways to take Tim out for airing each day. On the other hand, the Riverside Drive was close by and a beautiful area to take walks and for Tim to play.

Our stay in New York City was relatively brief as Martin and others doing research and translation work completed their designated tasks and the Navy Research unit closed.

Now we headed for Cambridge, Massachusetts, for Martin was appointed as an instructor (informant) of Japanese for a U.S.

*In 1989, Joyce Hirabayashi visited the site of the Topaz Relocation Center
in Utah, where her parents had been interned during World War II.
The plaque on the monument reads:*

TOPAZ 1942-1946
Site of Topaz, a World War II Internment Center

*In the never ending struggle for human dignity, there was enacted on this
spot an event of historic significance for a nation and its people.*

*During World War II this was the site of an internment camp, complete
with barbed wire fence and armed sentries, for 8,000 of the 110,000
Americans of Japanese ancestry, who for no justifiable reason, were
uprooted from their homes and interned by their own government. They
were the victims of wartime hysteria, racial animosity, and a serious
aberration of American jurisprudence.*

*That a nation dedicated to the principle of individualized freedom and
justice through law would, under the stress of war, allow this to happen –
and then recognizing the injustice of this action, hastened to soften the
effect of this action and make restitution. And that a whole generation of
a people, whose life and spirit was shattered and marred, would with
courage and hope and perseverance, fight back to re-establish themselves
in the American stream of life and were successful – are facts of sufficient
historic importance to be remembered forever.*

*So in this Bicentennial Year 1976, we dedicate this site as a reminder that
the lessons of history need always be heeded in forging a more perfect
form of human relationship.*

Military Government officers course at Harvard University. At Cambridge, we visited with a friend and former roommate of Martin's while he was attending the University of Washington. The friend who had been studying for the ministry at the University of Washington was now the pastor of a church in the outskirts of the city. Our move to Cambridge occurred in the autumn of 1944, and the fall colors in Massachusetts were more beautiful than any I had seen previously.

Finding suitable housing once again proved to be a problem for us. Martin found a place in a tenement area on the outskirts of Cambridge. At least it was a roof over our heads. We had to wait a few months or so to get in a Harvard University housing complex. Martin's sister Ruth who was with us decided to leave Boston to join her parents in Minneapolis, where they had relocated after leaving the Heart Mountain Relocation Center in Wyoming.

On August 14, 1945, the war with Japan finally ended. In the meantime, Martin received a telephone call from the War Department in Washington, D.C. asking if he would be interested in a job overseas. He was asked to go to Washington, D.C. for an interview. Before we knew it, Martin was on his way to Japan to research and survey the damage inflicted on Japan by the United States Armed Forces. His assignment was with the U.S. Strategic Bombing Survey Team. Because Tim and I did not want to stay in Cambridge, I packed our things and planned to join my parents in Minneapolis until Martin finished his work with the Bombing Survey Team.

Martin informed me by letter that the destruction in Tokyo was so great that he did not wish to stay there any longer than was necessary and would return to the United States as soon as he could. There was no housing in Tokyo as most buildings had been burned to the ground. He stayed in a U.S. military facility consisting of an office building converted for temporary housing.

Martin returned to Washington, D.C. after a few months in Tokyo to write reports utilizing data collected by the U.S. Strategic

Bombing Survey Team. His office was at Gravely Point in Virginia, just outside of Washington, D.C. Tim and I went to Washington, D.C. not to stay but just to see Martin, for I was on my way to Minneapolis. However, that did not happen. Tim and I stayed. Martin found a place in a cooperative housing unit near Thomas Circle which housed single people. We were to be the only married couple in the unit.

When Tim was three years old, we found a nursery school for him on Euclid Street in Washington, D.C. One summer, while I was working for the District of Columbia Public Library, I received a call from Martin and he asked me to meet him at the police station. He said that he would be there. On joining him, I saw our son, Tim, with the tip of his nose blackened and holding and eating an ice cream cone. Tim had apparently decided that he did not wish to be at the nursery school and took a street car to downtown Washington, D.C. The police noted that he was unaccompanied and thus took him into custody and asked him who his parents were, where they worked, and their home telephone number. He apparently provided that information because Martin, who happened to be at home, received the telephone call. The blackened nose was due to it being pressed against the display windows of stores which had items of interest for little children.

Following completion of his work with the U.S. Strategic Bombing Survey Team, Martin worked for a short period with a U.S. Government agency called the Washington Document Center (later it became part of the Central Intelligence Agency) while awaiting security clearance before being hired by the U.S. Department of State's Office of Research Intelligence. He was finally cleared for a job as research analyst.

Since we were living in downtown Washington, D.C. in temporary housing, we began to think about something more permanent. When the GI's returned home from World War II, there was a strong demand for affordable housing to take care of them. The National Housing Authority was established to assist in financing new private housing for GI's and other citizens. This program was an opportunity for us and we decided to buy a house. In September 1949, we moved out to Bethesda, Maryland, where Tim now could go to school without our being concerned about his safety or well-being. Nothing spectacular happened during the first seven years we were living there. We met our new neighbors, had coffees, took adult education classes, and lived a life not unlike that of others in our new neighborhood—low-cost housing units built on what had previously been a dairy farm area. Wives stayed at home to care for the children. Only those who had to work to make ends meet went out in the world seeking employment in those days.

Martin joined the new neighbors to establish the Ayrlawn Citizens Association to help get things done, such as negotiations with the builder or the city to install storm sewers, street lights, stop signs and other facilities to make the community function properly. Martin also started the Ayrlawn Newsletter not only to get the news of the community to the residents, but also to elicit community support for the Citizens Association's talks with the builder and local government officials.

Now we were settled for the rest of our lives, I thought, or as long as Martin worked for the State Department. I had to think about Tim's religious education and where he should attend Sunday School. In consideration, I thought of our beloved minister's wife who had attended Earlham College, a Quaker school. I also thought of Reverend West, a Congregational minister, and his sermons. In my last year at the University of Washington, I had stayed or boarded on the second floor of the Friends Meeting House (Quaker) just off campus, as war was declared. I felt the only place I could take Tim was the Quaker Meeting House. Just about this time, I learned that my college friend, a relative of Floyd Schmoe and the maid of honor at my wedding, was coming to Washington, D.C. Her husband was to head the Meeting House as Clerk. It was now an easy decision for me. I taught Sunday School classes and attended Sunday meetings (worship) and became part of the Meeting House. However, I could not forsake my own Reverend West whom I loved so much and talked to seriously, to become a Quaker; I am still a Congregationalist and also a Quaker at heart.

Now there were rumors circulating in the State Department about integrating the Civil Service people who worked there into the U.S. Foreign Service. It finally came to pass and after talking about the pros and cons of joining the Foreign Service, Martin made his plunge.

In those days, no Foreign Service officer was customarily assigned to a post of his or her parent's birthplace. Martin was one of the first to break the barrier. He was assigned to Tokyo as a Grade 4 Second Secretary officer with the title of economic-commercial officer.

Another move to be made. This time a house to sell and part of the furniture to be stored. We also had to decide what should be taken to the new post in Tokyo. By this time, Martin James, our second son, had become a part of the family.

We visited our parents in Minneapolis on the way to Japan since both parents had relocated there. Then, a stop in Los Angeles to visit with friends who were former fellow teachers at Boulder, Colorado; on to Honolulu and then to Wake Island, before we reached Tokyo on a twin engine propeller plane.

By the time we reached Tokyo, our son Jim had a high fever and I worried about entering Japan with some kind of a disease. Nothing happened and we were put up in a hotel until an apartment was located for us.

I can't say Japan was the beautiful place that my sister talked about after her return from Japan, where she had attended the U.S. Governors' Conference about a year before our assignment to Tokyo. The midnight trip from the Haneda Airport to Tokyo was dull and dreary like driving through a ghost town in one of those cowboy movies. I was ready to go back home. The culture shock was too much. The only thing that saved me was the friends we made back home in the State Department. Some had been assigned to Tokyo before us. It was good to see them and hear familiar voices. As time went on, we did a lot of things together on vacations and weekends.

The Embassy not only kept the men busy but the wives also had their work cut out for them. When Douglas MacArthur III, a nephew of General Douglas MacArthur, was assigned to Tokyo as the new American Ambassador, the real work began for the wives. The work revolved around protocol. The exacting Mrs. MacArthur, the daughter of former Vice President Alben Barkley of Kentucky, was a taskmaster in dealing with us who were for the most part neophytes as Foreign Service wives. Many, if not most, of us were new to the U.S. Foreign Service and were referred to as "integratees." We knew little about protocol. Even the U.S. Military Advisory Group (MAAG) members were occasionally called on the carpet by her. We all learned quickly but I can say thank goodness that we had the wife of a career diplomat to teach us the ins and outs of diplomatic service. I will always be thankful for her many contributions in that respect.

As wives of Embassy officers, we became members of the Wives Club which met once a month. MAAG wives were sometimes included in these meetings. The Wives Club sponsored a Japanese nursery school, financed in part by holding an open house event at the residence of the Ambassador. The Club members also undertook many other tasks and activities, including some for their own purposes such as cooking classes for Japanese and Chinese foods, flower arrangement classes, and *sumie* (brush painting) classes. But most importantly, we had to be available to the Ambassador and his wife to assist at dinners, receptions, and other Embassy events and activities.

During our first year on assignment in Tokyo, one of the more impressionable events was to be invited to go to the Imperial Palace to greet the Emperor and Empress on New Year's Day. A certain number of higher-ranking Foreign Service officers, plus Mili-

Joyce Hirabayashi with her sumie (brush painting) teacher, Mrs. Ota,
at the students' exhibit in Tokyo, Japan, circa 1959. Joyce's painting
of a crane is partially visible in the background (center).

tary Attaches and several others attached to the Embassy, were given
this honor. And we were included. We all met at the Ambassador's
residence and formed a line of cars according to the rank of the officers occupying them. We drove up to the Palace with crowds of people
lined up on both sides of the road to watch us as we went through the
gates into the Palace grounds.

For the New Year's affair at the Palace, we were expected
to adhere strictly to protocol with regard to dress and how we presented ourselves. The men wore morning coats. The protocol for
women's attire was more strict and elaborate. No white or red gowns

were allowed, gowns had to have long sleeves and a high neck line, and hats and gloves were in order. Representatives of each country were ordered to present themselves in the alphabetical order of the country names. Each Embassy representative entered the room of the Emperor's throne singularly and by rank. After entering the throne room, strict protocol on manners had to be observed. At no time were you permitted to turn your back to the royal family. To avoid a miscue, we practiced and talked about what was required at the Ambassador's Residence. After we had individually offered our New Year's greetings, consisting of a formal bow, we exited the room by giving once again a formal bow. We were then directed to another room where the New Year's food in boxes was given to each of us to take home. *Sake* was served at the event, and each of us took the *sake* cup home as a souvenir and as a remembrance of the occasion. Since we had two girls working for us at home, the New Year's food was given to them as a recognition of their part in the New Year's festivity. Since we were in Japan five years, we were privileged to go to the Palace each of those years.

As I recall it, the clothes which the Emperor and his family wore changed each year. The first year, the attire followed more of the traditional and elaborate clothing of historical significance. The youngest princess wore the traditional dress of a child, the other prin-cesses wore the *kimonos*. The Empress, on the other hand, had her traditional *kimono* for the occasion, whereas the Emperor wore West-ern clothes. By the fifth year (1961), all of the members of the Impe-rial Family had changed their attire to formal Western clothes.

American Embassy wives had volunteered to assist at the Japan Red Cross where one of the princesses was the Honorary Chair-person. When my turn came to offer volunteer assistance, I thought it might be wise to find out beforehand the location of the Red Cross building so as not to be delayed when the scheduled day arrived. On arrival at the address, I found no building with any Red Cross sign, or any building for that matter, so I parked my car and asked a police officer. He guided me to a police building where he called a central office and then handed me the phone. I asked where the Red Cross building was located and the police took the phone from me. When he received the response, he pointed to a building not far from there. My group of Embassy wives made it on time on the appointed day.

There were many dinners and receptions we gave in our home, as the occasion and Embassy responsibility required. Occasionally, we scheduled events at hotels managed by the U.S. military, where we could accommodate more people, particularly for receptions.

I took up *rozashi* (Japanese needlepoint) and studied at the residence of Mrs. Naokado Nishihara, the wife of a Ministry of Finance official, with an ex-baroness as an instructor. This was a real privilege for me as I had been invited to join the group by Ruth Trezise, the wife of the Counselor and later Minister of Economic Affairs for the U.S. Embassy. This was a very elite group. Martin's boss's wife and I were the only members of the group from our Embassy. When my mother visited Japan, I had the pleasure of introducing her, together with a professor from the University of Washington who was a friend of my sister, to the ex-baroness and Mrs. Nishihara.

During our Tokyo assignment, I invited my mother to come and visit us. This would make it possible for her to visit her family in Kyushu. I wrote in my invitation that if she did not wish to come alone, she could ask Martin's mother to come with her. That would enable them to see and do things in Tokyo together. Both of them did come and visited with us. They also visited their respective families during their stay. I asked both of them to limit their family visits to not more than two weeks. Mother went to Kyushu to visit her brother and sister who lived in different areas, as well as the home of her grandmother in Kagoshima. Mother indicated that she could have stayed longer than two weeks. Martin's mother's family lived in the outskirts of Matsumoto City in Nagano Prefecture, a place less distant than Kyushu. Her visit with her family and relatives was more brief as she returned within one week. She said that the visit was too much for her and pointed to the difficulty she had in sitting formally on her knees. She was a big woman physically, and I could see that it must have been hard on her as evidenced by the black and blue knees.

After the two mothers returned to Tokyo, I took them to a number of places in the nearby areas and also asked our son Tim to escort them around when I was not able to because of Embassy responsibilities. I believe the two mothers enjoyed their stay with us though it was all too brief.

Tim entered the eighth grade at a military school in the outskirts of Tokyo. The curriculum was a full year behind the schools in Montgomery County, Maryland, where Tim had attended previously. Tim thus was unhappy with the situation. The following year, we transferred him to the American School in Tokyo, which proved to be much more to his liking. Also, most of the American Embassy and American business people's children attended there. There was more camaraderie and competition among the students. Tim graduated from the American School in Japan (ASIJ) in 1961 and then continued his studies at the University of Colorado in Boulder, Colorado. Tim was born in Boulder and thus it was a kind of a homecoming. Jim, on the other hand, went to the St. Mary's School, a private parochial school for boys. He was chauffeured by mothers to and from school with other boys who lived in our housing compound.

During the period of our stay in Japan, there were several events of some historical significance. The present Emperor of Japan was married to his current Empress Michiko; the Japanese demonstrated against the planned visit of President Dwight Eisenhower and the trip was canceled; and the Japanese demonstrations against the planned signing of the U.S.-Japan Security Agreement led to the unfortunate death of a Japanese female student near the residence of the Prime Minister. A special memorial event in recognition of the student was held. In our Embassy, the staff members were asked to refrain from getting anywhere near the demonstrations. Contrary to these warnings, however, our son Tim, who was a photographer for his school's annual book, followed the demonstrations and took photos for "posterity."

A few months before Martin's tour of duty in Tokyo ended, his father and mother visited us. They also visited Martin's father's hometown of Hotaka, Nagano Prefecture. Upon their return from Hotaka, we had them join us for about ten days at a rented house near Lake Chuzenji at Nikko. We all enjoyed the rustic setting.

Now there was no time for me to visit Kyushu, home of my parents, and I was disappointed. Mother wanted me to go with her when she visited, but I could not go because I was needed in Tokyo!

A few weeks before our scheduled departure from Tokyo, we received word that Martin's next assignment would be in Surinam (Dutch Guiana). I certainly did not know my geography and I rushed to a reference book to locate the country. It was a disappointment— located ten degrees above the equator and the capital was at sea level. At one of the receptions we attended, Martin's boss took me aside and asked whether I was happy with the new assignment. I bluntly said no, that I preferred to go back to Washington, D.C. As it turned out, Martin was reassigned to Washington, D.C.

We bought a home in Bethesda, Maryland, a suburb of Washington, D.C. and again got ourselves settled. During our absence from Washington, D.C., the Washington-Tokyo Women's Club was formed with the wife of the Japanese Ambassador as Honorary President. Those of us who had served in Japan and returned to Washington, D.C. joined the Club. One year I served as Special Project Chairperson. I planned for the Japanese Embassy ladies to see the Republican and Democratic Party headquarters in Washington, D.C. At the last minute, the Republicans refused to allow us to see their headquarters. We were, however, permitted to see the Democratic Party's headquarters where they were very accommodating and nice to the group, and answered many questions raised by the Japanese visitors.

Another project which I chaired was to schedule the Japanese ladies to see the democratic process of handling votes at voting booths. One of the voting locations was at a school from which our son Tim had graduated. In response to my request to one of the school representatives, I was informed that they would be more than happy to have the Japanese ladies see democracy in action. Not only did the Japanese Embassy ladies come, but a number of the lower-ranked Embassy officers came along to observe the voting procedures. The people in charge of the voting booths seemed to be pleased to have the visitors and they answered questions posed by the Japanese ladies and the Embassy officers. This event was a big hit with the Japanese. After that, we had refreshments at our home, and the Japanese visitors talked and talked on and on about what they had observed.

On returning to Washington, D.C., we found that the pace of dinners and receptions to attend and host were considerably less than in Tokyo but enough to keep us busy. I also wanted to know and understand a little bit more about the history of the Department of State, not to mention learning more about other countries where we might find ourselves eventually assigned. I started to take courses at the University of Maryland, which I hoped would not take too much time, because there was still work to be done relating to Martin's new assignments in the Department of State and later with the Kennedy Round of Tariff Negotiations under the President's Special Trade Representative's Office.

In the Department of State, Martin was Chief Economist in the Office of the Far Eastern Affairs, where he dealt largely with officials of the Japanese Embassy and American business with complaints against Japan. Later (1964-67), Martin transferred to the Kennedy Round of Tariff Negotiations where he was asked to be the Chairman of the Country Team that had the responsibility of negotiating with Japan in GATT (General Agreement on Tariffs and Trade). Much of his preliminary work had to be done in Washington. Then he headed for Geneva, Switzerland. We agreed that we would rent our house during this expected short assignment. Jim and I remained at home during Martin's initial trip to Geneva, while Tim continued his schooling at the University of Colorado. I wasn't too anxious to go to Geneva early—Jim had to finish his schooling and I was taking a French language class at that time and I wanted to get as much time into it as I could. Martin felt lonely and came home to fetch us, since we were not making any moves.

Finally we rented our house. We bought tickets to go on the ship, the *Independence*. Martin had to pay for the family trip personally because his temporary assignment to Geneva did not include taking his family along. We were now on our way. We did a lot of sightseeing along the coast in the Mediterranean Sea—Casablanca; bus tour to Rabat; climbed Gibraltar (southern tip of Spain); toured Barcelona; weathered a storm in Sardinia; disembarked in Genoa—and finally reached Geneva. What a beautiful city! We stayed in a hotel until we found an apartment in Budé, located near the United Nations Headquarters and next to the Intercontinental Hotel, with a distant view of Mont Blanc.

This tour of duty for Martin was a holiday tour for me. No pressing things to be done. Weekends were mostly free. We did a lot of sightseeing, attended operas and symphonies and did a lot of eating of good Geneva food. We of course entertained the Japanese counterparts of Martin's negotiating team and friends from the U.S. Mission in Geneva from time to time, not to mention his team members from the Departments of Commerce, State, and Agriculture, the U.S. Tariff Commission, and others. We had occasions to see Roman ruins everywhere we went in Switzerland, Germany, France and of course Italy.

We made trips to Heidelburg, Wiesbaden, Frankfurt, Nuremberg, and many other places. One Easter vacation when Martin was busy with work, Jim was disappointed that he was not able to go anyplace on Easter like other students. So off we went, just Jim and I, to Wiesbaden, Germany, to see an opera and to do some shopping.

When Martin went to Paris to attend an OECD meeting as U.S. representative to work on some problem with the Japanese, I took Jim out of school on a Friday and we drove to Paris, staying overnight at Dijon in France. The following morning we saw three inches of snow on the ground. We made it to Paris and surprised Martin. We saw a little of Paris, stayed overnight on the West Bank, and then saw a bit more of the city before heading back to Geneva. It was an exciting weekend for Jim and the rest of us.

After Tim's graduation from the University of Colorado and before his induction into the U.S. Air Force, Tim visited us in Geneva but he took the Italian ship, the *Michelangelo*, which was to arrive in Genoa, Italy. Jim and I therefore went by car to Genoa to pick him up. Tim had taken a course in ROTC at the University of Colorado and was about to be called into service. But he asked for a delay to visit his parents and it was granted. While in Geneva, Tim took a course at the University of Geneva to learn a little bit more about the city and all of the many international organizations located there. In the late summer, Tim was called by the U.S. Air Force to go to Wiesbaden to be sworn in. Of course, I took him up there by car. While in Wiesbaden, we enjoyed a ballet together and then I left him at the Air Force base for them to take care of him.

With the Kennedy Round negotiations coming to an end, we headed back home by ship, the *Constitution*. Again we toured different cities where the ship docked, i.e., Nice, Barcelona, Gibraltar, Lisbon, etc. We sailed down the coast of North Africa to New York City and home.

This time Martin was detailed to the Special Trade Activities and Commercial Treaties Division (STA) of the Department of State in Washington, D.C. to work on various trade problems involving the United States and a host of other countries. With this job, his contacts widened even more as he held talks with representatives of nearly all of the trading countries. Also, our social obligations widened manyfold. One evening we were rushing from an embassy reception to an embassy dinner, and a police officer stopped us for speeding. We showed him our invitation and I said that we were late. The officer was most considerate. He commented that foreign diplomats get immunity from arrest. Even though we were Americans without diplomatic status while at home, he waved us on. He wished us well and said, "Drive carefully."

After serving two years in Washington, D.C., Martin was assigned to Helsinki, Finland. He was asked to report at his new post as soon as possible, since the man he was to replace had already left Helsinki. This did not give me time to plan. There were no schools in Helsinki for foreign children, i.e., English-speaking children at my son's level. Jim agreed to go with Dad to enter the Frankfurt Military School for American children. I thought it very brave of Jim. However, I accepted Jim's decision with some reservations.

Martin and Jim packed their bags to take care of their needs until the household items could be sent. But before the two weeks had passed, letters suddenly arrived in abundance from Jim. He felt the Frankfurt Military School was no place for him. There were drug problems and girls were becoming pregnant at the school. I was horrified and disappointed. I called Ruth Anna Davis Hadley, my maid of honor at the wedding, who was a dietitian at a Friends School in Philadelphia. I felt I could get Jim back to the United States and have him enrolled at a Quaker boarding school in Philadelphia. After talking with her, I was dismayed that even the Quaker Schools had problems with drugs. Therefore, I wrote to the International School in Geneva to see whether he could be accepted for enrollment. They were not accepting students since enrollment was closed, but they asked me to write for winter-spring semester admission, which I did.

We finally got Jim into the International School in Geneva. I took Jim from Helsinki, where he was visiting nearly every other week, to Frankfurt to pick up his belongings, and we took the train to Geneva. Since Jim would not use his French language at the railroad station, I had to try my Anglicized French, which Jim could not bear to hear. He practically disowned me—he walked away as far as possible so he did not hear me. Anyway, we arrived on the steps of the school.

I talked with the Headmaster to inform him of the physical allergy problems that Jim had. I wanted the school officials to be aware of them. On familiar grounds and with some of his past classmates also enrolled, he adjusted very nicely. Now, he came home on vacations and not every other weekend.

I finally sold our house in Bethesda, Maryland, cleaned the house for the new owners, and I was off to Finland.

Going to a new post meant for me another round of house hunting, meeting the head of each section or division, accepting social engagements, and the like. All I needed was a short vacation to get my breath before tackling the responsibilities of my new unpaid job.

The initial Strategic Arms Limitation Talks (SALT) between the Soviet Union and the United States had started just before I arrived in Helsinki. The Embassy was busy with officials from Washington, D.C. and the Finnish Government officials were going out of their way to be perfect hosts. They entertained all of the SALT representatives, both American and Russian, on an even basis so as not to give the wrong impression of bias. Our Ambassador, of course, also hosted the American SALT delegation. The American Ambassador had broken his leg just before the start of these SALT talks, as a result of an accident that occurred when he jumped from a boat on to the hard rocks on shore. Martin, therefore, was given the privilege and responsibility of escorting the American SALT delegates on the tours of Finland. Wives were invited and I joined the group.

This responsibility was extra—we still had other work to be done at the Embassy. For my part, in support of the members of the economic staff, I had to plan to hold a number of receptions. This planning was not easy, since Helsinki was so far from the rest of Europe, and yet I needed to obtain the necessary supplies. That was accomplished in part by placing food orders with the American Military Commissary in Bremerhaven, Germany, and having it shipped to Helsinki in bulk. With a bit of initial delay, I was able to get

*Joyce and Martin
Hirabayashi with
Ambassador Val Peterson
(middle) and other
section chiefs at the
U.S. Embassy in
Helsinki, Finland,
circa 1970.*

organized in a way to meet my social responsibilities and to contribute to the smooth and effective working relationships between and among the staff members.

The Ambassador asked me to help put together a Fourth-of-July picnic. He wanted to invite representatives from the Finnish Government, corporate executives, and other Finnish people with whom the U.S. Embassy had established friendly contacts, not to mention officials of other foreign embassies in Helsinki. I knew this would be a big job so I put my whole heart and soul into it. Since Jim would be home for the summer, I had him involved in it, too. Nearly all of the American Embassy personnel had a part in helping to put the thing together. I never saw such enthusiasm from all of them. After the event, the people whom I talked to had nice things to say. They had a great time as they were able to talk to guests at the same time they were making hamburgers and hot dogs, and to participate in our Independence Day activities.

In November 1970, I was asked to chair the Finnish-American Society's annual bazaar. All plans were completed and made ready for implementation, when, just a few days before the event, I received a call from my brother in Minnetonka, Minnesota. My mother had a stroke, and Sam didn't think she would be able to live very long and wanted me to come home immediately. Since the preparatory work for the bazaar was done, I was able to turn over the bazaar chair responsibilities to another person. Before I could leave, however, Sam called again and told me that Mother had passed away.

The Embassy people were very helpful and supportive. They notified the London Heathrow Airport personnel that I would be coming through. The Heathrow people helped me transfer from the Finnish Airline plane to the next plane for New York and thence to Minneapolis. Martin regrettably was unable to accompany me because of his official duties.

After returning to Helsinki, my life with Embassy activities continued to be full as we made many friends among the Finnish

people. But it was also time for us to think of Jim's college education. I had never heard of Franklin and Marshall, a small elite college in Pennsylvania, until the American Ambassador to Sweden visited Helsinki for an ambassadorial conference. I asked him about
that school which Jim had selected. I learned that it was a very fine
school. I was relieved.

Since Jim had full four years in college ahead of him, Martin felt that he, Martin, should stay overseas in the U.S. Foreign Service for another two years, or until the mandatory retirement age of
60. Financially, he thought we would be able to support Jim better
by doing so. He therefore asked for a direct transfer to another overseas post. That was granted and we were assigned to Stockholm,
Sweden.

The U.S. relationship with Sweden at that time was not very
good. Our Ambassador in Sweden was called home for consultation, in response to Swedish Prime Minister Olaf Palme's negative
comments on U.S. involvement in the Vietnam War. The
Ambassador's post, as well as the position of Deputy Chief of Mission (DCM) for our Embassy in Sweden, were vacant at the time that
we arrived there. As a result, the top two men, Economic and Political Section Heads, together with the Administrative Head, had to
keep the Embassy functioning. Martin headed the Economic Section. After about six months, the U.S. Government sent a new Ambassador and the relationship between the two countries was nor-
malized.

Our tour of duty in Sweden was also the time of the German Bader Meinhof terrorists, as well as the Japanese Red Guards,
roaming around Europe including the Scandinavian countries. The
Japanese Red Guards were spying on the Japanese Ambassador in
Sweden, we were told. The day after we had hosted a dinner in our
apartment for the Economic Counselor of the German Embassy, his
wife and some Swedish officials, the Bader Meinhof terrorist group
bombed the German Embassy in Stockholm, a building adjacent to
the American Embassy. Our guest for the previous evening, the Ger-

*Joyce and Martin
Hirabayashi at a farewell
party held in their honor
at the residence of
Dr. Jorma Pohjanpalo in
Helsinki, Finland, 1974.*

man Economic Counselor, and the German Military Attaché were killed. Although no specific reason for the bombing of the German Embassy was known, our own Embassy was required to heighten security, in part because the public and other criticisms of our Vietnam policies could make the Embassy a target for terrorists.

After two years in Sweden, it was time for Martin's retirement from the U.S. Foreign Service in 1976. Martin had heard from his sister in Minneapolis that his father was not doing too well living alone. Also, I heard from my brother in Minnetonka who had suffered a heart attack but was progressing nicely. We thought that we would go to Minneapolis to help out and then move back to Pennsylvania where we had bought land in a retirement complex. We are still here in the Twin Cities, and we still have the Pennsylvania land. Moving again did not appeal to me.

Before we really were settled, Martin started to hunt for something to do. He met Bill Ogden, the president of a consulting firm, International Finance and Management Group, Inc., and they seemed to hit it off. To this day, Martin goes down to his office once a week to see how things are and to pick up his mail.

Most of the work in our home in Edina was done gradually. I didn't have much energy. I also found out that my blood pressure was very high and it had to be controlled. Also, there was dental work to be done.

I needed to get away from stress and upheaval. I felt I was near the breaking point. I would do what I could for my brother, and Martin could help his father. I did not feel that I could take any responsibility for Martin's father. I was burned out!

It has been a long process of getting back on my feet. The responsibilities over 30 years with the U.S. Foreign Service and the State Department had taken their toll and I just couldn't and didn't want to do anything that brought on stress. I needed peace and time to be alone to heal my inner soul.

After nearly 15 years, I am now feeling like myself but I still enjoy the peace and quiet of my home.

The boys are on their own. Tim has been working for General Motors as an acoustical engineer in the Chevrolet and Pontiac Division at Milford Proving Grounds in Michigan. The younger son, Jim, is married to Sharon Matsumoto of Chicago, Illinois, and they have blessed us with a grandson, Scott, six years old now. They live in Alexandria, Virginia. Both of the boys visit us at least twice a year. We in turn have visited them in Washington, D.C. and Pleasant Ridge, Michigan.

Both Martin and I have always felt that our U.S. interests can best be maintained by continuing to keep good relations with Japan. I have encouraged and helped Martin to do anything we can in that direction since we moved here.

We had dinners for Japanese guests, including those from the Japan Productivity Center sponsored by the Minnesota International Center, when they visited Minnesota. We took care of the son of an old friend of Martin's who had come to Minnesota to study at the University of Minnesota-Crookston. The Minnesota International Center has often called on us for help in entertaining Japanese and other guests, and we have endeavored to respond positively.

Furthermore, when I took up quilting at a community center in Edina, the instructor wanted me to help a Japanese lady who was interested in quilting. Her husband was involved with the University of Minnesota. This led to getting a group of Japanese wives together at my home on a weekly basis to learn about quilting. Their husbands were affiliated with the University. This lasted for about one year.

Now since we are getting on in years, we have retired from most activities. Our time is taken up at the local YMCA in the morning; we walk or take short auto trips in the afternoon. We still enjoy the Minnesota Symphony Orchestra and the Minnesota Opera at the

Ordway Music Theatre. Also, attending art and cultural lectures at the Minneapolis Institute of Arts and listening to World Affairs luncheon speakers are part of our enjoyment. We enjoy the University of Minnesota Arboretum and try to get out there during good weather.

In the way of family affairs, our immediate family visits with us twice a year, as mentioned previously. I see my sister occasionally as we visit Seattle or she comes to Minneapolis. There is also a small group of former U.S. Foreign Service retirees living in the Twin Cities area who meet three or four times a year. And, the extended families of various relationships do get together in what we call "reunions."

I don't know whether our work with the U. S. Foreign Service has changed the world, but we have tried our best to make it a better place. I have enjoyed my part of the work. We have kept in touch with many of the people in Japan, Finland and Sweden. I have certainly tried to bring a better understanding of the United States to the people of those countries and others we have met.

Since we spent much of our lives overseas, our views and perspectives may be somewhat different from those of other Niseis in the United States. Nevertheless, I hope that other Niseis, Sanseis and Yonseis will look to the future and work toward strengthening the ties that bind our world. Working in a global world is not easy, but with each success, you will find the effort gratifying.

Reflections

As I look back on my life, I can see that world events played a major role in my life. I was not only reading newspapers, magazines and books, but also listening to the radio newscasts of world events.

Yes, World War II had a big impact on me. My life changed completely. It would never be the same. Many good things happened because of it.

After the War, President Truman desegregated the U.S. Army. This brought on many changes in civilian life, too. Housing, schooling, restaurants and other areas open to the public were desegregated. Opening eating places to all is one I remember best. We are still seeing changes to this day, i.e., gays and lesbians, AIDS patients, and others are being recognized in their own rights. President Truman's impact on life in the United States was significant in much the same way as President Gorbachev's decision to adopt capitalistic ways in the Soviet Union.

Also, my parents played a very important part in my life. We were a fairly close-knit family—in part because we were the only Japanese family in the community where we lived. My parents taught us Japanese words which were unique and not used by our friends in the country or out on the farm.

My parents' patience and wisdom, as well as their setting ethical values and stressing the importance of being truthful, helping others and thinking for myself, have all held me in good stead.

Both Martin and I worked for the communities in which we lived. We gave of ourselves wherever help was needed—schools, charities, voluntary organizations, etc. And, we never felt discriminated against in any of the places where we lived.

In our foreign service experience, we had many occasions to be thankful for our country and what it stands for. One experience I remember vividly occurred in Finland. It occurred one evening as our Ambassador Peterson, former five-time Governor of Nebraska, was leaving in his official car. I saw our U.S. flag on the side of the car. A flash of nostalgia and homesickness overcame me. I felt so proud to be an American. I stood there erect as the car passed by and I just had to salute the flag. I've always loved my country, but the full force of that feeling came upon me that evening.

Yes, I am proud that I am an American citizen. During World War II, given my heritage, unfortunate incidents could have hap-

Joyce and Martin Hirabayashi flanking his father, Toshiharu Hirabayashi, at his house in Minneapolis, Minnesota, 1976.

pened. But they did not. Thinking back to that unpredictable period of the war, it does bring back memories of what could have happened.

As noted earlier, I am proud of my parents and all that they have taught me. I hope that I have done the same for my children.

I am proud to have served my country as the wife of a U.S. Foreign Service Officer. In Japan, I was able to assist as a part of the team that helped Japan get back on her feet in the early days after the war (1956-1961).

I am proud to have served in Finland and Sweden with my husband. From that experience and others, I learned that people all over the world are not too different from each other. Their hopes and aspirations for a better life are similar.

During the years my husband and I served our country as a part of the U.S. Foreign Service, wives were a part of the team. The wives received no compensation—but they were expected to serve in many capacities as representatives of the Service. By the time we retired, nobody—not even the Ambassador—could ask the wives to perform duties of any kind. Today, most of the duties are performed by wives or staff members, but they are compensated. However, I think that the life just after World War II during the days of reconstruction of the national economies was much safer and satisfying even with all the responsibilities.

Minnesota has been good to us, too. We retired here in 1976 after 31 years in government. We like the climate, both winter and summer. The air is clean; wild animals and birds are nearby. There are many cultural happenings in both St. Paul and Minneapolis.

And, most importantly, we are near our parents. Both Martin's and my parents are buried at the Lakewood Cemetery in Minneapolis.